Frommer's®

PORTABLE

Australia's Great Barrier Reef

3rd Edition

by Lee Mylne

Here's what critics say about Frommer's:

"Amazingly easy to use. Very portable, very complete."

—*Booklist*

"Detailed, accurate, and easy-to-read information for all price ranges."

—*Glamour Magazine*

D0451625

Published by:

WILEY PUBLISHING, INC.

111 River St.
Hoboken, NJ 07030-5774

Copyright © 2005 Wiley Publishing, Inc., Hoboken, New Jersey. All rights reserved. No part of this publication may be reproduced, stored in a retrieval system or transmitted in any form or by any means, electronic, mechanical, photocopying, recording, scanning or otherwise, except as permitted under Sections 107 or 108 of the 1976 United States Copyright Act, without either the prior written permission of the Publisher, or authorization through payment of the appropriate per-copy fee to the Copyright Clearance Center, 222 Rosewood Drive, Danvers, MA 01923, 978/750-8400, fax 978/646-8600. Requests to the Publisher for permission should be addressed to the Legal Department, Wiley Publishing, Inc., 10475 Crosspoint Blvd., Indianapolis, IN 46256, 317/572-3447, fax 317/572-4355, E-Mail: brandreview@wiley.com.

Wiley and the Wiley Publishing logo are trademarks or registered trademarks of John Wiley & Sons, Inc. and/or its affiliates. Frommer's is a trademark or registered trademark of Arthur Frommer. Used under license. All other trademarks are the property of their respective owners. Wiley Publishing, Inc. is not associated with any product or vendor mentioned in this book.

ISBN 0-7645-7434-5

Editor: Kathleen Warnock
Production Editor: Ian Skinnari
Photo Editor: Richard Fox
Cartographer: Elizabeth Puhl
Production by Wiley Indianapolis Composition Services

For information on our other products and services or to obtain technical support, please contact our Customer Care Department within the U.S. at 800/762-2974, outside the U.S. at 317/572-3993 or fax 317/572-4002.

Wiley also publishes its books in a variety of electronic formats. Some content that appears in print may not be available in electronic formats.

Manufactured in the United States of America

5   4   3   2   1

Contents

List of Maps

ABOUT THE AUTHOR

Lee Mylne is a freelance travel writer who writes for a broad range of publications, including the national travel trade magazine, *Travel Week Australia*. Born and raised in New Zealand, she traveled widely before finally figuring out she could make a living out of it. Mylne has lived in Australia for the past 18 years and is a Full Member of the Australian Society of Travel Writers. She is also co-author of *Frommer's Australia 2005* and *Frommer's Australia from $50 a Day*.

AN INVITATION TO THE READER

In researching this book, we discovered many wonderful places—hotels, restaurants, shops, and more. We're sure you'll find others. Please tell us about them, so we can share the information with your fellow travelers in upcoming editions. If you were disappointed with a recommendation, we'd love to know that, too. Please write to:

> *Frommer's Australia's Portable Great Barrier Reef,* 3rd Edition
> Wiley Publishing, Inc. • 111 River St. • Hoboken, NJ 07030-5774

AN ADDITIONAL NOTE

Please be advised that travel information is subject to change at any time—and this is especially true of prices. We therefore suggest that you write or call ahead for confirmation when making your travel plans. The authors, editors, and publisher cannot be held responsible for the experiences of readers while traveling. Your safety is important to us, however, so we encourage you to stay alert and be aware of your surroundings. Keep a close eye on cameras, purses, and wallets, all favorite targets of thieves and pickpockets.

FROMMER'S STAR RATINGS, ICONS & ABBREVIATIONS

Every hotel, restaurant, and attraction listing in this guide has been ranked for quality, value, service, amenities, and special features using a **star-rating system.** In country, state, and regional guides, we also rate towns and regions to help you narrow down your choices and budget your time accordingly. Hotels and restaurants are rated on a scale of zero (recommended) to three stars (exceptional). Attractions, shopping, nightlife, towns, and regions are rated according to the following scale: zero stars (recommended), one star (highly recommended), two stars (very highly recommended), and three stars (must-see).

In addition to the star-rating system, we also use **seven feature icons** that point you to the great deals, in-the-know advice, and unique experiences that separate travelers from tourists. Throughout the book, look for:

Finds	Special finds—those places only insiders know about
Fun Fact	Fun facts—details that make travelers more informed and their trips more fun
Kids	Best bets for kids and advice for the whole family
Moments	Special moments—those experiences that memories are made of
Overrated	Places or experiences not worth your time or money
Tips	Insider tips—great ways to save time and money
Value	Great values—where to get the best deals

The following **abbreviations** are used for credit cards:

AE	American Express	DISC	Discover	V	Visa
DC	Diners Club	MC	MasterCard		

FROMMERS.COM

Now that you have the guidebook to a great trip, visit our website at **www. frommers.com** for travel information on more than 3,000 destinations. With features updated regularly, we give you instant access to the most current trip-planning information available. At Frommers.com, you'll also find the best prices on airfares, accommodations, and car rentals—and you can even book travel online through our travel booking partners. At Frommers. com, you'll also find the following:

- Online updates to our most popular guidebooks
- Vacation sweepstakes and contest giveaways
- Newsletter highlighting the hottest travel trends
- Online travel message boards with featured travel discussions

Introducing Australia's Great Barrier Reef

The statistics are formidable, but nothing can prepare you for the reality of the Reef. Experienced divers on their first time here are as awed as snorkelers who've donned mask and fins for the first time.

The Great Barrier Reef stretches more than 2,000km (1,250 miles) along the east coast of northern Australia. It is home to 1,500 kinds of fish, 400 species of corals, 4,000 kinds of clams and snails, and countless sponges, worms, starfish, and sea urchins. It covers an area bigger than the size of England, Scotland, and Wales, a mere 348,700 sq. km (134,633 sq. miles). And if that's not enough, try this: it's the only living thing on Earth visible from the moon. Some call it the Eighth Wonder of the World.

So where to start? Take heart—it may be awesome in scale, but a trip to the Great Barrier Reef is entirely manageable with good planning. That's where this book comes in, designed to give you the lowdown on some of the best sites to snorkel and dive this magnificent piece of nature and to provide tips on how to make the most of your experience. We tell you about the top dive and snorkel sites, as well as some remote spots rarely explored by travelers. We walk you through everything from how to fit your snorkel mask to how to pick a dive course, and recommend the best boats for exploring the Reef, from day-trip vessels to dedicated live-aboard dive boats. We tell you about some of the wonderful creatures you will see (and the few scary ones to avoid!). We recommend places to stay, from inexpensive

⸜Fun Fact⸝ Reef Eco-Facts

The Great Barrier Reef is a huge conglomeration of tiny animals called coral polyps. Coral polyps are tiny soft animals that coat themselves in limestone, and as they die, their bodies cement to form coral reef, onto which more living coral grows. Reefs need warm, clear, shallow water in which to thrive.

Australia

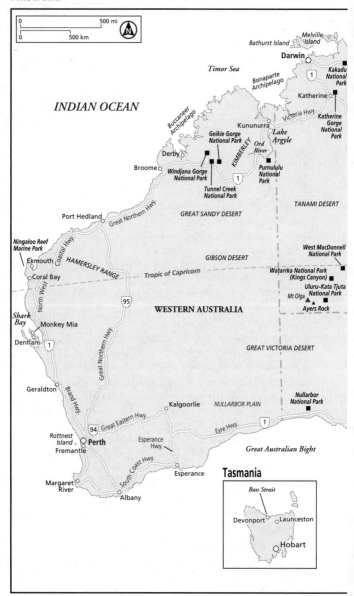

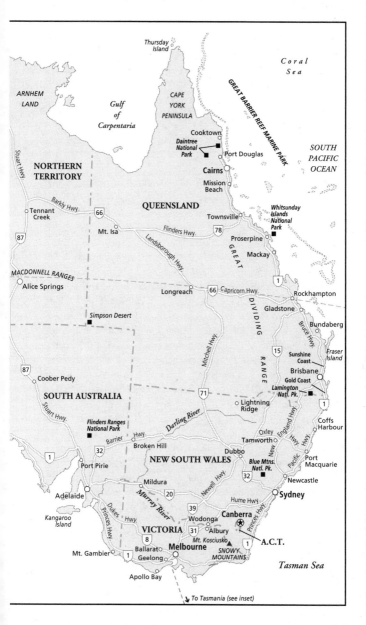

Thursday
Island

Coral Sea

ARNHEM
LAND

Gulf of Carpentaria

CAPE
YORK
PENINSULA

GREAT BARRIER REEF MARINE PARK

Cooktown
Daintree National Park
Port Douglas

Cairns
Mission Beach

SOUTH
PACIFIC
OCEAN

NORTHERN
TERRITORY

Barkly Hwy.
66

QUEENSLAND

Whitsunday Islands National Park

Tennant
Creek

Mt. Isa
Flinders Hwy.
78
Townsville
Proserpine
Mackay

87

Landsborough Hwy.

MACDONNELL RANGES
Alice Springs

Longreach
66 Capricorn Hwy.
Rockhampton
Gladstone

G
R
E
A
T

D
I
V
I
D
I
N
G

R
A
N
G
E

Stuart Hwy.

Simpson Desert

Bundaberg

Bruce Hwy.

Fraser Island

87
Coober Pedy

15
Sunshine Coast
Brisbane
Gold Coast
Lamington Natl. Pk.

SOUTH AUSTRALIA

71

Lightning Ridge

New England Hwy.

Coffs Harbour

Flinders Ranges National Park

Barrier Hwy.

Darling River

Mitchell Hwy.

Stuart Hwy.

1
Port Pirie

32
Broken Hill

NEW SOUTH WALES
Dubbo
Blue Mtns. Natl. Pk.

Oxley Hwy.
Tamworth

Pacific Hwy.

Port Macquarie

Adelaide

Mildura
20

Newell Hwy.

32

Newcastle

1

Hume Hwy.

Sydney

Kangaroo Island

Murray River

39
Wodonga

Canberra

Dukes Hwy.

Princes Hwy.

VICTORIA
8
Ballarat

31
Albury
Mt. Kosciusko

Princes Hwy.

1 A.C.T.

Mt. Gambier
1
Melbourne
Geelong

SNOWY MOUNTAINS

Tasman Sea

Apollo Bay

To Tasmania (see inset)

3

(Fun Fact The Sex Life of Coral

Never underestimate the effect of a full moon! For coral it sets the mood about once a year, between the third and sixth nights after the November full moon. At this time, coral polyps produce male and female eggs that get released into the water, creating a "soup" where they meet, float away, and settle to create a new piece of coral. The process is called "coral spawning," and dive boats conduct nighttime trips to see it happen.

B&Bs to glamorous Great Barrier Reef island resorts. And recognizing that even die-hard snorkelers and divers want to take a break from the water once in a while, we cover the best stuff to do on dry land, such as four-wheel-drive safaris into a World Heritage–listed rainforest or visiting a turtle rookery.

The Great Barrier Reef, which is made up of approximately 2,900 individual reefs, is enclosed within the World Heritage–listed **Great Barrier Reef Marine Park.** There are three kinds of reef on the Great Barrier Reef—fringe, ribbon, and platform. **Fringe reef** grows along the mainland and island shores. **Ribbon reefs** are long, thin "streamers," found only north of Cairns. Divers love these for the amazing variety of life found on the long continuous reef walls. **Platform reefs,** or patch reefs, are splotches of coral that emerge off the continental shelf all along the Queensland coast. Platform reefs, some of which are more than 130m (426 ft.) tall—taller than the pyramids in Egypt— are by far the most common kind of reef. There are nearly 1,000 islands in the Great Barrier Reef Marine Park. The islands are either "continental," meaning they are part of the Australian landmass, or "cays," which are piles of crushed dead coral and sand amassed over time by water action, sometimes vegetated with scrubby trees or rainforest. Cays are surrounded with sensational coral and fish life, whereas the coral around continental islands ranges from terrific to nonexistent. There are 618 continental islands and 300 cays in the marine park.

To see the Reef, you can snorkel it, fish it (recreational fishing is permitted in most zones), fly over it, sail in it, and dive it. Most of the Reef lies an average of 65km (40 miles) off the coast, though isolated patch reefs and island-fringing reefs lie closer to the mainland.

Whether you snorkel or dive, you will see green and purple clams, pink sponges, red starfish, purple sea urchins, and myriad fish ranging in color from electric blue to neon yellow. You'll see richly colored *nudibranchs* (they're sort of like shellfish without the shell), Christmas tree worms, giant clams, and Spanish dancers (little flatworms that swim by waving their frilly "wings" that look like a flamenco dancer's skirt). At many reefs, you can pat and hand-feed big, friendly *Maori wrasse* (you may know these as "Napoleon fish"). You may see harmless reef sharks, giant manta rays (most common Nov–Apr), and big green loggerhead or hawksbill sea turtles. Divers will see moray eels, and often grouper hiding under rocks, and bigger fish such as barracuda, tuna, and the occasional whale or hammerhead shark. En route to the Reef, you may see dolphins and, more rarely, dugongs (also called sea cows) from the boat. Between July and September it's common to spot humpback whales; occasionally snorkelers and divers encounter them underwater, and divers even hear them singing sometimes. Divers may see dwarf minke whales around the ribbon reefs and the Whitsunday Islands in June and July.

Back to School: Reef Teach

What can a crazy Irishman tell us about the Great Barrier Reef? Lots, if he's enthusiastic marine biologist and scuba diver Paddy Colwell. Paddy conducts a wonderfully entertaining Reef briefing and slide-show presentation in Cairns called **Reef Teach** ℛ (℗ **07/4031 7794**). Paddy tells you everything you need to know about the Reef before you visit it, from how coral grows, to some of the dangerous critters to avoid, to some simple but "must-have" tips on how to take successful underwater photos. Presentations take place Monday through Saturday, starting at 6:15pm in a large "classroom" at 14 Spence St. (at Abbott St.), Cairns. The session ends around 8:30pm. The cost is A$13 (US$10) adults and A$6 (US$4.80) children under 14.

By day, Paddy does what he loves most—diving—and you can join him. He is a dive instructor qualified in all four major scuba systems: PADI, NAUI, SSI, and BSAC. He goes out on whatever dive boat takes his fancy most days, taking along customers who want to soak up his knowledge and use him as what amounts to a free dive guide. Ring him a day or two before your Reef trip and see what boat he's planning to dive, then contact the boat and book a place.

Water temperature on the Great Barrier Reef rarely drops below 66°F (19°C) in the midwinter month of July, and can get to 82°F (28°C) or even higher in high summer in February. The norm is around 73° to 79°F (23°–26°C). A low tide and a sunny day are what you're hoping for when you snorkel. Choppy water and strong currents can make snorkeling more difficult. After rain, the water silts up slightly with runoff from the mainland, although visibility will still be good. On a neap (extra-low) tide, the outgoing water rushes off the Reef, creating a waterfall effect.

1 The Regions in Brief: Choosing a Gateway to the Reef

Lots of visitors to Australia believe that Cairns is the best place from which to access the Reef. Not so. Cairns is a fine place from which to see it; but the quality of the coral is just as good off any town down the Queensland coast, so don't worry too much about which part of the Reef is "best." The outer Reef is pretty much equidistant from any point along the coast—about 90 minutes by motorized catamaran. It is closest at Mission Beach (an hour away) and farthest away at Townsville and Bundaberg (more like 2½ hr. away).

The main gateways, taken north to south, are Port Douglas, Cairns, Mission Beach, Townsville, the Whitsunday Islands, Rockhampton, and Bundaberg. Heron Island off Gladstone is on the Reef itself.

PORT DOUGLAS

The picturesque rainforest fishing town of Port Douglas has plentiful reefs offshore, which most boats take about 90 minutes to reach. It's a 30-minute motorized boat trip or a 1-hour to 90-minute sail from Port Douglas to the **Low Isles,** two pretty, uninhabited sandy cays surrounded by coral and fish you can snorkel over. "Port," as the locals call it, has only about a dozen or so dive and snorkel boats, but the choice is big enough and the standard of boats is high. Only one live-aboard diving vessel makes trips from Port; most live-aboard boats depart from Cairns.

Port is about an hour's drive north of Cairns, and many Cairns-based tour operators will pick you up here, usually for an extra A$10 (US$8) or A$20 (US$16). Port has more charm and better restaurants than Cairns, a lovely beach, and a championship golf course. It's also the gateway to the **Daintree rainforest.** See chapter 4.

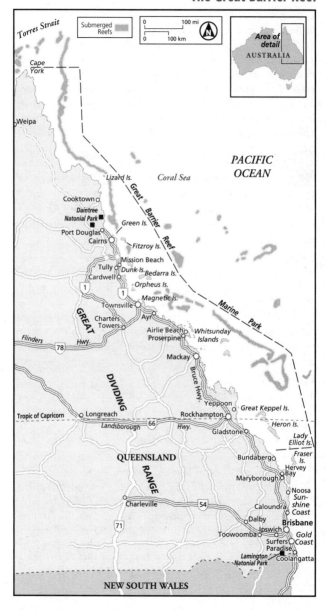

CAIRNS

Several large catamarans, a few sailing vessels, and many small dive boats make day trips from Cairns to the reefs offshore. Most live-aboard dive boats running trips to the Great Barrier Reef (and to the diving beyond the Reef in the Coral Sea) depart from Cairns. **Lizard Island,** 240km (149 miles) to the north, and **Green Island,** 27km (17 miles) to the east, have some of the best snorkeling to be found anywhere on the Reef. Lizard Island is the only place from which you can make a diving day trip to renowned **Cod Hole** ⚓. Fitzroy Island, 35km (22 miles) east, is not a top snorkel spot, but has some good diving. Cairns lacks the palm-tree-studded charm of Port Douglas, but the airport is here and the city has a wide choice of Reef cruises, land-based tours, and accommodations. This is also where most dive schools are. You can explore the rainforest town of **Kuranda** on a day trip. See chapter 3 for complete coverage.

MISSION BEACH

This collection of jungle hamlets hidden along pristine white beaches is really a place you come to escape the tourist hordes, not a prime Reef destination. Nonetheless, from Mission Beach or neighboring **Dunk** and **Bedarra** island resorts just offshore, you can visit **Beaver Cay** on the Great Barrier Reef on a day trip. Mission Beach is a nice spot for snorkelers, but divers should probably consider other destinations. No live-aboard vessels operate out of Mission Beach.

TOWNSVILLE

Although Townsville is one of the points farthest from the Great Barrier Reef, don't dismiss it out of hand. It offers Australia's best wreck dive, the **SS *Yongala*** ⚓, and its reefs, although distant, offer good diving, often on big drop-offs with fish to match. Diving in these waters is generally for the more experienced scuba diver, although snorkelers and novice divers will find plenty to suit them in the shallow reefs around **Magnetic Island,** an inexpensive resort island just 8km (5 miles) offshore. The city has a commercial diving school that teaches a huge range of specialty diving skills.

The city is home to the headquarters of the Great Barrier Reef Marine Park Authority, whose premises, **Reef HQ,** are well worth a visit. Townsville is a modern, unprepossessing place without the tropical appeal, endless tours, and pretty beaches of Cairns and Port Douglas. See chapter 5 for complete coverage.

> *Tips* **Beware of the Stingers**
>
> North of Gladstone, deadly box jellyfish known as "stingers" put a stop to all swimming on the mainland in summer from October to May. Never swim in unprotected seas at that time. Most popular beaches have net enclosures for safe swimming. If you love swimming, you don't want to swim in nets, and you're visiting in stinger season, head to an island or choose a hotel with a pool. The islands are less likely to be a problem, as stingers tend to hug the shore, but there are no guarantees! The tiny Irakandji jellyfish is small enough to slip through some stinger nets. Ask advice from the locals or the lifesavers on duty. Some places have "stinger suits" you can hire.

THE WHITSUNDAY ISLANDS

The beautiful Whitsundays are just as good a stepping stone to the outer Great Barrier Reef as Cairns. Some people even think they're better, because while the outer Reef is about the same distance from the mainland here as it is at Cairns, most of the islands also have some additional fringing reef around their shores. There are also good reefs between the islands you can visit on boat trips. A small range of good dive schools, live-aboard boats, and snorkel/dive day trips operate from both the mainland and the region's popular island resorts. The Whitsundays are also prime sailing territory. You can snorkel and make dives on many crewed sailing vacations. The Whitsundays are far enough south to miss the worst of the hot, humid wet season suffered by Cairns, Port Douglas, and Townsville between November and March. See chapter 6 for complete coverage.

THE CENTRAL & SOUTHERN REEF ISLANDS

The Great Barrier Reef in this region attracts far fewer visitors than North Queensland. This is due more to the area's lack of tourism infrastructure than to a lack of reefs. That said, the region is home to the brightest stars in the Great Barrier Reef firmament, **Heron Island,** a coral cay surrounded by acres of coral and home to some of the Reef's top dive sites, and nearby **Wilson Island.** From **Rockhampton** to the north, you can visit **Great Keppel Island,** where snorkel and diving trips around the island's fringing reefs are geared toward beginner divers. Snorkelers and experienced divers will enjoy taking day trips from the mainland to the many reefs in these parts that are mostly unexplored by visitors. From **Bundaberg** in the south, you can join a snorkel/dive day trip or a live-aboard boat to explore the excellent and untouched Bunker Group islands and reefs. This region is home to the southernmost Great Barrier Reef resort island, **Lady Elliot Island,** a basic resort whose dive sites are renowned for good coral and marine life, especially manta rays.

Rockhampton, Gladstone, and Bundaberg are rural towns with only a handful of attractions to explore. The scenery in these parts is eucalyptus bushland, not the rainforest vistas you enjoy farther north.

2 Which Great Barrier Reef Resort Is Right for You?

Choosing the right resort can be a tricky business; the Reef is home to about 15 major resorts of varying levels of luxury and comfort. Much will depend on your tastes, budget and interests—if you want to dive, you will want a resort with easy access to the reef, or boats that go to the reef; if not, you may settle for something where you can get away from it all with a book and a long drink.

The jewels of the reef are undoubtedly Heron and Wilson islands, the most southerly islands of the Great Barrier Reef. They are both right on the reef—just get in the water and you're there. Superb diving and snorkeling, sea turtles nesting, a range of low-key activities and—in Heron's case—newly renovated accommodations make these two a "must" in my book. Heron Island is accessed from Gladstone in Central Queensland, and Wilson Island from Heron.

In the far north, there are four major island resorts off Cairns. Lizard and Bedarra are the epitome of luxury, with lodge-style rooms and villas beloved by the rich and famous. Lizard has excellent coral, but it is limited at Bedarra, where the emphasis is on utter privacy for no more than 30 people. Green Island is very close to Cairns and has stylish rooms and good diving. For those at the other end of the budget, Fitzroy offers simple cabins and bunkhouses.

From Townsville, you can choose between the "suburban" style of Magnetic Island, just a stone's throw from the city and offering a large range of motels, hotels, apartments and camping facilities, or the simple but pricey exclusivity of Orpheus (which can also be reached by air from Cairns).

The Whitsunday Island resorts offer the biggest choice of all, with access from Airlie Beach on the mainland or through Hamilton Island airport. Hayman is Australia's most luxurious resort, where you may find yourself rubbing shoulders with world leaders and foreign royalty, but there are plenty of other options if you're not in that league. Hamilton Island is popular with families and has a range of accommodations including hotel rooms, apartments, and *Bures* (a South Pacific-style beach dwelling).

There's limited access to coral from Hamilton, so this is perhaps not the best choice for serious divers, but there is a huge range of water sports and other activities. Long Island has three resorts from the simple but comfortable cabins at Whitsunday Wilderness Lodge to the noisy fun of Club Crocodile and the romantic luxury of Peppers Palm Bay. South Molle and Dunk islands are popular with families and have activities for kids, but limited coral viewing. Hook Island has basic cabins and dorm beds and is popular with students.

Off the Capricorn coast, further south, there are two islands to choose from besides Heron Island. On Great Keppel Island, you will find plenty of action, particularly if you're 18 to 35, and a big range of water sports and activities. But there are no trips to the Outer Reef from Great Keppel. Lady Elliot is, like Heron, right on the reef, but has very basic lodge-style rooms.

All island resorts offer day trips to the Outer Reef, except Great Keppel. From Orpheus, they are charter-only, and from Long Island they are by seaplane only, making it a more expensive proposition.

3 Picking a Boat: Day-Trip or Live-Aboard, Big or Small?

An almost endless variety of day-trip dive boats and live-aboard vessels ply the Reef.

You will experience the Reef's wonders in full if you take a day trip from the mainland or from an island resort. Extended dive or snorkel trips on live-aboard vessels allow you to see more in quantity, but not necessarily more in quality. True, you need to travel on a live-aboard boat to access some sites, such as the wonderful Ribbon Reefs off Port Douglas/Cairns, the shark diving and dramatic drop-offs of the Coral Sea, and renowned Cod Hole off Lizard Island north of Cairns (though Cod Hole is accessible on a day trip if you stay at Lizard Island's very expensive resort). But a day trip will do you fine, whether you dive or snorkel.

Most snorkelers and many divers visit the Reef by taking a full-day trip on one of the big, 400-plus-passenger motorized catamarans that operate out of Cairns, Port Douglas, Townsville, Mission Beach, the Whitsunday mainland and islands, and Bundaberg. These are typically air-conditioned and have a bar, videos, and educational material onboard, and a marine biologist who gives an introductory lecture on the Reef en route. The boats tie up at private permanent pontoons anchored to a platform reef. The pontoons usually have glass-bottom boats and/or semi-submersibles, dry underwater viewing platforms, sun decks, shaded seats, and (sometimes cold) freshwater showers. Four hundred passengers may sound like a lot, but the big boats actually offer a fairly personalized experience. Most people enjoy the big boats because they are more spacious and comfortable, and you can relax on the pontoon between activities.

An alternative to the "big" boats are the multitude of medium-size and smaller boats that take anywhere from around 30 to 100 passengers. Midsize and smaller boats visit two or three Reef sites. Another advantage is that the crew gives you more personal attention; and you have the coral pretty much to yourself. The drawbacks? You have only the deck of the boat to sit on when you get out of the water. Boats of this size are pretty zippy, just about matching the big boats for speed. Small or medium-size boats operate from Port Douglas, Cairns, and the Whitsunday Islands.

If you're not agile, it's best to take a medium-size or large vessel. Most small boats and yachts do not have a lot of seating, and are more difficult to move around on. Often smaller boats and yachts have only a string of marine cable serving as a guardrail, so they're not ideal for little kids.

If you only have 1 day to spend on the Reef, or if you have your heart set on a particular boat, book ahead, as it is possible for a boat to get booked up days in advance. If you don't really mind which vessel you travel with, leave it until you get to Australia. There are so many boats that you can always find a place on one, even in peak season. If you stroll along the marina after about 5pm, when the boats return for the day, you can choose the one you like the best. Live-aboard vacations should always be booked in advance.

Tips **Contacts or Glasses?**

Contact lenses are fine to wear under your mask when snorkeling or diving, although there is a small risk you will lose them in the water. If you wear glasses, travel with a boat that offers **prescription masks;** most do. Some charge an extra A$5–A$10 (US$4–US$8) for them. If you have small children, check that your chosen boat carries **kid-size snorkel gear.**

Snorkelers are often welcome to travel on live-aboard dive boats at a reduced price. This is a good option if you're traveling with a friend who dives, but you don't. Check the itinerary and the boat's facilities to make sure the dive sites are snorkelable (they usually are) and that the boat is pleasant enough for you to spend time on while your buddy dives. Some live-aboard boats are built for super-keen divers who care only about what's under the water, not whether there is a deck for sunbathing or comfortable cabins.

Every boat, big or small, goes to its own area of reef, many miles apart, so you will not encounter passengers from any other vessel. Sure, you encounter the other snorkelers from your own vessel, but the snorkeling area is usually so big you won't feel crowded.

DAY TRIPS TO THE REEF

The fare for most day trips typically includes your snorkel gear—fins, mask, and snorkel—a plentiful buffet lunch, morning and afternoon refreshments, and, on the big boats that have pontoons, free use of the underwater viewing chambers, glass-bottomed boat rides and/or semi-submersible rides. On most boats, a marine naturalist or marine biologist presents a short talk on the Reef's ecology. Aussie boat crews are almost unfailingly good-humored and extremely safety conscious. Typically, about 20% to 30% of passengers are divers, and the rest are snorkelers. Many people enjoy their day on the Reef so much that they book a second trip a day or two later, often aboard the same vessel. *Note:* Almost no boats travel to the Reef on Christmas Day, December 25; FantaSea Cruises in the Whitsunday Islands is one that does.

Expect to pay around A$80 (US$64) per person in a small 30-passenger boat, A$110 (US$88) on a medium-size 100-passenger boat, or A$160 (US$128) on a big 300-passenger motorized cat. Introductory and certified dives cost extra. Expect to pay around A$90 to $110 (US$72–$88) for an introductory dive or A$60 to $100 (US$48–$80) for a certified dive. Sometimes dives are included in a day package, which can be a good value. Some boats charge A$5 to $11 (US$4–$8.80) extra for a half-wet suit, which you will probably want June through August in the Whitsundays north to Port Douglas, and April through September in the Central and Southern Reef areas. Take one if you're inclined to feel the cold at all. A wet suit is a good idea even in summer, as they aid your buoyancy and help protect you from sunburn, coral cuts, and stings from animals and plants.

The Reef Tax

Every passenger over 4 years of age must pay a A$4.50 (US$3.60) Environmental Management Charge (EMC), commonly called "reef tax," on every visit to the Great Barrier Reef with a commercial boat or dive operator. This money goes toward Reef management and conservation. Some operators include it in their prices; most collect it from you onboard.

The A$4.50 (US$3.60) tax is a daily charge, so you will pay it again if you take a second day trip to the Reef. Divers and snorkelers on extended trips of more than 3 days pay a maximum reef tax of A$12 (US$9.60). You may find the cost varies with each tour operator, sometimes being as high as A$6 (US$4.80). This is because some operators add GST (Goods & Services Tax payable to the government) and an administration fee to the base A$4.50.

If your cruise offers a **snorkel safari** ⭐, take it! These small-group expeditions led by a marine biologist show you stuff you would never find on your own. They are worth the extra cost of A$20 (US$16) or so. Quite a few boats offer free snorkel safaris.

Helicopter and/or seaplane flights to the Reef are available from Port Douglas, Cairns, and the Whitsundays, sometimes as a fly/cruise option incorporated with a boat's day trip. Cheap they're not, but they offer spectacular views of the coral and are good if you know you're going to get seasick on a boat or if you're really short on time.

On a day trip, bring a hat, sunscreen, a swimsuit (called "swimmers" or "bathers" in Australia), sunglasses, a towel, a change of underwear so you're not sitting in a wet swimsuit all the way home, a sweater (even in summer because it can get breezy on deck), and cash or a credit card for purchasing dives, disposable underwater cameras, possibly a video of your day, chocolate bars, and so on.

A day trip to the Reef offers you a great opportunity to go **diving** ⭐—even if you've never dived before. Just about all day-trip and live-aboard boats offer **introductory dives** ⭐ for around A$60 to $100 (US$48–$80). These allow anyone to dive to a shallow depth, usually between 6m and 12m (20–40 ft.) in the company of an instructor. You complete a medical questionnaire and a 30-minute briefing session on the boat. Then you make a quick practical lesson in shallow water or just under the surface, doing mask-clearing and regulator-clearing exercises. Then it's time for a 20- to 40-minute foray into a magical underwater world. Most people are thrilled but terrified on their first dive, so the instructor usually keeps in physical contact with you, by either holding your hand or swimming directly above or below you until you feel ready to break loose. They will never stray more than a short distance from your side. Introductory dives are also called "resort" dives, because many resorts offer a similar thing, giving you a couple of hours' instruction in the resort pool before taking you to a nearby reef to dive.

A MULTIDAY CRUISE ALONG THE REEF

The 150-passenger **M.V. *Reef Endeavour*** makes 3- and 4-night (or a combined 7-night) forays from Cairns along the Great Barrier Reef, calling at islands, coral cays, and outer reefs. A 4-day northbound itinerary takes you to tropical Cooktown, the coral cays of Two Isles, Lizard Island, and the fabulous Ribbon Reef No. 5 on the outer reef. A 3-night southbound cruise takes you to Fitzroy Island with its lush rainforest and prolific bird life, snorkeling and diving on Hedley Reef, up the Hinchinbrook Channel and to Dunk Island. Diving is available for certified divers only (A$90/US$72 for a 40-min. dive), but the reef sites are really chosen more for snorkelers. The ship has a naturalist and dive master onboard, glass-bottom and dive boats, a sun deck, a pool, two Jacuzzis, a sauna, a cocktail lounge, and live entertainment. All 75 large cabins—with air-conditioning, telephones, and bathrooms with hair dryers—are on the outside, with sea views. Fares start at A$1,235 (US$988) for the 3-night trip and A$1,646 (US$1,317) for 4 nights, per person, twin-share. The cruise departs weekly; northbound on Mondays and southbound on Fridays. Book through **Captain Cook Cruises** (© **1866/331 3365** in the U.S. and Canada, 01483/222 093 in the U.K., 09/478 6959 in New Zealand, or 02/9206 1122 Sydney sales office; www.captaincook. com.au).

Tips **Feeling Green?**

If you are inclined to be seasick, come prepared with medication or acupressure wristbands. Some boats sell a ginger-based antiseasickness pill, but it doesn't always work! Buy medication from a pharmacy, as boats are not allowed to sell drugs, and take your medication about 30 minutes before you set sail; once you're underway, it's generally too late. Kwell is the brand that most often seems to be recommended by Australian pharmacies, and it is least likely to make you drowsy.

4 Tips for Divers & Snorkelers

DIVING THE REEF

A typical day trip will include two dives. Generally you have to make these in the company of a dive master, but some boats allow you to dive unguided with a buddy. **Mike Ball Dive Expeditions** (see chapters 3 and 5) allows experienced divers over 21 to make solo dives, assuming the company thinks your skills and the dive conditions are up to it. The majority of boats offer videos (for around A$60/US$48) of your dive, guided dives for about A$20 (US$16) extra, and underwater camera hire for about A$80 (US$64). Most dive boats, even the big live-aboard vessels, welcome beginners who want to take a first-time dive in the company of an instructor. Most dives are between about 10m and 18m (40 and 80 ft.).

Virtually all day-trip boats and live-aboard vessels rent complete sets of dive gear, and most visiting divers choose to rent. However, every boat will let you bring your own. Tanks and weights are always supplied. You can expect to save about A$20 (US$16) on quoted day-trip prices if you have your own gear. Queensland law requires all divers to dive with a second, alternative air source. American dive gear is virtually identical to Australian gear, with two main exceptions. The first is that Australia works in metric measurements, so your dive depth is measured in meters. One meter equals 3.28 feet; the maximum permitted dive depth of 60 feet for a diver with open-water certification works out to 18 meters in Australia. The second major difference between American and Aussie gear is that air pressure is measured in PSI in the United States, and "Bar" in Australia. A full tank of 3,000 PSI is roughly equivalent to 200 Bar. If you bring your own gear and you have a European air source, you will need to purchase a converter. A 3mm (⅛-in.) wetsuit is fine year-round, except on the Central Coast and Southern reefs in winter (June–Aug or Sept), when you will need a 5mm suit.

Don't forget to bring your "C" certification card. It's also a good idea to bring along your dive log. Most international dive certificates, including PADI, NAUI, SSI, and BSAC, are recognized in Australia. If you're over 55 years old, check that your chosen boat is willing to let you dive. They may not be insured to accept you.

LEARNING TO DIVE

Dive schools are located in most Great Barrier Reef gateways and on most island resorts.

Beginners' learn-to-dive courses are known as "open-water certification"; this qualifies you to dive anywhere in the world to a depth of 18m (60 ft.). Open-water certification courses typically require 2 days of theory in a pool at the dive company's premises on land, followed by 2 or 3 days diving in the open ocean. A 4-day course usually includes four dives, the minimum required for certification, while a 5-day course gets you nine dives including a night dive. Some dive schools provide the final "at sea" days by making day trips from the mainland or island; others send you out on their liveaboard vessels. Take that into account when comparing prices, as you will need to budget for accommodations and meals on land if the course is the day-trip variety. Diver training and safety standards in Australia are of a high standard, and the courses are all fairly similar, no matter which dive school you choose. Expect to pay A$550 to $600 (US$440–$480) for a 5-day course with a live-aboard component. Budget for your medical certificate (see below), two passport photographs of yourself, and possibly a refundable deposit for course textbooks and materials.

Most dive schools offer courses through advanced, rescue, and dive master, right up to Instructor level. Advanced certification qualifies you to dive to 30m (100 ft.) and introduces you to some specialized areas of diving. Some schools also do short specialty courses such as "Underwater Naturalist" or "Wreck Diver." Most schools on the Great Barrier Reef teach PADI qualifications. Most companies' open-water certification courses commence every day, or at least several times a week.

Travelers pressed for time can do a referral course, where you study your theory work at home, do a few hours of pool work at a dive center in your home country, and then spend 2 or 3 days on the Great Barrier Reef doing your qualifying dives. Expect the dive instructor to grill you on your theory again before you hit the water. Many Great Barrier Reef dive schools offer these courses.

To undertake a dive course in Australia, you'll need a **medical certificate,** which must come from an *Australian* doctor trained in hyperbaric medicine, specifically stating that you are fit for scuba diving. See "Diving & Snorkeling Safety" below for conditions that might preclude you from diving. Virtually all dive schools will arrange the exam for you; expect to pay around $50 (US$40) for it. Remember to allow time to complete the medical before you commence your course. You also need to be able to swim 200m (650 ft.).

Look But Don't Touch

Coral is a delicate creature. Soft corals can withstand a caress from your fingers, but hard corals cannot. Touching the soft little polyps that poke out of hard coral's limestone casing is enough to kill them, especially if you have sunscreen on your fingers. Try never to stand on coral or to kick it while snorkeling.

The Great Barrier Reef is a Marine Park, and removing coral (living or dead), shells, or any other natural item is an offense.

Litter and inorganic matter lost or thrown overboard is a *major* threat to marine life.

The minimum age for learning to dive is 12, with no maximum age limit.

Dive schools appear under the relevant regional chapters.

SNORKELING THE REEF

Don't think snorkeling is the poor cousin to diving. The coral's rich colors need lots of light, so the brightest marine life is right under the surface. Snorkeling is easy to master. You see most and feel more comfortable if you look 45 degrees ahead when snorkeling, not straight down or straight ahead. To keep your mask from filling with water, keep all your hair out of it. Fit the mask's strap high on the back of your head, not low. Flippers should fit closely, but a little too big is better than a little too tight. Kick with long, slow movements from the waist, not from the knees.

While the crew on big boats are usually happy to tutor you in snorkeling, as a rule the crew on smaller boats are more solicitous, simply because they have more time to be. If you are a first-time snorkeler, Port Douglas has a perfect boat for you—snorkeling specialist **Wavelength** (see chapter 4), whose crew get into the water with you to teach you the ropes. Another tip for beginning swimmers or snorkelers is to choose a cay (like Michaelmas Cay, Upolu Cay or Green Island off Cairns, the Low Isles off Port Douglas, Beaver Cay off Mission Beach, or Heron Island off Gladstone) if you can't swim well. You can wade into the coral off the shore. All boats post snorkeling scouts to watch for anyone in trouble and to count heads periodically. While not all boats have flotation vests for snorkelers, virtually all have some kind of **flotation device,** usually a 2m (7-ft.) colored foam tube that you tuck across your chest under your arms. If you think you will have trouble staying above water without a flotation device, check which aids your boat offers before booking.

5 Diving & Snorkeling Safety

HEALTH HAZARDS

Some health conditions will prevent you from making a dive, due to Queensland's medical diving regulations. You are unlikely to pass a dive medical if you suffer from asthma, pneumothorax, epilepsy, fainting spells, brain or nervous-system disorders, heart disease, diabetes requiring insulin, a perforated ear drum, or if you have had heart surgery or are pregnant. Other conditions that may prevent your diving are bronchitis or chest complaints, blood-pressure difficulties, lung disease, ear problems, or recent illnesses or surgery. Many boats will ask you to complete a medical questionnaire onboard, which the dive master will assess. If you think there is a risk you may be rejected for diving, check with the dive master at the time you book your place on the boat. They can run your condition by their dive doctors, or refer you to a doctor for a medical examination before you take the boat trip. If you are taking medication (apart from the contraceptive pill), bring a letter from your doctor stating you may dive. That helps the dive master give you the okay to hit the water.

Diving safety standards are extremely high in Australia, and accidents are rare. Nonetheless, when diving, you will be asked to sign a disclaimer form releasing the dive company from indemnity for any injury to you. One of the things the form will have you state is that you are aware that in the event of an accident requiring recompression, the nearest recompression chamber may be a long way away. For example, from Cairns and Port Douglas, the nearest one is in Townsville, about 450km (279 miles) south of Cairns. Most boats sell a A$16 (US$13) insurance policy onboard, covering you for medical evacuation and diving-related medical treatment in the case of a diving accident. The "Health & Insurance" section in chapter 2 has more details on travel and diving insurance.

Remember, you can fly before you dive, but you must complete your last dive at least 24 hours before you fly to an altitude of 300m or more (about 1,000 ft.). This catches a lot of people off guard when they are preparing to fly the day after a visit to the Reef.

DEADLY & DANGEROUS!

Aussies love regaling wide-eyed visitors with tales of all the critters that can have you sent home in a coffin from Down Under. Don't get too alarmed. Most deadly Aussie animals are more scared of you than you are of them.

If you have the uncommon misfortune to be bitten or stung by a dangerous creature:

1. Keep calm and immobile.
2. Apply first aid (see below).
3. Send for medical help *immediately.*

Here is a rundown of the main scary creatures you may encounter on north Queensland beaches and the Great Barrier Reef. This is not an exhaustive list. A good rule of thumb is this: Don't touch or pick up any marine plant or animal you don't know to be safe.

"Stingers" (also called box jellyfish, or sea wasp): The sting of this pale, hard-to-spot jellyfish, about 20cm (8 in.) across with tentacles up to 4m (13 ft.) long, has killed more than 70 people in northern Australian seas since 1900. Children, who may die within minutes of the sting, are the most common victims. Found in mainland waters, rivers, and mangroves north of the Tropic of Capricorn (which cuts through Rockhampton), stingers' presence puts a stop to ocean swimming from September or October to April or May—throughout summer, in other words. During these times, swim only in areas that are guarded by safety nets, erected at the most popular beaches.

Until recently, it was thought that because stingers die and break up outside calm coastal waters, it was completely safe to swim year-round off islands and reefs. This conventional wisdom has been challenged in recent years with two deaths caused by stings from the thimble-size Irakandji jellyfish. Although the risk is small, it does exist on the islands and you should take advice from local lifeguards before entering the water during stinger season. The Irakandji is also small enough to sneak through the mesh of stinger nets.

What to Do: A sting causes shock to the heart (that's what kills you), breathing difficulties, red blood cell damage, and red/brown/purple welts on the skin. Apply vinegar to the tentacles to disable them, and then remove the tentacles. Local councils leave bottles of vinegar on popular beaches for this purpose. Touching the tentacles without vinegar will cause more poison to be released. The welts will be scars if you do not take anti-venom. Apply mouth-to-mouth resuscitation and/or cardiac massage if breathing is difficult.

Blue-ringed Octopus: Kids are easily tempted to pick up this pretty little brown octopus covered with bright blue circles. Up to 20cm (8 in.) across, it is common all over Australia, often washed up in tidal rock pools. It can inject venom by biting with its sharp beak, a bite you may not feel. The venom kills by paralysis.

What to Do: Apply the pressure first-aid method (see below). Apply mouth-to-mouth resuscitation if breathing is difficult.

Stonefish: Looking *exactly* like the rough brown rock or coral it's sitting on, this prickly-looking fish has 13 spines along its back, which it will inject into your hand or foot if you handle or stand on it. The pain is strong enough to bring on a state of shock and collapse. Although not all victims die, death is easily caused by heart muscle damage. Stonefish wounds are deep and tear your flesh, so foreign matter easily gets stuck in them. It is not unknown for victims to die of tetanus later, instead of the sting.

Common all along the Queensland coast, stonefish also come in a grayish species that buries itself in sand on shallow tidal flats. Stonefish grow up to about 45cm (18 in.) long, but they can be a lot smaller. Rubber-soled gym shoes are no protection against the spines. The safest way to avoid them is to *never* stand on or touch rocks in the water, and avoid wading in the water on tidal flats.

What to Do: Immerse the sting in hot water, which usually minimizes the pain. Using a pressure bandage is not a good idea, as this is one case where you want the venom to spread to decrease the pain at the wound's site. Apply mouth-to-mouth resuscitation and/or cardiac massage if breathing is difficult.

Stingrays: You will likely see at least a few of Australia's many ray species, either on the Reef or feeding at high tide at the water's edge on the beach. Because they lightly bury themselves in the sand, they can be impossible to spot. A sting occurs when you stand on or threaten the animal and it flicks its spiny tail at you, injecting venom. Shuffle your feet in the sand and you're less likely to stand on them. While the stings are by no means always life threatening, in extreme cases they can cause organ rupture. Tetanus can infect the wound.

What to Do: Treat as you would a stonefish sting (see above).

Sea Snakes: All Australia's sea snake species are venomous, and 16 species of them live on the Reef. Divers are more likely to encounter them. Sea snakes are curious by nature, so one may swim up to you for a closer look; but they are unlikely to bite unless you scare them. This may be an old wives' tale, but a dive operator told me that a sea snake would need to bite you, say, on the skin flap between your fingers to get a good grip, as they cannot open their jaws wide enough to bite a human being's leg or arm easily. No snorkeler or diver has died of a sea snake bite on the Great Barrier Reef.

What to Do: Apply the pressure first-aid method (see below) and keep the victim still.

Cone Shells: While not a famous name on the "deadly creatures" list, many Aussie species of cone shell—a long shellfish shaped like a blunted cone, up to 30cm (1 ft.) long—pose a danger. You will likely come across them buried in the sand under the water. Pick one up or stand on it, and it can "bite" you with its harpoon-like teeth about 1cm (½ in.) long at the end of its long, fleshy snout. The venom causes pain, then numbness, then a slow paralysis that starts with a tingling around the mouth, then breathing difficulties, coma, and possibly death.

What to Do: Apply the pressure first-aid method (see below) and keep the victim still. Apply mouth-to-mouth resuscitation if breathing is difficult.

BUT WHAT ABOUT SHARKS?

"Don't worry, the crocs ate 'em all" is a common reply to this question from Queensland boat operators with a dented sense of humor. Seriously, sharks are not a great threat. Black-tipped and white-tipped reef sharks are common and generally harmless. Great whites do exist in north Queensland, but sightings are very rare; their home is really the cold, deep Southern Ocean. Dangerous tiger sharks are common in north Queensland's warm shallow waters, but again, snorkelers and divers rarely see them. Hammerheads, another potentially dangerous species, are often seen by divers, almost never by snorkelers; they usually swim away from people. Sharks are generally scared away by crowds of people.

SO WHAT ABOUT CROCS?

Estuarine crocodiles (known in Australia as saltwater crocodiles) inhabit the mainland rivers of north Queensland as far south as

---

Tips **The Pressure First Aid Method**

Immobilize the wounded part of the body and apply a wide, tight pressure bandage—not a tourniquet—to the whole limb if possible. This keeps the venom under the bandage and stops it from spreading to organs. Don't remove the victim's clothes unless you can do so easily, as moving encourages the venom to travel. A pressure bandage can remain comfortably on the limb indefinitely, unlike a tourniquet, which causes nerve and artery damage and begins to kill tissue after about 20 minutes. Sources include *Venomous Creatures of Australia* by Dr. Struan K. Sutherland (Oxford University Press, revised edition 1988).

Tips **Ouch! Reef Safety Warnings**

Coral is sharp; coral cuts aren't dangerous but they're painful, and they can get infected quickly. Clean any wounds carefully, and rinse with fresh water. Ask your cruise-boat crew for antiseptic cream, and apply it to grazes as soon as you leave the water.

The Australian sun burns you fast. You're facing down when you snorkel, so put sunscreen on your back, neck, the backs of your legs—especially behind your knees—and behind your ears. It stays on best if you apply it a good 20 minutes before you enter the water. Reapply when you leave the water. Wearing a T-shirt in the water is good protection against the sun.

If you lose your group or buddy while diving, search for *1 minute only,* then surface and signal for help or swim to the boat. International marine safety signals are as follows: Placing one or both hands on your head means "I'm okay." Raising an arm means "I'm not about to go toes up, but I need some assistance." Waving both arms frantically means "Get me out of the water this second!"

Rockhampton, and possibly even farther south. Despite their name, saltwater crocodiles make their home in *freshwater* rivers. They can and do swim in the ocean and, on a very few occasions, have been spotted on the Reef. Your chance of meeting a crocodile on the Reef is very small. Great Barrier Reef islands are regarded as croc-free, as none has the long, deep, still, murky rivers that crocs like.

"Salties" are dangerous, move with great speed and ferocity, and can be hidden 1 inch beneath the surface of a muddy rainforest river. Unlike most deadly Aussie animals who want to avoid you, crocs are only too happy to meet you. They can't run for more than a few meters, so they use surprise to attack, sometimes leaping a long way out of the water to snare their prey. When near mainland waterways, mangroves or estuaries in north Queensland, *never* swim in the water; don't stand on logs over the water; don't lean over the side of a boat; don't stand at the water's edge, especially if you are fishing; don't clean fish or throw fish remains into the river (bury them instead); and camp at least 25m (82 ft.) from the water's edge.

2

Planning Your Trip: The Basics

This chapter aims to answer the practical questions that may pop up as you're planning your trip to the Great Barrier Reef: How will you get there, how much will it cost, and other pesky details. We've done the legwork—ferreting out ways to nail down smart deals on airfares, listing package companies, and more—so you won't have to.

1 Visitor Information

The **Australian Tourist Commission (ATC)** is the best source of information on traveling Down Under. Its website, **www.australia. com**, has more than 10,000 pages of listings for tour operators, hotels, car-rental companies, specialist travel outfitters, public holidays, maps, distance charts, suggested itineraries, and much more. It provides you with information tailored to travelers from your country of origin, including good-value packages and deals. By signing up for the free online Travel Club, you will be e-mailed newsletters with hot deals, major events, and the like. The ATC only operates a website to dispense information, not telephone lines. The ATC also maintains a network of "Aussie Specialist" travel agents in cities across the United States, Canada, the United Kingdom, New Zealand, and other countries. These agents are trained in booking the best destinations, hotels, deals, and tours in Oz. Get a referral to the nearest Aussie Specialists by clicking the "Talk to An Aussie Specialist" button on the ATC website.

If you are not online and want information on snorkeling or diving the Great Barrier Reef, you are probably better off using other sources such as this guidebook, word-of-mouth recommendations, magazine articles, or travel agents. Choose a destination, and then either contact the snorkel/dive operators recommended in this guide, or contact the **nearest local tourist office** for a list of dive operators in that area. The contact details for visitor centers appear under "Visitor Information" in each destination chapter in this book. **Dive Queensland** (the Queensland Dive Tourism Association; ✆ **07/4051 1510;** www.dive-queensland.com.au) puts you in touch with member dive operators in that state who stick to a code of ethics. That's not to say that companies who are not members are not reputable or professional. Virtually every dive company in Queensland has high safety standards.

Government marketing bureau **Tourism Queensland** operates a good website at www.queensland-holidays.com.au (click the "North American Site" tab on the home page for advice tailored to American travelers) that contains links to snorkel and scuba dive operators.

Diversion Dive Travel & Training (© **07/4039 0200;** www.diversionoz.com) is a Cairns-based travel agent that specializes in dive holidays on the Great Barrier Reef, as well as in Australia's many other good dive locations. It books day-trip cruises and diving holidays on live-aboard vessels, as well as dive courses (its proprietors are both dive instructors so they have a feel for the right course), island resorts with diving, accommodations, and nondiving tours. It also sells DAN (Divers Alert Network) insurance.

You'll also find information via the **Great Barrier Reef Visitors Bureau,** a private company offering itinerary planning and booking services for a wide range of accommodations and tours throughout north Queensland. Contact them at © **07/3876 4644,** fax 07/3876 4645, or online at www.great-barrier-reef.com.

Keen divers may find these books helpful: *Peter Stone's Dive Australia* is a 608-page guidebook to more than 2,000 dive sites, plus some dive operators, all over Australia, including the Great Barrier Reef. It is published by Australian dive publisher **Oceans Enterprises** (© **03/5182 5108;** www.oceans.com.au). For readers outside Australia, the latest edition (1999) costs US$35, including postage. The best guidebooks to dive sites on the Great Barrier Reef are author Tom Byron's series of Dive Guides to the "Southern Great Barrier Reef," the "Central Great Barrier Reef," "Cairns and Northern Great Barrier Reef," and "Whitsunday Islands." They are available from Oceans Enterprises (above) for between A$26 and $32 (US$21 and $26).

USEFUL WEBSITES

We refer you to many useful websites throughout this book. Here are some additional general ones you may find helpful:

Great Barrier Reef Marine Park Authority   Townsville is the headquarters of this governmental body, which is responsible for the Reef's ecological and commercial well-being. A visit to its showcase, **Reef HQ** ⨝ (see chapter 5), is a superb introduction to this underwater fairyland.

www.gbrmpa.gov.au

Australian Bureau of Meteorology   How cold does it really get in Cairns? Find out here, and check forecasts, average temperatures and rainfall, and other climatic considerations for just about any point in Australia you care to visit.

www.bom.gov.au

Australian Embassy, Washington, D.C.   While not aimed only at vacationers, this site posts loads of links to sites on tourism, as well as cultural and educational matters; briefings on the economy, trade, sport, geography, and the Aussie people; events listings; and more. It's written with North Americans in mind.

www.austemb.org

Queensland Bed & Breakfast Association   More than 100 properties, some of them lovely old timber Queenslander houses with wide verandas, can be located and booked here.

www.bnb.au.com

Bed & Breakfast and Farmstay Association of Far North Queensland   Link to the websites of B&Bs and farmstays in and around Cairns, Port Douglas and the Daintree rainforest area, Mission Beach, and Townsville.

www.bnbnq.com.au

Cairns Online   A detailed source for travelers containing links to the websites of a huge range of fishing charters, cruise boats, yachting trips, wildlife attractions, rainforest safaris, tour operators, accommodations, and more. It covers not only Cairns but Kuranda, Port Douglas, and the Daintree as well.

www.cairns.aust.com

Environmental Protection Agency   This site has descriptions of all Queensland's national parks, including major things to see and do in each one, hiking-trail descriptions, campsites and fees, tips on exploring, when to go, visitor facilities, and more.

www.epa.qld.gov.au

Tourism Tropical North Queensland   If you're visiting Cairns, Port Douglas, Mission Beach, or other parts of north Queensland, north Queensland's official tourism marketing site links you to websites of Great Barrier Reef cruises, dive operators, 4WD rainforest safaris, tour providers, accommodations, and more. It has tips on getting around north Queensland and suggested itineraries.

www.tropicalaustralia.com.au

2 Entry Requirements & Customs

ENTRY REQUIREMENTS

Along with a current passport valid for the duration of your stay, the Australian government requires a visa from visitors of every nation, except New Zealand, to be issued before you arrive. If you are a short-term visitor, the process is quick and easy and can be done in a few minutes on the Internet (for a small cost), using the Australian government's new Electronic Travel Authority (ETA). This is an electronic visa that takes the place of a stamp in your passport.

You can apply for an ETA yourself, or get your travel agent or airline to do it for you when you book your plane ticket (they may charge you extra to do this).

Apply online at **www.eta.immi.gov.au**. There is a A$20 (US$16) charge, which you can pay for by credit card (AE, DC MC, or V). If you do not have a criminal conviction and are in good health, your ETA should be approved in less than 30 seconds. You can also apply for an ETA at Australian embassies, high commissions, and consulates (see below).

Tourists should apply for a Visitor ETA. It's free and valid for as many visits to Australia as you like of up to 3 months each within a 1-year period. Tourists may not work in Australia, so if you are visiting for business, you have two choices: apply for a free Short Validity Business ETA, which is valid for a single visit of 3 months within a 1-year period, or pay A$65 (US$52) to apply for a Long Validity Business ETA, which entitles you to as many 3-month stays in Australia as you like for the life of your passport. Children traveling on their parent's passport must have their own ETA.

If your travel agent, airline, or cruise ship is not connected to the ETA system, you will still need to apply for a visa the old-fashioned way—by taking or mailing your passport, a completed visa application form, and the appropriate payment to your nearest Australian embassy or consulate. In the United States, Canada, the United Kingdom, Ireland, and many other countries, most agents and airlines are ETA-compatible, but your cruise lines may not be yet. You will also need to do it this way if you are something other than a tourist or a business traveler—for example, a student studying in Australia; a business person staying longer than 3 months; a long-term resident; a sportsperson; a member of the media; a performer; or a member of a social group or cultural exchange. If you fall into one of these categories, you will need to apply for a Temporary Residence visa. There is a A$65 (US$52) processing fee for non-ETA tourist and business visas for stays of up to 3 months, and A$165 (US$132) for business visas for stays between 3 months and 4 years. Non-ETA visa application fees for other kinds of travelers vary, from nil to thousands of dollars. Contact the nearest Australian embassy, consulate, or high commission to check what forms of payment they accept.

Apply for non-ETA visas at Australian embassies, consulates, and high commissions. In the United States, apply to the Australian Embassy, 1601 Massachusetts Ave. NW, Washington, DC 20036 (© **202/797 3000;** dimia-washington@dfat.gov.au). The website of the Australian Embassy in North America is www.austemb.org. In Canada, contact the Australian High Commission, 50 O'Connor St., No. 710, Ottawa, ON K1P 6L2 (© **1888/990-8888;** www.ahc-ottawa.org). For business-visa inquiries in the United States and Canada, call © **800/579-7664.** In the United Kingdom and Ireland, contact the Australian High Commission, Australia House, The Strand, London WC2B 4LA (© **020/09065 508900** for 24-hr. recorded information, or 020/7379 4334; www.australia.org.uk). There is no counter service at the High Commission in London, and you should obtain an application form for a non-ETA visa by post or via the Internet at the Australian Department of Immigration and Multicultural Affairs website (www.immi.gov.au). This site also has a good explanation of the ETA system.

Allow at least a month for processing of non-ETA visas.

CUSTOMS & QUARANTINE

WHAT YOU CAN BRING IN   The duty-free allowance in Australia is A$400 (US$320) or, for those under 18, A$200 (US$160). Anyone over 18 can bring in no more than 250 cigarettes or 250 grams of cigars or other tobacco products, 1.125 liters (41 fl. oz.) of alcohol, and "dutiable goods" to the value of A$400 (US$320), or A$200 (US$160) if you are under 18. "Dutiable goods" are luxury items like perfume concentrate, watches, jewelry, furs, plus gifts of any kind. Keep this in mind if you come bearing presents for family and friends in Australia; gifts given to you also count toward the dutiable limit. Personal goods you're taking with you when you leave are usually exempt from duty but if you are returning with valuable goods that you already own, you should file form B263. Customs officers do not collect duty of less than A$50 (US$40) as long as you declared the goods in the first place. A helpful brochure, available from Australian consulates or Customs offices, is *Know Before You Go.* For more information, contact **Australian Customs**

Services, GPO Box 8, Sydney NSW 2001 (© **1300/363 263** in Australia or 02/6275-6666), or check out www.customs.gov.au.

Cash in any currency, and other currency instruments such as traveler's checks, under a value of A$10,000 need not be declared. Firearms in Australia are strictly controlled; contact the nearest Australian diplomatic post for advice on importing a handgun.

Australia is a signatory to the Convention on International Trade in Endangered Species (CITES), which restricts or bans the import of products made from protected wildlife. Examples of the numerous restricted items are coral, giant clam, wild cats, monkey, zebra, crocodile or alligator, bear, some types of caviar, American ginseng, and orchid products. Banned items include ivory, tortoise (marine turtle) shell, products made from rhinoceros or tiger, and sturgeon caviar. Bear this in mind if you stop in other countries en route to Australia where souvenirs from items such as these may be widely sold. Australian authorities may seize and not return the items to you.

Because Australia is an island, it is free of many agricultural and livestock diseases. To keep it that way, strict quarantine applies to importing plants, animals, and their products, including food. "Sniffer" dogs are used at airports to detect these products (as well as drugs). Some items may be held for treatment and returned to you; others may be confiscated; others may be held over for you to take with you when you leave the country. Amnesty trash bins are available before you reach the immigration counters in airport arrivals halls for items such as fruit. Don't be alarmed if, just before landing, the flight attendants spray the aircraft cabin (with products approved by the World Health Organization) to kill potentially disease-bearing insects that entered the plane in a foreign country. For more information on what is and is not allowed entry, contact the nearest Australian embassy or consulate, or contact **Australia's Department of Agriculture, Fisheries and Forestry,** which runs the Australian Quarantine and Inspection Service (© **02/6272 3933;** www.affa.gov.au). Its website contains a list of many restricted or banned foodstuffs, animal and plant products, and other items.

WHAT YOU CAN TAKE HOME   Check with your country's Customs or Foreign Affairs department for the latest guidelines—including information on items that are not allowed to be brought into your home country—just before you leave home.

Returning **U.S. citizens** who have been away for at least 48 hours are allowed to bring back, once every 30 days, $800 worth of merchandise duty-free. You'll be charged a flat rate of 4% duty on the next $1,000 worth of purchases. Be sure to have your receipts handy. On mailed gifts, the duty-free limit is $200. You cannot bring fresh foodstuffs into the United States; tinned foods, however, are allowed. For more information, contact the **U.S. Customs Service,** 1300 Pennsylvania Ave. NW, Washington, DC 20229 (*©* **202/354-1000**) and request the free pamphlet *Know Before You Go.* It's also available on the Web at www.customs.gov. (Click on "Travel" then "Know Before You Go Online Brochure.")

For a clear summary of **Canadian** rules, write for the booklet *I Declare,* issued by the **Canada Border Services Agency** (*©* **800/461-9999** in Canada, or 204/983-3500; www.cbsa-asfc.gc.ca). Canada allows its citizens a C$750 exemption, and you're allowed to bring back duty-free 1 carton of cigarettes, 1 can of tobacco, 40 imperial ounces of liquor, and 50 cigars. In addition, you're allowed to mail gifts to Canada valued at less than C$60 a day, provided they're unsolicited and don't contain alcohol or tobacco (write on the package "Unsolicited gift, under $60 value"). All valuables should be declared before departure from Canada, including serial numbers of valuables you already own, such as expensive cameras. *Note:* The $750 exemption can only be used once a year and only after an absence of 7 days.

U.K. citizens returning from a non-EU country have a Customs allowance of 200 cigarettes; 50 cigars; 250 grams of smoking tobacco; 2 liters of still table wine; 1 liter of spirits or strong liqueurs (over 22% volume); 2 liters of fortified wine, sparkling wine or other liqueurs; 60cc (ml) perfume; 250cc (ml) of toilet water; and £145 worth of all other goods, including gifts and souvenirs. People under 17 cannot have the tobacco or alcohol allowance. For more information, contact HM Customs & Excise at *©* **0845/010 9000** (from outside the U.K., 020/8929 0152), or consult their website at www.hmce.gov.uk.

For New Zealand Customs information, contact **New Zealand Customs,** The Customhouse, 17–21 Whitmore St., Box 2218, Wellington (*©* **04/473 6099** or 0800/428 786; www.customs.govt.nz).

3 Money

CASH & CURRENCY

The Australian dollar is divided into 100 cents. Coins come in 5¢, 10¢, 20¢, and 50¢ pieces (all silver in color) and $1 and $2 pieces (gold in color). The 50-cent piece is 12-sided. Prices ending in a

The Australian Dollar, the U.S. Dollar & the British Pound

For U.S. Readers   The rate of exchange used to calculate the dollar values given in this book was US$1 = approximately A$1.25 (or A$1 = US 80¢).

For British Readers   The rate of exchange used to calculate the pound values in the accompanying table was £1 = A$2.45 (or A$1 = 40p).

Note: International exchange rates can fluctuate markedly. Check the latest rate when you plan your trip. The table below, and all the prices in this book, should be used only as a guide.

A$	US$	UK£	A$	US$	UK£
0.25	0.20	0.10	30.00	24.00	12.00
0.50	0.40	0.20	35.00	28.00	14.00
1.00	0.80	0.40	40.00	32.00	16.00
2.00	1.60	0.80	45.00	36.00	18.00
3.00	2.40	1.20	50.00	40.00	20.00
4.00	3.20	1.60	55.00	44.00	22.00
5.00	4.00	2.00	60.00	48.00	24.00
6.00	4.80	2.40	65.00	52.00	26.00
7.00	5.60	2.80	70.00	56.00	28.00
8.00	6.40	3.20	75.00	60.00	30.00
9.00	7.20	3.60	80.00	64.00	32.00
10.00	8.00	4.00	85.00	68.00	34.00
15.00	12.00	6.00	90.00	72.00	36.00
20.00	16.00	8.00	95.00	76.00	38.00
25.00	20.00	10.00	100.00	80.00	40.00

variant of 1¢ and 2¢ (for example, 78¢ or $2.71), are rounded up or down to the nearest 5¢. Bank notes come in denominations of $5, $10, $20, $50, and $100.

ATMs

Most ATMs in Australia will be linked to a network that most likely includes your bank at home. **Cirrus** (℗ 800/424-7787; www.mastercard.com) and **PLUS** (℗ 800/843-7587; www.visa.com) are the two most popular networks in the United States; call or check online for ATM locations at your destination. Be sure you know your four-digit PIN before you leave home and be sure to find out your daily withdrawal limit before you depart. You can also get cash advances on your credit card at an ATM. Keep in mind that

What Things Cost in Cairns	US$
Taxi from airport to downtown Cairns	12.00
Local bus from downtown to Trinity Beach	4.00
Double at Shangri-La The Marina (deluxe)	368.00
Double at Cairns Plaza Hotel (moderate)	104.00–116.00
Double at Lilybank Bed & Breakfast (inexpensive)	70.00–88.00
Dinner for one, without wine, at Fishlips (deluxe)	40.00
Dinner for one, without wine, at Perrotta's (moderate)	20.00
Glass of beer (10 oz.)	2.10
Coca-Cola	1.60
Cup of coffee	2.00
Admission to Tjapukai Aboriginal Cultural Park	23.00
Roll of ASA 100 Kodacolor film, 36 exposures	6.85
Movie ticket	8.80

credit-card companies try to protect themselves from theft by limiting the funds someone can withdraw away from home. It's therefore best to call your credit-card company before you leave and let them know where you're going and how much you plan to spend. You'll get the best exchange rate if you withdraw money from an ATM, but keep in mind that many banks impose a fee every time a card is used at an ATM in a different city or bank. On top of this, the bank from which you withdraw cash may charge its own fee.

In Outback areas, carry cash and a credit card because ATMs can be conspicuous by their absence in small country towns, and shopkeepers in remote parts may not cash traveler's checks.

CREDIT CARDS

Visa and MasterCard are universally accepted in Australia, but American Express and Diners Club are considerably less so. Always carry a little cash, because many merchants in Australia will not take cards for purchases under A$15 (US$12) or so. If your credit card is linked to your bank account, it is good for withdrawing emergency cash from an ATM (keep in mind that interest starts accruing immediately on credit-card cash advances).

Almost every credit-card company has a toll-free number that you can call if your wallet or purse is stolen. Here are the Australia-wide numbers for the three major cards: **American Express** (© **1300/132 639**), **MasterCard** (© **1800/120 113**), and **Visa** (© **1800/805 341**).

Report your stolen wallet to the police, because your credit-card company may require a police report number.

TRAVELER'S CHECKS

Major towns and cities in Australia have 24-hour ATMs, and virtually every establishment, even Outback gas stations, accepts credit cards. Traveler's checks are not nearly as widely accepted.

If you do buy checks, get them in Australian dollars. Checks in U.S. dollars are widely accepted at banks, big hotels, currency exchanges, and shops in major tourist regions used to selling to customers from overseas, but most other shops, restaurants, and businesses will have no idea what the current exchange rate is when you present a U.S. check. Another advantage of Australian-dollar checks is that two of the largest Aussie banks, ANZ and Westpac, cash them free. It will cost you around A$5 to $11 (US$4–$8.80) to cash checks in foreign currency at most Australian banks.

Keep a record of your checks' serial numbers, separately from the checks of course. To report lost or stolen American Express traveler's checks, call ⓒ **1300/132 639** anywhere in Australia.

4 When to Go

When it is winter in the Northern Hemisphere, Australia is basking in the Southern Hemisphere's summer, and vice versa. Midwinter in Australia is July and August, and the hottest months are November through March. Remember, unlike in the Northern Hemisphere, the farther south you go in Australia, the colder it gets.

HIGH & LOW TRAVEL SEASONS

It might surprise you to learn that the peak travel season in the most popular parts of Australia, including most of the Great Barrier Reef, is winter—that is, June, July, and August. Airfares to Australia offered by U.S. airlines are lowest from mid-April to late August.

Diving high season on the Great Barrier Reef is from June to December; peak visibility is August through January. However, the marine life will wow you any time, and visibility is good year-round.

The best time to visit **Cairns, Port Douglas, Mission Beach,** and **Townsville** is from April to September or October, when daytime temperatures are around 66° to 89°F (19°–31°C) and it rarely rains. Maybe take a sweater in June, July, and August. These 3 months are the busiest in these parts, so you'll need to book accommodations and tours in advance—you can look forward to paying higher accommodation rates then, too. From October/November to March, north

Queensland suffers a summertime Wet Season. It is just too hot, too humid, too rainy, or all three, to do much comfortably then (although Townsville, being in a rain shadow, misses the worst of the rain).

Any time is a good time to visit the **Whitsunday Islands.** Winter is pleasantly warm, requiring the odd sweater by day, maybe a light jacket at night. **Central and Southern Queensland** can be chilly in winter, enough to need trousers and a sweater, but still warm enough to snorkel and dive with a wetsuit. Summer from the Whitsundays and southward is still very hot and humid, but not unbearably so, and the Wet Season does not spread this far south. No part of the Great Barrier Reef is immune to cyclones between around November and March, but they're rare enough that you shouldn't let that put you off.

Try to avoid Australia from Boxing Day (Dec 26) to the end of January, when Aussies take their summer vacations. Hotel rooms and seats on planes are as scarce as hen's teeth, and it's a rare airline or hotel that will discount even one dollar off their full tariffs.

Cairns' Average Temperatures (°F) and Rainfall

	Jan	Feb	Mar	Apr	May	Jun	Jul	Aug	Sep	Oct	Nov	Dec
Max (°F)	88	88	88	84	82	79	79	81	82	84	88	88
Max (°C)	31	31	31	29	28	26	26	27	28	29	31	31
Min (°F)	75	75	73	72	68	64	63	63	66	70	72	73
Min (°C)	24	24	23	22	20	18	17	17	19	21	22	23
Days of rain	18	19	19	18	14	10	9	8	8	8	10	14

Source: Australian Bureau of Meteorology

HOLIDAYS

In addition to the period from December 26 to the end of January, when Aussies take their summer vacations, the 4 days at Easter (Good Friday–Easter Monday) and all school holiday periods are very busy, so book ahead. The school year in Australia is broken into four semesters, with 2-week holidays falling around the last half of April, the last week of June and the first week of July, and the last week of September and the first week of October. Some states break at slightly different dates.

Almost everything shuts down on Boxing Day (Dec 26) and Good Friday, and much is closed New Year's Day, Easter Sunday, and Easter Monday. Most things are closed until 1pm, if not all day, on Anzac Day, a World War I commemorative day on April 25.

Among other major public holidays in Queensland are Australia Day (Jan 26), Labour Day (1st Mon in May), and Queen's Birthday (2nd Mon in June).

5 Health & Insurance

You don't have a lot to worry about healthwise on a trip to Australia. Medical and hygiene standards are high. No vaccinations are needed to enter the country unless you have been in a yellow-fever danger zone—that is, South America or Africa—in the past 6 days.

WHAT TO DO IF YOU GET SICK AWAY FROM HOME

If you worry about getting sick away from home, you may want to consider medical travel insurance (see the section on insurance below). In most cases, however, your existing health plan will provide all the coverage you need. Be sure to carry your identification card in your wallet.

If you suffer from a chronic illness, consult your doctor before your departure. For conditions like epilepsy, diabetes, or heart problems, wear a **Medic Alert Identification Tag** (© **800/432 5378;** www.medicalert.org), which will alert doctors to your condition and give them access to your records through Medic Alert's 24-hour hot line. Membership is US$35, then US$20 for annual renewal.

Pack prescription medications in your carry-on luggage, and carry prescription medications in their original containers. Also bring along copies of your prescriptions in case you lose your pills or run out. Carry the generic name of prescription medicines, in case a local pharmacist is unfamiliar with the brand name. If you need more medication while you're in Australia, you will need to get an Australian doctor to write the prescription for you. Doctors are listed under "M" for Medical Practitioners in the Australian Yellow Pages.

And don't forget sunglasses and an extra pair of contact lenses or prescription glasses.

WARNING: SUNSHINE MAY BE HAZARDOUS TO YOUR HEALTH

There's a reason Australians have the world's highest death rate from skin cancer—the country's intense sunlight. Limit your exposure to the sun, especially during the first few days of your trip, and always avoid it from 11am to 3pm in summer and 10am to 2pm in winter. Use a broad-spectrum sunscreen with a high protection factor (SPF 30+). Wear a broad-brimmed hat that covers the back of your neck, ears, and face (not a baseball cap), and a long-sleeved shirt. Kids need more protection than adults do.

Don't even think about coming to Oz without sunglasses, or you'll spend your entire vacation with your eyes shut!

INSURANCE

There are three kinds of travel insurance: trip-cancellation, medical, and lost-luggage coverage. Rule number one: Check your existing policies before you buy any additional coverage.

The cost of travel insurance varies, depending on the cost and length of your trip, your age and overall health, and the type of trip. Insurance for extreme sports or adventure travel, for example, will cost more than coverage for a cruise. Some insurers provide packages for specialty vacations, such as skiing or backpacking. More dangerous activities may be excluded from basic policies.

For information, contact one of the following popular insurers:

- **Access America** (℃ 866/807-3982; www.accessamerica.com)
- **Travel Guard International** (℃ 800/826-4919; www.travel guard.com)
- **Travel Insured International** (℃ 800/243-3174; www.travel insured.com)
- **Travelex Insurance Services** (℃ 888/457-4602; www.travelex-insurance.com)
- **Columbus Direct** (℃ 0845/330-8518 in London; www.columbusdirect.com) insures residents of the U.K. and Europe as well as some other countries; only for travel originating from the U.K.

TRIP-CANCELLATION INSURANCE

There are three major types of trip-cancellation insurance—one, in the event that you pre-pay a cruise or tour that gets canceled, and you can't get your money back; a second when you or someone in your family gets sick or dies, and you can't travel (but you may not be covered for a pre-existing condition); and a third, when bad weather makes travel impossible. Some insurers provide coverage for events like jury duty; natural disasters close to home, like floods or fire; even the loss of a job. A few have added provisions for cancellations due to terrorist activities. Always check the fine print before signing on, and don't buy trip-cancellation insurance from the tour operator that may be responsible for the cancellation; buy it only from a reputable travel insurance agency. Don't overbuy. You won't be reimbursed for more than the cost of your trip.

MEDICAL INSURANCE

Most health insurance policies cover you if you get sick away from home—but do check, particularly if your insurance is with an HMO. With the exception of certain HMOs and Medicare/Medicaid, your medical insurance should cover medical treatment—even hospital care—overseas. However, most out-of-country hospitals make you pay your bills up front, and send you a refund after you've returned home and filed the necessary paperwork. Members of **Blue Cross/ Blue Shield** can now use their cards at select hospitals in most major cities worldwide (☏ **800/810-BLUE** or www.bluecares.com for a list of hospitals).

Some credit cards (American Express and certain gold and platinum Visa and MasterCards, for example) offer automatic flight insurance against death or dismemberment in case of an airplane crash if you charged the cost of your ticket.

If you require additional insurance, try one of the following companies:

- **MEDEX International,** P.O. Box 19056 Baltimore, MD 21284 (☏ **410/453-6300;** fax 410/453-6301; www.medexassist.com)
- **Travel Assistance International** (☏ **800/821-2828;** www.travel assistance.com), P.O. Box 668, Millersville, MD 21108; for general information on services, call the company's Worldwide Assistance Services, Inc., at ☏ **800/643-5525**).

The cost of travel medical insurance varies widely. Check your existing policies before you buy additional coverage. Also, check to see if your insurance covers you for emergency medical evacuation: If you have to buy a one-way same-day ticket home and forfeit your nonrefundable round-trip ticket, you may be out big bucks.

Medical care in Australia is expensive. One of the most potentially financially ruinous situations arising from getting sick in Australia is the need to be evacuated to your home country. Your policy should cover the cost to fly you back home in a stretcher, along with a nurse, should that be necessary. A stretcher takes up three coach-class seats, plus you may need extra seats for a nurse and medical equipment.

Australia has a reciprocal medical-care agreement with Great Britain and a limited agreement with Ireland and New Zealand. Under this, travelers are covered for medical expenses for immediately necessary treatment in a public hospital (but not evacuation to your home country, ambulances, funerals, and dental care) by Australia's national health system, called Medicare like it is in the United States. It's still crucial to buy insurance, though, because Australia's national health-care system typically covers only 85%, sometimes much less, of treatment; you will not be covered for treatment in a private hospital; and evacuation insurance is a must.

> ## *Tips* Insurance for Divers
>
> If you plan to **scuba dive**, check that your policy does not clas-
> sify scuba diving as a dangerous sport, and exclude it. For
> more health tips on diving, see the "Health Hazards" section
> in chapter 1. The **Divers' Alert Network (DAN)** (© **800/446-
> 2671;** www.diversalertnetwork.org) insures scuba divers and
> provides a diving medical-emergency hot line in **Australia**
> (©**1800/088 200**). Its website is an excellent source of dive
> medical information.

Most foreign students must take out the Australian government's
Overseas Student Health Cover as a condition of entry.

LOST-LUGGAGE INSURANCE

On international flights (including U.S. portions of international
trips), baggage is limited to approximately $9.05 per pound, up to
approximately $635 per checked bag. If you plan to check items
more valuable than the standard liability, see if your valuables are
covered by your homeowner's policy, get baggage insurance as part
of your travel-insurance package, or buy Travel Guard's "BagTrak"
product. Don't buy insurance at the airport, as it's usually over-
priced. Be sure to take any valuables or irreplaceable items with you
in your carry-on luggage, as many valuables (including books,
money, and electronics) aren't covered by airline policies.

   If your luggage is lost, immediately file a lost-luggage claim at the
airport, detailing the luggage contents. For most airlines, you must
report delayed, damaged, or lost baggage within 4 hours of arrival.

   If you file a lost luggage claim, be prepared to answer detailed
questions about the contents of your baggage, and be sure to file a
claim immediately, as most airlines enforce a 21-day deadline.
Before you leave home, compile an inventory of all packed items
and a rough estimate of the total value to ensure you're properly
compensated if your luggage is lost. You will only be reimbursed for
what you lost, no more. Once you've filed a complaint, persist in
securing your reimbursement; there is no law governing the length
of time it takes for a carrier to reimburse you. The airlines are
required to deliver luggage, once found, directly to your house or
destination free of charge. If your bag is delayed or lost, the airline
may reimburse you for reasonable expenses, such as a toothbrush or
a set of clothes, but the airline is under no legal obligation to do so.

Lost luggage may also be covered by your homeowner's or renter's policy. Many platinum and gold credit cards cover you as well. If you choose to purchase additional lost-luggage insurance, be sure not to buy more than you need. Buy in advance from the insurer or a trusted agent (prices will be much higher at the airport).

6 Tips for Travelers with Special Needs

FOR TRAVELERS WITH DISABILITIES   For information on all kinds of facilities and services in Australia for people with disabilities (not just travel-related organizations), contact **National Information Communication Awareness Network (NICAN),** P.O. Box 407, Curtin, ACT 2605 (✆ **1800/806 769** voice and TTY in Australia, or 02/6285 3713; www.nican.com.au). This free service can put you in touch with accessible accommodations and attractions throughout Australia, as well as with travel agents and tour operators who understand your needs. TTY facilities in Australia are still limited largely to government services, unfortunately.

Tusa Dive in Cairns (see chapter 3) conducts **dive courses** for people with disabilities. Specialist diving travel agent Cairns-based DIVErsion Dive Travel & Training (www.diversionoz.com) offers **IAHD (International Association for Handicapped Divers)** dive instruction. It can also set you up with a dive buddy, or make travel arrangements for your Reef holiday that have the facilities you need.

FOR GAY & LESBIAN TRAVELERS   Australia is pretty gay-friendly, especially in large cities. Noosa, on Queensland's Sunshine Coast, is a favored destination for revelers after the Sydney Mardi Gras, and there are a couple of resorts in north Queensland catering to gay and lesbian travelers.

Liberty Resort at Kuranda near Cairns (✆ **1800/007 556** in Australia, or 07/4093 7556; www.libertyresort.com.au), opened in late 2002, billing itself as the world's most luxurious gay and lesbian resort. It has 56 villas, 8 apartments, and an 80-bed backpacker hostel set on 3.2 hectares (8 acres) of tropical rainforest. **Turtle Cove Resort** (✆ **1300/727 979** in Australia, or 07/4059 1800; www.turtle cove.com.au), on a private beach between Cairns and Port Douglas, is another well-known resort for lesbians and gay men.

The **International Gay & Lesbian Travel Association (IGLTA)** (✆ **800/448-8550** or 954/776-2626; www.iglta.org) is the trade association for the gay and lesbian travel industry, and offers an online directory of gay and lesbian-friendly travel businesses; go to their website and click on "Members." Gay & Lesbian Tourism Australia (www.galta.com.au) also has listings of useful businesses in each state.

FOR SENIORS   Seniors—often referred to as "pensioners" by Aussies—visiting Australia don't always qualify for the discounted entry prices to tours, attractions, and events that Australian seniors enjoy, but mostly they do. The best ID to bring is something that shows your date of birth, or something that marks you as an "official" senior, like a membership card from AARP.

Members of **AARP** (formerly known as the American Association of Retired Persons), 601 E St. NW, Washington, DC 20049 (© **800/ 867-2277;** www.aarp.org), get discounts on hotels, airfares, and car rentals. AARP offers members a wide range of benefits, including *AARP: The Magazine* and a monthly newsletter. Anyone over 50 can join.

Elderhostel (© **877/426-8056;** www.elderhostel.org) arranges study programs for those age 55 and over (and a spouse or companion of any age) in the United States and in more than 80 countries around the world, including Australia. Most courses last 5 to 7 days in the United States (2–4 weeks abroad), and many include airfare, accommodations in university dormitories or modest inns, meals, and tuition.

There is no upper age limit for snorkeling, diving, or learning to dive, but it's a good idea to tell your boat operator/dive school your age. Some may require you to have a letter from your doctor, or a medical certificate, stating you are fit to snorkel or dive. Some boats impose an upper age limit of 70 years on snorkeling and diving.

FOR FAMILIES   International airlines and domestic airlines within Australia charge 75% of the adult fare for kids under 12. Most charge 10% for infants under 2 not occupying a seat. As a general rule, Great Barrier Reef boat cruise operators, as well as attractions and tour operators, charge around half-price for kids under 12 or 14. Kids of any age can snorkel; travel with the many boats that provide kid-size snorkel gear. Children must be age 12 or older to dive, or to learn to dive.

Rascals in Paradise (© **415/921-7000;** www.rascalsinparadise. com) sells family vacation packages to Australia. Many of the island resorts in Queensland have great kids' clubs and almost all Australian hotels will arrange babysitting given a day's notice.

FOR STUDENTS   If you're planning to travel to Australia, you'd be wise to arm yourself with an **International Student Identity**

Card (ISIC), which offers substantial savings on rail passes, plane tickets, and entrance fees. It also provides you with basic health and life insurance and a 24-hour help line. The card is available for $22 from **STA Travel** (℗ **800/781-4040,** and if you're not in North America there's probably a local number in your country; www.sta travel.com), the biggest student travel agency in the world. If you're no longer a student but are still under 26, you can get an **International Youth Travel Card (IYTC)** for the same price from the same people, which entitles you to some discounts (but not on museum admissions).

Travel CUTS (℗ **800/592 2887;** www.travelcuts.com) offers similar services for both Canadians and U.S. residents. Irish students should turn to **USIT** (℗ **0818/200-020** or 01/602 1777; www.usitnow.ie).

The **Australian Youth Hostels Association** (YHA; ℗ **02/9261 1111;** www.yha.com.au), which is the Australian arm of Hostelling International, has more than 140 hostels in Australia. Rates range from A$10 to A$31 (US$8–$25). You don't have to join the association to stay at its hostels, but members receive discounted rates and myriad other discounts—on car rental, bus travel, and tours, for example—that can repay the membership fee many times over. It's best to join before you arrive in Australia. In the United States, contact **Hostelling International** (℗ **301/495-1240;** www.hiayh.org). The 12-month membership is free if you are 17 or under, US$28 if you are 18 to 54, and US$18 if you are 55 or older.

Students receive discounts of about 25% on some Great Barrier Reef day trips, but as a general rule, you won't get discounts on live-aboard snorkeling and diving trips, or on dive courses.

7 Booking a Package or Escorted Tour

It's possible to buy a package tour to Australia that includes airfare and, say, 5 nights in a decent hotel for less than the cost of the airfare alone. Because each element of a package—airfare, hotel, tour, car rental—costs the package company much less than if you had booked the same components yourself, packages are a terrific value and well worth investigating.

The airlines themselves are often a good source of package tours. Check newspaper ads, the Internet, or your travel agent. **Austravel** (℗ **800/633-3404** in the U.S. and Canada, or 0870/166 2020 in the U.K.; www.austravel.net) is one American company offering independent packages Down Under. **Austravel** (℗ **800/633-3404** in the

U.S. and Canada or 0870/166 2020 in the U.K.; www.austravel. net) is an American company offering independent packages Down Under. The following companies offer both independent and escorted tours: **ATS Tours** (© **800/423-2880** in the U.S. and Canada; www. atstours.com); **Collette Vacations** (© **401/727 9000** in the U.S., 800/468 5955 in Canada, or 0800/6921 888 in the U.K.; www. collettevacations.com); **Goway** (© **800/387-8850** in the U.S. and Canada; www.goway.com); **Maupintour** (© **800/255-4266** in the U.S. and Canada; www.maupintour.com); **Qantas Vacations** (© **800/348-8145** in the U.S. or 800/348-8137 in Canada; www. qantasvacations.com); **Sunbeam Tours** (© **800/955-1818** in the U.S. and Canada; www.sunbeamtours.com); **Swain Australia Tours** (© **800/22-SWAIN** in the U.S. and Canada; www.swainaustralia. com); Swain Australia's budget-travel division, **Downunder Direct** (© **800/642-6224** in the U.S. and Canada; www.downunderdirect. com); and **United Vacations** (© **888/854-3899** in the U.S. and Canada; www.unitedvacations.com). Swain Australia is operated and largely staffed by Aussies. Collette Vacations, Inta-Aussie South Pacific, Sunbeam Tours, Swain Australia, and Goway have offices in Australia.

8 Flying to Australia

Australia is a long haul from anywhere except New Zealand. Sydney is a nearly 15-hour non-stop flight from Los Angeles, longer if you come via Honolulu. From the East Coast, add 5½ hours. If you're coming from the States via Auckland, add transit time in New Zealand plus another 3 hours for the Auckland–Sydney leg. If you are coming from the United Kingdom, brace yourself for a flight of more or less 12 hours from London to Asia; then possibly a long day in transit, because flights to Australia have a nasty habit of arriving in Asia early in the morning and departing around midnight; and finally the 8- to 9-hour flight to Australia. If you're coming from Europe and you have a long layover in Asia, I recommend you book a day room at a hotel with a 6pm checkout. Wandering around a humid, crowded city at 2pm when your body thinks it's 3am is not fun.

Sydney, Cairns, Melbourne, Brisbane, Adelaide, Darwin, and Perth are all international gateways, but most airlines fly only into Sydney, and a few fly to Melbourne.

THE MAJOR CARRIERS

Here are toll-free reservation numbers and websites for the major international airlines serving Australia. The "13" prefix in Australia means the number is charged at the cost of a local call from any-where in the country.

MAJOR CARRIERS FLYING FROM NORTH AMERICA

- **Air Canada** (© **888/247-2262** in the U.S. and Canada, 02/ 2848 5757 in Sydney, or 1300/655 767 from elsewhere in Australia; www.aircanada.ca)
- **Air New Zealand** (© **800/262-1234** in the U.S., 310/615-1111 in the Los Angeles area, 800/663-5494 in Canada or 13 24 76 in Australia; www.airnewzealand.com)
- **Qantas** (© **800/227-4500** in the U.S. and Canada or 13 13 13 in Australia; www.qantas.com.au)
- **United Airlines** (© **800/538-2929** in the U.S. and Canada or 13 17 77 in Australia; www.united.com or www.united.ca)

MAJOR CARRIERS FLYING FROM THE U.K.

- **British Airways** (© **0870/850 9850** in the U.K., 1800/626 747 in Ireland, or 1300/767 177 in Australia; www.british airways.com)
- **Cathay Pacific** (© **020/8834 8888** in the U.K. or 13 17 47 in Australia; www.cathaypacific.com/uk)
- **Malaysia Airlines** (© **0870/607 9090** in the U.K. and Ireland or 13 26 27 in Australia; www.malaysiaairlines.com.my or www.malaysiaairlineseurope.com)
- **Qantas** (© **0845/774 7767** in the U.K. or 13 13 13 in Australia; www.qantas.com.au)
- **Singapore Airlines** (© **0870/608 8886** in the U.K. or 13 10 11 in Australia; www.singaporeair.com/uk)
- **Thai Airways International** (© **0870/6060 911** in the U.K. or 1300/651 960 in Australia; www.thaiair.com)

FINDING THE BEST AIRFARE

If you're flying from the United States, keep in mind that the air-lines' low season is from mid-April to the end of August—which also happens to be the best time to visit the Great Barrier Reef! High season is December through February, and shoulder season is Sep-tember through November, and again from March to mid-April.

Keep an eye out for special deals offered throughout the year. Unexpected lows in airline passenger loads often lead airlines to put cheap offers on the market. The catch is these usually have a short lead time, requiring you to travel in the next 6 weeks or so. Some deals involve taking a circuitous route, via Fiji or Japan, for instance.

Some travel agents specializing in cheap fares include **Austravel** (*ⓒ* **800/633-3404** in the U.S. and Canada or 0870/166 2020 in the U.K.; www.austravel.net); **Downunder Direct,** a division of Swain Australia (*ⓒ* **800/642-6224** in the U.S. and Canada; www.downunderdirect.com); and **Goway** (*ⓒ* **800/387-8850** in the U.S. and Canada; www.goway.com).

Consolidators, also known as bucket shops, are a good place to find low fares. Consolidators buy seats in bulk from the airlines and then sell them to the public at prices usually below even the airlines' discounted rates. Their small ads usually run in Sunday newspaper travel sections. And before you pay, request a confirmation number from the consolidator and then call the airline to confirm your seat. Be aware that bucket shop tickets are usually nonrefundable or rigged with stiff cancellation penalties, often as high as 50% to 75% of the ticket price. Protect yourself by paying with a credit card rather than cash. Keep in mind that if there's an airline sale going on, or if it's high season, you can often get the same or better rates by contacting the airlines directly, so do some comparison shopping before you buy. Also check out the name of the airline; you may not want to fly on some obscure Third World airline, even if you're saving $10. And check whether you're flying on a charter or a scheduled airline; the latter is more expensive but more reliable.

Several reliable consolidators are worldwide and available on the Net. **STA Travel** (*ⓒ* **800/781-4040;** www.statravel.com) is now the world's leader in student travel, thanks to their purchase of Council Travel. It also offers good fares for travelers of all ages.

The TravelHub (*ⓒ* **888/AIR-FARE;** www.travelhub.com) represents nearly 1,000 travel agencies, many of whom offer consolidator and discount fares. Other reliable consolidators include **1-800-FLY-CHEAP** (www.1800flycheap.com and the **Smart Traveller** (*ⓒ* **800/448-3338** in the U.S., or 305/448-3338), which rebate part of their commissions to you.

You can also use Internet-based travel agencies for cheap fares. The "big three" online travel agencies—**Expedia.com, Travelocity.com,** and **Orbitz.com**—sell most of the air tickets bought on the Internet. (Canadian travelers should try expedia.ca and Travelocity.ca; U.K. residents can go for expedia.co.uk and opodo.co.uk.) Each has different deals with the airlines and may offer different fares on the same flights, so it's wise to shop around. Expedia and Travelocity will also send you **e-mail notification** when a cheap fare becomes available to your favorite destination. Of the smaller travel agency websites, **SideStep** (www.sidestep.com) has gotten the best reviews from Frommer's authors. It's a browser add-on that purports to "search 140 sites at once," but in reality only beats competitors' fares as often as other sites do.

Other sites worth taking a peek at are sites selling off excess airline or hotel room inventory for travelers prepared to take to the air at short notice, such as **www.lastminute.com**, **www.moments-notice. com**, **www.priceline.com**, and **www.hotwire.com**.

9 Getting Around Queensland

BY AIR

Qantas (© **13 13 13** in Australia; www.qantas.com.au) and its subsidiary **QantasLink** serve most coastal towns from Brisbane, and a few from Cairns. **Virgin Blue** (© **13 67 89** in Australia; www.virgin blue.com.au) services Brisbane, Cairns, Townsville, Mackay, Proserpine on the Whitsunday Coast, Rockhampton, Gold Coast, and Maroochydore on the Sunshine Coast.

BY TRAIN

Queensland Rail's **Traveltrain** (© **13 22 32** in Australia; www.travel train.qr.com.au), operates two trains on the Brisbane–Cairns route: *The Sunlander* runs twice a week from Brisbane to Cairns offering a choice of the premium, all-inclusive Queenslander Class; single, double or triple berth sleepers; or economy seats. Two services also run as far as Townsville on this route without Queenslander Class. The high-speed *Tilt Train* operates three weekly trips on the same route in less time—by about 8 hours—with business-class–style seating. Tilt Trains also service Rockhampton daily from Brisbane. Traveltrain also operates trains to Outback towns. All Traveltrain and most Countrylink long-distance trains stop at most towns en route, so they're useful for exploring the eastern states. Ask about Traveltrain packages including accommodation and/or sightseeing.

Outside Australia, the umbrella organization Rail Australia (www.railaustralia.com.au) handles inquiries and makes reservations for most long-distance trains through its overseas agents: **ATS Tours** (© **310/643 0044**) in the U.S.; **Goway** (© **416/322 1034**) in Canada; **International Rail** (© **0870/751 5000**) in the U.K.; and **Tranz Scenic** (© **03/339 3809**) in New Zealand. Make train reservations well in advance, if possible.

BY BUS

Bus travel in Australia is a big step up from the low-rent affair it can be in the U.S. Unlike Australia's train service, there are few places the extensive bus network won't take you. Buses are all nonsmoking.

Australia has two national coach operators: **Greyhound Pioneer Australia** (✆ **13 20 30** in Australia, or 07/4690-9888; www. greyhound.com.au; no relation to Greyhound in the U.S.) and **McCafferty's** (✆ **13 14 99** in Australia, or 07/4690-9888; www. mccaffertys.com.au). McCafferty's bought Greyhound Pioneer a few years ago (hence the same telephone number, above). While the coach lines operate as separate brands and on their own networks, pass products are combined and can be used interchangeably. The coaches and service standards of both companies are identical. Both companies offer multiple daily services between Brisbane and Cairns stopping at just about all towns en route. McCafferty's/Greyhound Pioneer has many international agents, including **Inta-Aussie South Pacific** (✆ **310/568-2060**) in the United States, **Goway** (✆ **800/ 387-8850**) in Canada, and **Bridge the World** (✆ **020/7911 0900**) in the United Kingdom.

BY CAR

The Bruce Highway links coastal towns between Brisbane and Cairns. It is mostly a narrow two-lane highway, bordered by euca-lyptus bushland most of the way, but from Mackay north you will pass through sugar cane fields, adding some variety to the trip.

Tourism Queensland publishes regional motoring guides. All you are likely to need, however, is a state map from the **Royal Automobile Club of Queensland (RACQ)**, 300 St. Pauls Terrace, Fortitude Valley, QLD 4006 (✆ **13 19 05** in Australia, or 07/3359 4422; www.racq.com.au). A more convenient city office is in the General Post Office building at 261 Queen St., Brisbane (✆ **07/3872 8465**). Its Cairns office is at Shop 50X in the Stockland Shopping Centre, Mulgrave Rd., Earlville (✆ **07/4033 6433**). For **road condition** reports, call ✆ **1300/130 595** (recorded message). The state's **Department of Natural Resources** (✆ **07/3896 3216**) publishes an excellent range of "Sunmap" maps that highlight tourist attractions and national parks, although they are of limited use as road maps. You can get them at newsagents and gas stations throughout the state.

DRIVING DOWN UNDER

Australians drive on the left. Your current driver's license or an inter-national driver's permit is fine in every state of Australia. By law you must carry your license with you when driving. The minimum driving age is 16 or 17, depending on which state you visit, but some rental-car companies require you to be 21, or even 26 sometimes if you want to rent a 4WD vehicle. The maximum permitted blood alcohol level when driving is 0.05. The police set up random breath-testing units (RBTs) in cunningly disguised and unlikely places all the time, so it is easy to get caught. You will face a court appearance if you do. The speed limit is 50kmph (31 mph) or 60kmph (37.5 mph) in urban areas and 100kmph (63 mph) or 110kmph (69 mph) in most country areas. Speed-limit signs are black numbers circled in red on a white background. Drivers and passengers, including taxi passengers, must wear a seatbelt. Damage to a rental car caused by an animal (hitting a kangaroo, for instance) is not covered by car-rental companies' insurance policies (which should give you an inkling of how common an occurrence this is), nor is driving on an unpaved road—and Australia has a lot of those.

The price of petrol (gasoline) will elicit a cry of dismay from Americans and a whoop of delight from Brits. Prices go up and down a lot, but very roughly, you're looking at around A90¢ a liter (or US$2.72 per U.S. gal.) for unleaded petrol in coastal Queensland, more in Outback areas. One U.S. gallon equals 3.78 liters.

The emergency breakdown assistance telephone number for every Australian auto club is ⓒ **13 11 11** from anywhere in Australia, billed as a local call. If you are not a member of an auto club back home that has a reciprocal agreement with the Australian clubs, you can join the Australian club on the spot and they will come tow or repair your car. This costs around A$80 (US$64), not a big price to pay when you're stranded. In the Outback, the charge may be considerably higher.

The "big four" car-rental companies all have extensive networks across Australia:

- **Avis** (ⓒ **13 63 33** in Australia, www.avis.com.au; 800/230-4898 in the U.S., www.avis.com; 800/272-5871 in Canada; 0870/6060 100 in the U.K. and Ireland, www.avis.co.uk; 0800/655-111 in New Zealand, www.avis.co.nz)
- **Budget** (ⓒ **1300/362 848** in Australia, www.budget.com.au; 800/527-0700 in the U.S., www.budget.com; 800/268-8900 in Canada, www.budget.ca; 01344/484 100 in the U.K., www.budget-uk.com; 906/627 711 in Ireland, www.budget-ireland.com; 0800/652 227 in New Zealand, www.budget.co.nz)

- **Hertz** (𝄞 **13 30 39** in Australia, www.hertz.com.au; 800/654-3131 in the U.S., www.hertz.com; 800/263-0600 in English or 800/263-0678 in French in Canada, or 416/620-9620 in Toronto, www.hertz.ca; 020/7026 0077 in the U.K., www.hertz.co.uk; 1/676 7476 in Ireland; 0800/654 321 in New Zealand)
- **Thrifty** (𝄞 **1300/367 227** in Australia, www.thrifty.com.au; 800/229 0984 in the U.S. and Canada, www.thrifty.com; 0800/783 0405 in the U.K., www.thrifty.co.uk; 1800/51 5800 in Ireland, www.thrifty.ie; 0800/73 7070 in New Zealand, www.thrifty.co.nz).

FAST FACTS: Australia

American Express For all travel-related inquiries regarding any American Express service, including reporting a lost card, call 𝄞 **1300/132 639.** To report lost or stolen traveler's checks, call (𝄞 **1800/251 902**).

Business Hours Banks are open Monday through Thursday from 9:30am to 4pm, and until 5pm on Friday. General business hours are Monday through Friday from 8:30am to 5:30pm. Shopping hours are usually from 8:30am to 5:30pm weekdays and from 9am to 4pm or 5pm on Saturday. Some shops close Sundays, although major department stores and shops in major cities and tourist centers are open 7 days. Late-night shopping to 9pm operates in most towns either Thursday or Friday night.

Climate See "When to Go," earlier in this chapter.

Currency See "Money," earlier in this chapter.

Customs See "Entry Requirements & Customs," earlier in this chapter.

Dates Australians write their dates day, month, year: March 6, 1958, is 06/03/58.

Drugstores These are called "chemists" or "pharmacies." Australian pharmacists are permitted to fill only prescriptions written by Australian doctors.

Electricity The current is 240 volts AC, 50 hertz. Sockets take two or three flat, not rounded, prongs. North Americans and Europeans will need to buy a converter before they leave home (Australian stores sell only converters for Aussie appliances). Some hotels have 110V outlets for electric shavers or dual voltage and some will lend converters, but don't count on it. Power does not start automatically when you plug in an appliance; you need to flick the switch beside the socket to the "on" position.

Embassies/Consulates Most diplomatic posts are in Canberra: **British High Commission,** Commonwealth Avenue, Canberra, ACT 2600 (℃ **02/6270 6666**); **Embassy of Ireland,** 20 Arkana St., Yarralumla, ACT 2600 (℃ **02/6273 3022**); **High Commission of Canada,** Commonwealth Avenue, Yarralumla, ACT 2600 (℃ **02/6270 4000**); **New Zealand High Commission,** Commonwealth Avenue, Canberra, ACT 2600 (℃ **02/6270 4211**); and the **United States Embassy,** 21 Moonah Place, Yarralumla, ACT 2600 (℃ **02/6214 5600**).

Emergencies Dial ℃ **000** anywhere in Australia for police, ambulance, or the fire department. This is a free call from public and private telephones and needs no coins.

Holidays See "When to Go," earlier in this chapter.

Information See "Visitor Information," earlier this chapter.

Internet Access Internet access is available just about everywhere, including some of the smallest Outback towns, which generally have at least one cybercafe and/or coin-operated machines, which are also available at larger airports. Major tourist towns such as Cairns have whole streets full of cybercafes.

Liquor Laws Hours vary, but most pubs are open daily from around 10am or noon to 10pm or midnight. The drinking age is 18. Alcohol is sold only in liquor stores, or "bottle shops" attached to a pub, rarely in supermarkets.

Mail A postcard costs A$1 (US80¢) to the United States, Canada, the United Kingdom, or New Zealand.

Police Dial ℃ **000** anywhere in Australia. This is a free call and requires no coins.

Safety Violent crime is uncommon. Guns are strictly controlled. Purse-snatchers are the same threat in capital cities and tourist areas that they are all over the world.

Smoking Smoking in most public areas, such as museums, cinemas, and theaters, is restricted or banned. Increasingly

Oz restaurants are totally banning smoking, though in many states restaurants have smoking and nonsmoking sections. Most hotels have smoking and nonsmoking rooms. Australian aircraft are completely nonsmoking, as are all airport buildings.

Telephones The primary telecommunications network in Australia is Telstra (www.telstra.com).

Mobile Calls: Cellular or "mobile" telephones are available for daily rental at major airports and in big cities, and increasingly from car- and campervan-rental companies. The cell network is digital, not analog. Calls to, or from, a mobile telephone are generally more expensive than a call to, or from, a fixed telephone—A60¢ a minute is a ballpark guide, although the price varies widely depending on the telephone company, the time of day, the distance between caller and recipient, and the pricing plan on the telephone used to make the call.

To call Australia: If you're calling Sydney from the United States:

1. Dial the international access code: 011
2. Dial the country code 61
3. Dial the city code 2 (drop the 0 from any area code given in this book) and then the number. So the whole number you'd dial would be 011-61-2-0000-0000.

To make international calls: To make international calls from Australia, first dial 0011 and then the country code (U.S. or Canada 1, U.K. 44, Ireland 353, New Zealand 64). Next dial the area code and number. For example, if you wanted to call the British Embassy in Washington, D.C., you would dial 0011-1-202-588-7800. For other codes, call © **1222** or look in the back of the Australian White Pages.

To make a long-distance call within Australia: Dial the two-digit area code, followed by the number you are calling. Australia's area codes are New South Wales and the A.C.T. (02); Victoria and Tasmania (03); Queensland (07); and South Australia, Western Australia, and the Northern Territory (08). Long-distance calls within Australia are usually cheaper at night and on weekends. You do not have to dial the area code if calling long-distance within the same state, for example from Brisbane to Cairns.

To make a local call in Australia: Local calls in Australia are untimed and cost a flat A40¢ from a public phone, or A25¢, sometimes a little less, from a private phone in a home or office. Many phones these days do not accept coins, so you should consider buying a phone card. The cards typically contain a prepaid allotment of call time for local, long-distance, international, and cellphone calls. They are widely sold at newsagents. Telstra's PhoneAway phone card can also be used to call Australia from more than 45 overseas countries, including the United States and the United Kingdom. PhoneAway cards have a personalized Voicemail voice and fax box. They are sold at newsagents, Telstra shops, and Australia Post outlets. Australia's second major telecommunications network, Optus, sells a similar card at Optus stores, Australia Post post offices, newsagents, Kmart, and other outlets.

For directory assistance: Dial 🕿 **12455** if you're looking for a number inside Australia, and dial 1225 for numbers to all other countries.

For operator assistance: To reach the operator for help making a call, dial 🕿 **1234.** To make a collect call, called a "reverse charges" call in Australia, call 🕿 **12550.**

Toll-free numbers: Numbers beginning with 1800 within Australia are toll-free, but calling a 1-800 number in the States from Australia is not toll-free. In fact, it costs the same as an overseas call. Numbers starting with 13 or 1300 in Australia are charged at the local fee of A25¢ from anywhere in Australia. Numbers beginning with 1900 (or 1901 or 1902 and so on) are pay-for-service lines and you will be charged as much as A$5 (US$4) a minute.

Time Zone Eastern Standard Time (EST, also written as AEST sometimes) covers Queensland, New South Wales, the Australian Capital Territory, Victoria, and Tasmania. Central Standard Time is used in the Northern Territory and South Australia, and Western Standard Time (WST) is the standard in Western Australia. When it's noon in New South Wales, the A.C.T., Victoria, Queensland, and Tasmania, it's 11:30am in South Australia and the Northern Territory and 10am in Western Australia. All states except Queensland, the Northern Territory, and Western Australia observe daylight saving time, usually from the last Sunday in October (the first Sun in Oct in Tasmania's case) to the last Sunday in March. However, not all states switch over to daylight saving on the same day or in the same week.

The east coast of Australia is GMT (Greenwich Mean Time) plus 10 hours. When it is noon on the east coast, it is 2am in London that morning, and 6pm in Los Angeles and 9pm in New York the previous night. These times are based on standard time, so allow for daylight saving in the Australian summer, or in the country you are calling. New Zealand is 2 hours ahead of the east coast of Australia, except during daylight saving, when it is 3 hours ahead of Queensland.

Tipping Tipping is not expected in Australia. It is usual to tip around 5% or round up to the nearest A$10 for a substantial meal in a restaurant (but not for a casual sandwich and cup of coffee). Some passengers round up to the nearest dollar in a cab, but it's okay to insist on every last piece of change back from the driver. Tipping bellboys and porters is sometimes done but no one tips bar staff, barbers, or hairdressers.

Useful Phone Numbers
- U.S. Dept. of State Travel Advisory: ℂ 202-647-5225 (manned 24 hr.)
- U.S. Passport Agency: ℂ 877-487-2778
- U.S. Embassy in Australia: ℂ 02/6214 5600
- Canadian High Commission in Australia: ℂ 02/6270 4000
- U.K. High Commission in Australia: ℂ 02/6270 6666
- Irish Embassy in Australia: ℂ 02/6273 3022
- New Zealand High Commission in Australia: ℂ 02/6270 4211
- U.S. Centers for Disease Control International Traveler's Hotline: ℂ 877-FYI-TRIP

Water Water is fine to drink everywhere.

Cairns

This part of Australia is the only place in the world where two World Heritage–listed attractions—the Great Barrier Reef and the Wet Tropics Rainforest—lie side by side. In parts of the far north, the rainforest touches the reef, reaching right down to sandy beaches from which you can snorkel the reef. Cairns is the gateway to these natural attractions, plus to man-made tourist attractions such as the Skyrail Rainforest Cableway. It's also a stepping-stone to islands of the Great Barrier Reef and the grasslands of the Gulf Savannah.

When international tourism to the Great Barrier Reef boomed a decade or two ago, Cairns boomed with it. The result is that this small sugar-farming town now boasts five-star hotels, island resorts off shore, big Reef-cruise catamarans in the harbor, and too many souvenir shops.

The 110-million-year-old rainforest, the Daintree, where plants that are fossils elsewhere in the world exist in living color, is just a couple of hours north of Cairns. The Daintree is part of the Wet Tropics, a World Heritage–listed area that stretches from north of Townsville to south of Cooktown, beyond Cairns, and houses half of Australia's animal and plant species.

Although it has a few charming colonial-era civic buildings and is edged by green mountains, downtown Cairns has little to get excited about. The shopping is lackluster; make no mistake, you are here for the out-of-town attractions. The "city" beach is a 4,000-sq.-m (43,000-sq.-ft.) man-made saltwater lagoon and beach on the Esplanade, with the real thing at the "northern beaches" a short drive from Cairns. If you are spending more than a day or two in the area, consider basing yourself at one of the northern beaches, in Kuranda or Port Douglas (see chapter 4), an hour's drive north. While prices will be higher in the peak season (Australian winter and early spring, July–Oct), the town has affordable accommodations year-round.

1 Essentials

GETTING THERE   By Plane   Qantas (© **13 13 13** in Australia) has direct flights throughout the day to Cairns from Sydney and Brisbane, and at least one flight a day from Darwin and Perth. From Melbourne you can fly direct some days, but most flights connect through Sydney or Brisbane. **QantasLink** also flies from Townsville, Hamilton Island in the Whitsundays, Alice Springs, and Uluru (Ayers Rock). **Virgin Blue** (© **13 67 89** in Australia) flies to Cairns direct from Brisbane, Sydney, and Melbourne. Several international carriers fly to Cairns from various Asian cities, and from New Zealand. **Jetstar** (© **13 15 38** in Australia) flies from Brisbane twice a day. New Qantas international subsidiary **Australian Airlines** (© **1300/799 798** in Australia) also links Cairns with Sydney and the Gold Coast.

Cairns Airport is 8km (5 miles) north of downtown, and a 5-minute walk or a A$2 (US$1.60) shuttle ride separates the domestic and international terminals. Both terminals' arrivals hall have showers, baby-change rooms, ATMs, currency exchange, accommodations boards with free booking telephones, booking counters for coaches, and taxi and limousine ranks. Both terminals have lockers big enough for a suitcase that cost from A$6 to $12 (US$4.80–$9.60) per day. Baggage trolleys are free for arriving international passengers, and $2 (US$1.60) for everyone else. The **Australia Coach** (© **07/4048 8355**) shuttle, which costs A$7.50 (US$6) adults, A$3.50 (US$2.80) children 3 to 12, meets major flights at both terminals for transfers to city hotels. **Sun Palm Express Coaches** (© **07/4099 4992**) provides transfers from the airport to the city and northern beaches. The one-way fare is A$13 (US$10) adults and A$7.50 (US$6) children 4 to 14 to the city, and A$15 (US$12) adults and A$7.50 (US$6) children to Palm Cove.

A taxi from the airport costs around A$15 (US$12) to the city, A$30 (US$24) to Trinity Beach, and A$40 (US$32) to Palm Cove. Call **Black & White Taxis** (© **13 10 08** in Australia).

Avis, Budget, Hertz, and **Thrifty** all have car-rental offices at the domestic and international terminals (see "Getting Around," below).

By Train   Long-distance trains operate from Brisbane several times a week. Queensland Rail's **Traveltrain** (© **13 22 32** in Queensland; www.qr.com.au) operates the services. The new 160kmph (99mph) Tilt Train takes about 25 hours and costs A$280 (US$224) for a business class fare between Brisbane and Cairns. Northbound services leave Brisbane at 6.25pm on Mondays, Wednesdays, and Fridays;

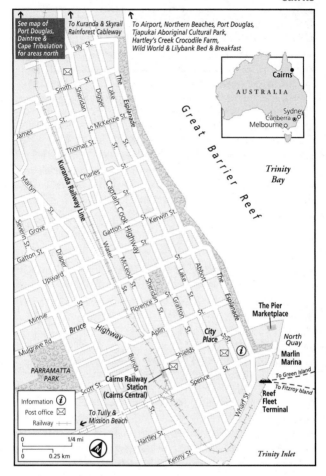

To Kuranda & Skyrail Rainforest Cableway

See map of Port Douglas, Daintree & Cape Tribulation for areas north

To Airport, Northern Beaches, Port Douglas, Tjapukai Aboriginal Cultural Park, Hartley's Creek Crocodile Farm, Wild World & Lilybank Bed & Breakfast

AUSTRALIA
Cairns
Sydney
Canberra
Melbourne

Great Barrier Reef

Trinity Bay

Lily St.
Smith St.
Sheridan St.
Lake St.
Digger St.
The Esplanade
McKenzie St.
James
Thomas St.
Charles
Kuranda Railway Line
Captain Cook Highway
Kerwin St.
Gatton St.
Water St.
Marryn
Grove
Severin St.
Gatton St.
Draper
Upward
McLeod St.
Sheridan St.
Grafton St.
Florence St.
Abbott St.
Lake St.
The Esplanade
Minnie
Bruce Highway
Aplin
City Place
The Pier Marketplace
North Quay
Marlin Marina
Mulgrave Rd.
Bunda
Shields
Spence St.
To Green Island
To Fitzroy Island
PARRAMATTA PARK
Cairns Railway Station (Cairns Central)
Scott St.
Wharf St.
Reef Fleet Terminal
To Tully & Mission Beach
Hartley St.
Kenny St.
Trinity Inlet

Information ⓘ
Post office ✉
Railway ┼┼┼

0   1/4 mi
0   0.25 km

southbound services depart Cairns at 8.15am on Wednesdays, Fridays, and Sundays. The train features luxury "business class" seating, with an entertainment system for each seat including multiple movie and audio channels.

The Sunlander, which runs twice a week between Brisbane and Cairns, takes 32 hours and costs A$187 (US$150) for a sitting berth, A$240 (US$192) for an economy-class sleeper, A$377 (US$302) for a first-class sleeper, or A$646 (US$517) for the all-inclusive Queenslander class. Trains pull into the Cairns Central terminal

> ### _Tips_ **Staying Connected**
>
> You can surf the Web and check your e-mail at **The Inbox Café**, 119 Abbot St. (© **07/4041 4677**; fax 07/4041 4322), for A$1.50 (US$1.20) for 15 minutes, A$2.50 (US$2) for 30 minutes, or A$4 (US$3.20) an hour. It's open daily from 7am to midnight. The Inbox Café, which has 7 computers on line, all with broadband, CD burners and live web-cam, is Cairns's only licensed Internet cafe. The cafe food is by the **Red Ochre Grill** (see "Where to Dine," later in this chapter). It's fresh, tasty, and affordable, with breakfast available all day. There is a bar with lots of newspapers and magazines, and resident DJs play groovy tunes to set a relaxed mood with an extra beat on weekend nights.

(© **13 22 32** in Australia for reservations or inquiries 24 hr. a day, or 07/4036 9249 for the terminal from 8am–6pm, 07/4036 9203 after hours) on Bunda Street in the center of town. The station has no showers, lockers, or currency exchange, but you will find 24-hour ATMs outside the Cairns Central mall, right above the terminal.

By Bus   McCafferty's (© **13 14 99,** or 07/4051 5899 for Cairns terminal) and **Greyhound Pioneer** (© **13 20 30,** or 07/4051 5899 for terminal) buses pull into Trinity Wharf Centre on Wharf Street in the center of town. Buses travel from the south via all towns and cities on the Bruce Highway, and from the west from Alice Springs and Darwin via Tennant Creek on the Stuart Highway and the Outback mining town of Mt. Isa to Townsville, where they join the Bruce Highway and head north. The 46-hour Sydney-Cairns trip costs A$278 (US$222), the 29½-hour trip from Brisbane is A$188 (US$150), and from Darwin, the journey takes about 38 hours and costs A$400 (US$320).

By Car   The **Bruce Highway** from Brisbane enters Cairns from the south. To reach the northern beaches or Port Douglas from Cairns, take **Sheridan Street** in the city center, which becomes the **Captain Cook Highway.** The nearest highway from the west joins the coast in Townsville.

VISITOR INFORMATION   **Tourism Tropical North Queensland** is at 51 The Esplanade, Cairns, QLD 4870 (© **07/4051 3588;** fax 07/4051 0127; www.tropicalaustralia.com). Its information center is a particularly good source of information on Great Barrier Reef dive and snorkel boats. It is also a good one-stop shop for information on other tour operators, not just in Cairns and its environs, but also in Mission Beach, Port Douglas and the Daintree rainforest, Cooktown and Cape York to the north, and Outback Queensland to the west. It's open daily from 8:30am to 5:30pm, and 10am to 2pm on public holidays. Closed Christmas.

Another useful website is Cairns Online at **www.cairns.aust.com**. Oodles of free tourist guides are available at the airport, in your hotel lobby, and from tour desks.

CITY LAYOUT   A major redevelopment of the Cairns Esplanade, completed in 2003, has transformed the face of the city. The focal point is a 4,000-sq.-m (40,000-sq.-ft.) saltwater swimming lagoon with a wide sandy beach and surrounding parkland with public artworks and picnic areas. Suspended over the mudflats and providing a platform for bird-watching, a timber boardwalk runs 600m (1,800 ft.) along the waterfront, and is lit for nighttime use. A walkway links the Esplanade to the **Reef Fleet Terminal,** the departure point for Great Barrier Reef boats.

Downtown Cairns is on a grid 5 blocks deep, bounded in the east by the Esplanade on the water, and in the west by McLeod Street, where the train station and the Cairns Central shopping mall are located. In between are shops, offices, and restaurants.

Heading 15 minutes north from the city along the Captain Cook Highway, you come to the **northern beaches:** Holloway's Beach, Yorkey's Knob, Trinity Beach, Kewarra Beach, Clifton Beach, Palm Cove, and Ellis Beach.

GETTING AROUND   By Bus   Sunbus (© **07/4057 7411**) buses depart City Place Mall at the intersection of Lake and Shields streets. Buy all tickets and passes on board, and try to have correct change. You can hail buses anywhere it's convenient for the driver to stop. Buses 2 and 2A travel to Trinity Beach; and 1 and 1X (weekend express) travel to Palm Cove. The "N" route runs along the highway from the city to Palm Cove until 2:25am on Friday and Saturday nights, stopping at all beaches in between. Most other buses run from early morning until almost midnight.

By Car   Avis (© 07/4051 5911), **Budget** (© 07/4051 9222), **Hertz** (© 07/4051 6399), and **Thrifty** (© 07/4051 8099) all have offices in Cairns city and at the airport. One of the biggest local outfits, **Sugarland Car Rentals** (© 07/4052 1300; www.sugarland. com.au) has reasonable rates, 19 vehicle types including 4WDs (four-wheel-drives), and offices in Cairns and Mission Beach. **Britz Australia** (© 1800/33 1454 in Australia or 07/4032 2611), **Budget Campervan Rentals** (© 07/4032 2065), and **Maui Rentals** (© 07/4032 2065, or 1300/363 800 in Australia) rent motor-homes. Britz and most major rental-car companies rent four-wheel-drives.

By Taxi & Limo   Call **Black & White Taxis** at © **13 10 08.**

2 Diving & Snorkeling the Reef

MAJOR REEF SITES

Approximately 20 reefs lie within a 90-minute to 2-hour boat ride from Cairns. These are the reefs most commonly visited by snorkelers and divers on day trips, because they are so close and so pretty. Some reefs are small coral "bommies," or outcrops, that you can swim completely around in a matter of minutes, whereas others are miles wide. Some reefs have more than one good dive site; Norman Reef, for example, has at least four. Three of the most popular reefs with both snorkelers and divers are **Hastings, Saxon,** and **Norman** ⚑, which are all within a short boat ride of one another. Each has a wonderful array of coral, big colorful reef fish, schools of pretty rainbow-hued small reef fish, and the odd giant clam. Green sea turtles and white-tip reef sharks are common, especially at Saxon, though you will not necessarily spot one every day. Divers may see a moray eel and a grouper or two, barracuda, reef sharks, eagle and blue-spotted rays, and octopus. Norman is an especially lovely reef with several nice sites. South Norman has sloping coral shelves. If you are an experienced diver and like swim-throughs, The Caves at Norman is a good spot; it has boulder and plate corals and crays.

Some of the best diving anywhere on the Great Barrier Reef is on the **Ribbon Reefs** ⚑ on the outer Reef edge, which fringes the continental shelf off Cairns and Port Douglas. Glorious coral walls, abundant fish, and pinnacles make these a rich, colorful dive area with lots of variety. The currents can be stronger here, because the reefs are the last stop between the open sea, so drift dives are a possibility. The Ribbon Reefs are beyond the reach of day boats, but are commonly visited by live-aboard boats (see later in this chapter). For divers, the experts at **Taka Dive Australia** (© **07/4051 8722;** www.taka.com.au) recommend **Steve's Bommie** and **Dynamite Pass.** Dynamite Pass is a channel where barracuda, trevally, grouper, mackerel, and tuna gather to feed in the current. Black coral trees and sea whips grow on the walls, patrolled by eagle rays and reef sharks. Steve's Bommie is a coral outcrop in 30m (98 ft.) of water, topped with barracudas, and covered in colorful coral and small marine life. You can swim through a tunnel here amid crowds of fish.

Cairns's most famous dive site is **Cod Hole** ⚓, where you can hand-feed giant potato cod as big as you, or bigger. The site also has Maori wrasse, moray eels, and coral trout. Cod Hole is about 20km (12½ miles) off Lizard Island, 240km (149 miles) north of Cairns, so it is not a day trip, unless you are staying at exclusive Lizard Island (see "Where to Stay," later in this chapter). However, it is a popular stop with just about every live-aboard vessel, often combined in a trip to the Ribbon Reefs lasting about 4 days, or in a trip to the Coral Sea (see below) lasting between 4 and 7 days. Either itinerary makes an excellent dive vacation.

Keen divers looking for adventure in far-flung latitudes can visit the **Far Northern** region of the Great Barrier Reef, much further north than most dive boats venture. Up in this large region you will find a choice of good sites, little explored by the average diver. Visibility is always clear. Graham McCallum, who has skippered dive boats on the Reef for many years, recommends the following sites: **Silvertip City** on Mantis Reef has sharks, pelagics (a sportfish), potato cod, and beautiful lionfish that patrol a wall up to 46m (150 ft.) deep. Another goodie is the **Magic Cave** swim-through adorned with lots of colorful fans, soft corals, and small reef fish. Sleeping turtles are often spotted in caves on the reefs off **Raine Island,** the world's biggest green turtle rookery. Visibility averages 24m (80 ft.) at Rainbow Wall, a colorful wall that makes a nice gentle drift dive with the incoming tide.

Some 100 to 200km (63–126 miles) east of Cairns, out in the **Coral Sea,** isolated mountains covered in reefs rise more than a kilometer (more than half a mile) from the ocean floor to make excellent diving. Although not within the Great Barrier Reef Marine Park, the Coral Sea is discussed here because it is often combined into a single live-aboard trip that also takes in Cod Hole and the Ribbon Reefs. The trip usually takes 4 to 7 days. As well as showing you amazing huge schools of pelagic and reef fish big and small, a wide range of corals, and excellent gorgonian fans, the area is a prime place to spot sharks. The most popular site is **Osprey Reef,** a 100-sq.-km (39-sq.-mile) reef with 1,000m (3,300-ft.) drop-offs, renowned for its year-round visibility of up to 70m (230 ft.). The highlight of most Osprey Reef itineraries is a **shark feeding** session. White-tip reef sharks are common, but the area is also home to gray reef shark, silvertips, and hammerheads. Green turtles, tuna, barracuda, potato cod, mantas, and grouper are also common.

Closer to shore, Cairns has several coral cays and reef-fringed islands within the **Great Barrier Reef Marine Park.** Less than an hour from the city wharf, **Green Island** is a 15-hectare (37-acre) coral cay with snorkeling equal to that on the Great Barrier Reef. It is also a popular diving spot. You can visit it in half a day if time is short. The sailing boat *Ocean Free* (see later in this chapter) makes a snorkel/dive day trip that moors off the island, and the "Exploring the Islands" section later in this chapter has details on other day trips to the island.

The **Frankland Islands** is a pristine group of uninhabited rain-forested isles edged with sandy beaches, reefs, and fish 45km (28 miles) south of Cairns. The islands are a rookery for **green sea turtles,** which snorkelers and divers often spot in the water. In February and March, you may even be lucky enough to see dozens of baby turtles hatching in the sand. **Michaelmas Cay** and **Upolu Cay** are two pretty coral sand blips, 30km (19 miles) and 25km (16 miles) off Cairns, surrounded by reefs. Michaelmas is vegetated and is home to 27,000 sea birds; you may spot *dugongs* (manatees) off Upolu. Michaelmas and Upolu are great for snorkelers and introductory divers, but experienced divers are probably better off visiting the sites at such reefs as Norman, Hastings, or Saxon.

DAY-TRIP DIVE & SNORKEL BOATS

The prices quoted below include all snorkel and dive gear, unless otherwise specified, and lunch. Departure times given here are the time the boat heads out to sea; plan to board about 30 minutes earlier on a medium-size boat, and as much as 45 minutes earlier on the big 300-passenger boats.

Remember to add the A$4.50 (US$3.60) Environmental Management Charge, or "reef tax," to the fare of every passenger over 4 years old.

Fun Fact **Send a Letter from the Sea!**

Australia's only "floating post office" is on Agincourt Reef, about 72km (45 miles) offshore from Port Douglas. It was established by Quicksilver Connections, and your letter or postcard will be stamped with a special postmark from the Great Barrier Reef.

EXPENSIVE BOATS

Two companies in Cairns operate 30m (100-ft.) and larger motorized catamarans, each carrying about 300 passengers to the Reef: **Sunlover Cruises** (© **1800/810 512** in Australia, or 07/4050 1333; www.sunlover.com.au) and **Great Adventures** (© **07/4044 9944;** www.greatadventures.com.au). Their boats have two or three large levels of indoor seating and sunny outdoor seating. Sunlover makes two daily cruises: one via Palm Cove Jetty to Arlington Reef, and one to Moore Reef. Both give you about 4 hours on the reef. Once it reaches the Reef, the boat moors at its own pontoon, which has shaded tables and chairs, an underwater observatory, free semi-submersible and glass-bottom boat rides, cold freshwater showers, a marine life touch tank, and a tiny sea enclosure for little kids. Moore Reef has a lovely variety of coral on its flat top and its steep walls, a few giant clams, and a good range of fish life. Safety standards were excellent: The crew gives a very informative snorkel briefing, all snorkelers are encouraged to wear a lifejacket (many smaller boats do not offer these), and the snorkel area is roped off with buoys and rest stations. Despite the defined snorkeling area, it's easy to escape the crowds. At the end of the snorkel safari, the crew feed large schnapper, which you can watch from the deck or from the underwater theatre. There's an excellent Reef talk, and videos of your day are sold on board.

The trip to Moore Reef is A$179 (US$143) for adults, A$90 (US$72) for kids ages 4 to 14, or A$448 (US$358) for a family of four. Diving is pricey, though, and costs an extra A$107 (US$86) for either an introductory dive, or a guided certified dive. The Arlington Reef trip is similar, but slightly less expensive at A$142 (US$114) for adults, A$71 (US$57) for kids, and A$355 (US$284) for a family of four. A guided snorkel safari is A$20 (US$16). Pickups from city and northern beaches hotels cost A$8 (US$6.40) per person, from Port Douglas they cost A$13 (US$10) per person. Both boats depart daily from Cairns' Reef Fleet Terminal at 10am, returning at 5pm or 5:30pm. Lockers are available at the wharf for A$4 (US$3.20); towels are also available for rent. *A tip:* Book the snorkel safari the moment you board, as places are limited and fill up fast.

Sunlover also has special packages that include such features as a ride on Skyrail, a visit to Kuranda and Rainforestation, and a day on the Atherton Tablelands.

Great Adventures (© **1800/079 080** in Australia, or 07/4044 9944; www.greatadventures.com.au) is the other big operator in

Cairns. Its day trips are similar to Sunlover's in the kind of boats, number of passengers, traveling times, and activities. It visits a pontoon on Norman or Moore reefs, where you get at least 3 hours. The day costs A$162 (US$130) adults, A$84 (US$67) children ages 4 to 14, and A$414 (US$331) for a family of four. Hotel transfers are available from Cairns, the northern beaches, and Port Douglas for an extra charge. Guided snorkel tours are A$30 (US$24) extra, introductory dives are A$125 (US$100) extra, and certified dives cost A$80 (US$64) for one dive, A$125 (US$100) for two. Great Adventures' trips run daily and depart at 10:30am. Great Adventures also has a trip departing at 8:30am that spends around 2 hours on Green Island en route. This cruise runs daily and costs A$182 (US$146) adults, A$94 (US$75) kids, or A$464 (US$371) families.

A pleasant alternative to a big motorized catamaran is a big sailing catamaran operated by **Ocean Spirit Cruises** (© **1800/644 227** in Australia or 07/4031 2920; www.oceanspirit.com.au). Its two smart white sailing catamarans take 150 or 100 passengers to Michaelmas Cay or Upolu Cay, respectively. If you choose Upolu Cay, you will also have time at Oyster Reef on the way. The trip includes a 2-hour sail to your destination, free use of snorkel equipment and guided beach walk (on Michaelmas only), a marine biology presentation, semisubmersible or glass bottom boat rides, lunch, and a free glass of bubbly and live music on the way home. You get 4 hours on the Reef. The trip to Michaelmas Cay is A$169 (US$135) for adults and A$88 (US$70) for children 4 to 14. The trip to Upolu Cay costs A$99 (US$79) for adults, A$76 (US$61) for kids. Transfers from Cairns and the northern beaches are A$12/US$9.60 (free on the Upolo Cay trip), or A$39 (US$31) per person from Port Douglas. Introductory dives cost A$95 (US$76) at Michaelmas Cay and A$64 (US$51) at Upolu; certified divers pay A$65 (US$52) for one or A$110 (US$88) for two, all gear included, at Michaelmas Cay, and A$45 (US$36) for one and A$70 (US$56) for two at Upolu. The boats depart Reef Fleet Terminal at 8:30am daily.

If you're staying in Cairns, remember you can transfer to Port Douglas to join the Reef boats operating from that town. You can even board the Port Douglas–based **Quicksilver Wavepiercers** (see chapter 4) in Cairns or Palm Cove, cruise up to Port Douglas to pick up the passengers there, then head out to the Reef. You transfer back to Cairns by Wavepiercer or coach, or you can stay on in Port Douglas. The fare for the whole day from Cairns or Palm Cove

---

> ### *Tips* Diving Made Easy
>
> Can't swim? Don't want to get your hair wet? Don't worry—
> you can still get underwater and see the wonders of the Reef.
> Several companies are now offering the chance to don a "dive
> helmet" and "walk" underwater. Similar to the old-style diving
> helmets, which allow you to "breathe" underwater, the helmet
> has air pumped into it by a hose. You walk into the water to a
> depth of about 4 meters, accompanied by instructors, and the
> reef is right before you. With **Quicksilver Cruises** it's called
> "Ocean Walker," with **Sunlover Cruises** and at **Green Island
> Resort** it's "Sea Walker." You must be 10 or 12 years or older,
> and the cost is about A$130 (US$104) for 20 minutes.

---

is A$190 (US$152) adults, A$98 (US$78) kids 4 to 14. A second
child travels free in a family package.

Frankland Islands Cruise & Dive (✆ **1800/079 039** in Australia, or 07/4031 6300; www.franklandislands.com) is the only
company with a permit to visit the Frankland Islands. It takes a
maximum of 100 passengers in a 24m (79-ft.) catamaran on daily
trips to Normanby Island within the Frankland group. The trip
includes easy walks among the island's rainforest and tidal flats and
educational underwater snorkel trails on the Reef. The trip includes
free glass-bottom boat rides, and a gourmet beach barbecue lunch.
Snorkeling can be done from right off the beach. Snorkeling
instruction and a snorkel safari are included. You get about 5 hours
on the island. The tour begins and ends with a cruise along the Mulgrave River to learn about the riverine ecosystem, which is vital to
the Reef's well being. The trip costs A$139 (US$111) for adults,
A$70 (US$56) for children 4 to 14, and A$348 (US$278) for a
family of four. Introductory diving is A$90 (US$72) extra, or A$60
(US$48) for the second dive; certified diving is A$60 (US$48), or
A$55 (US$44) for the second dive. The price includes round-trip
hotel transfers. You'll be picked up from your Cairns or northern
beaches hotel by 7:15am. You return between 5:30 and 6pm. The
boat departs a riverside landing 45km (28 miles) south of Cairns at
8:50am, arriving at Normanby Island at 9:45am. Wear old shoes as
you will get them wet. The company also does 2-day packages.

MODERATELY PRICED BOATS
Medium-size, moderately priced, fast-paced motorized boats that take
from 50 to 100 passengers are the most common kind of day-trip

vessel operating in Cairns. They typically take about 90 minutes or 1¾ hours to get to the Reef, and usually visit two, sometimes three, different Reef sites in a day. Most have shaded indoor seating and limited sunny outdoor seating. Space can be tight, especially on the outdoor deck, but the boats are generally pretty comfortable. One of the best also happens to be one of the cheapest—the *Osprey V,* described in the "Inexpensive" section, below.

Another boat with a good reputation in this category is *Sea Quest,* a modern 21m (68-ft.) mono-hull operated by **Deep Sea Divers Den** (© 07/4046 7333; www.divers-den.com). It carries a maximum 43 passengers (of which a maximum of 35 are divers) to 2 sites out of a possible 18. Cruises depart Marlin Marina daily at 8:30am and return around 4:30pm. The cost is A$95 (US$76) for snorkelers, A$160 (US$128) for certified divers with two unguided dives, or A$190 (US$152) with a dive guide, and A$145 (US$116) for first-time divers. Rates include round-trip hotel pickups from the city and northern beaches, and a wet suit. The crew offers free, guided snorkel tours, sells a video of your day, and rents underwater cameras. Unusual for a day-trip boat, this one has hot showers.

INEXPENSIVE BOATS

The medium-size *Osprey V,* operated by **Down Under Dive** (© 1800/079 099 in Australia, or 07/4052 8300; www.downunder dive.com.au) comes highly recommended by those who've experienced it. That's not only because it visits two great Reef sites (North Norman and Saxon), but because it also has an unfailingly good-humored crew, who finish your day with them with a riotous cheer and a handshake from the entire crew as you disembark. The 30m (98-ft.) catamaran was delivered new in August 2000, equipped with all-new dive gear. It is one of the fastest boats on the Reef, giving you 5 hours on the coral.

Osprey V is a good choice for first-timers. Both snorkelers and certified divers receive an extremely thorough briefing, and safety is paramount. Every passenger is assigned a safety number on boarding (most other boats simply perform a head count), snorkelers are asked to look up at the boat every 3 or 4 minutes to check its location, a "heads-up" whistle system alerts snorkelers to any announcements, and the lifeguards are rigorous about whistling back snorkelers who stray more than 100m (328 ft.) from the boat. Less-confident snorkelers are offered supervision and life jackets. Introductory dives cost A$130 (US$104) for one dive, A$165 (US$132) for two, and A$185 (US$148) for three. Pre-book your dive, or you'll pay A$20 (US$16) extra if you book once aboard. Certified divers may dive without a guide; dive guides cost A$10 (US$8) extra per dive. The day costs just A$95 (US$76) for snorkelers; certified divers pay A$130 (US$104) for two dives or A$150 (US$120) for three, including a free snorkel safari. A pass for a family of four covering two kids ages 4 to 14 costs A$270 (US$216). Wet suits are A$5 (US$4) for snorkelers, free for divers. Round-trip transfers from your hotel cost A$7 (US$5.60), or A$12 (US$9.60) from the northern beaches. A barbecue lunch is served. The boat does not produce videos of your day, or rent underwater cameras. It departs Marlin Marina every day at 8:30am and returns around 5pm. Ask about packages that combine the Reef trip with excursions to Kuranda (see "A Rainforest Village: A Side Trip to Kuranda," later in this chapter), tandem skydiving, whitewater rafting, or a 4WD safari through the Daintree rainforest (see chapter 4).

Most boats at the budget end of the market tend to be sailing boats, on which deck space is limited. Many don't have seats; so they may not be a good choice if you're unfit or not prepared to do a bit of clambering. Sailing boats are also usually not as fast as motorized vessels, so they usually stick to a single Reef site at closer-in spots like Upolu Cay and Green Island.

An exception is *Passions of Paradise II* (© 1800/111-346 in Australia or 07/4050 0676; www.passionsofparadise.com), a new A$1.5-million (US$1.2 million) 25m (81-ft.) sailing catamaran that visits both the Outer Reef and Upolu Cay daily for A$89 (US$71) adults, A$55 (US$44) children aged 4 to 12. The boat, launched in November 2002, is one of the fastest and most modern sailing catamarans in Australia and because it is designed to sail in all weathers, is ideal for passengers who want to sail—you'll be encouraged to get into the whole spirit of the thing. First stop on the trip is Paradise Reef (or what the locals call Breaking Patches) where you'll have exclusive use of the reef, which means fewer crowds and better-protected coral. It's an excellent reef for snorkeling and diving, and there are free snorkel safaris and the chance to do introductory and certified diving during your 3½ hours there. On the return journey, you'll have about an hour or so at Upolu Cay where you can get off the boat, sunbake on the cay, swim in the shallow waters, and snorkel. *Passions of Paradise II* is unique among the sailboats in that you get to experience both the Outer Barrier Reef and a coral cay.

One of the nicest day trips is offered by *Ocean Free* (© 07/4041 1118; www.oceanfree.com.au), a 19m (63-ft.) schooner that motor-sails to a private mooring at Pinnacle Reef, 1km (½ mile) off Green Island. It carries a maximum of 35 passengers daily and has a marine naturalist on board. After a morning snorkel or dive and lunch, you can spend the whole afternoon on Green Island, or have an hour on the island and get taken back to the mooring by the tender boat for more snorkeling and diving. The boat returns home under sail, which you can take a hand in if you like, while enjoying a free glass of wine and a cake/fruit/cheese platter. You get about 4½ hours on the Reef. The boat allocates one dive instructor to every two or three first-time divers, compared to most boats' diver-to-instructor ratio of 4 to 1. If you're super-nervous, they will give you an instructor to yourself. Certified divers also enjoy a low diver-to-guide ratio of 4 to 1. The boat has life jackets for snorkelers. A snorkel safari is included in the price of A$89 (US$71) adults, A$60 (US$48) children 4 to 12, or A$268 (US$214) for a family of four. Introductory dives are A$70 (US$56) for one, or A$105 (US$84) for two. Certified dives are A$50 (US$40) for one, or A$70 (US$56) for two. A dive guide is free. The boat departs Marlin Marina at 8:30am and gets back between 5:30 and 6pm.

Another good inexpensive choice is **Seahorse** (© **07/4041 1919;** www.seahorsedive.com.au), a new 20-passenger sailing catamaran that visits Upolu Cay daily for A$89 (US$71) adults and A$55 (US$44) kids 4–14. A snorkel safari is included, and they also offer introductory dives for A$65 (US$52) and certified diving for A$45 (US$36), with guide. Wetsuit hire is A$6 (US$4.80). *Seahorse* is known for its friendly crew, and offers pick-ups from the city for A$6 (US$4.80) or from the northern beaches for A$12 (US$9.60). It leaves Marlin Marina at 8:55am and returns around 6pm.

LIVE-ABOARD EXCURSIONS

The most lavish live-aboard vessel operating out of Cairns is the *Nimrod Explorer,* operated by **Explorer Ventures** (© **800/322 3577** in the U.S., or 07/4031 5566 in Australia; www.explorer ventures.com). The 20m (65-ft.) catamaran accommodates a maximum of 18 passengers in smart wood-paneled double or quad-share air-conditioned cabins. All have en suite bathrooms, and portholes or windows. The roomy lounge has a stereo and a book/video/game library, and there is outdoor deck space for relaxing and barbecues. Photographers can rent underwater cameras and videos and process and edit the results on board. The boat visits Cod Hole, the Ribbon Reefs, and the Coral Sea, as well as occasionally the Far Northern Reefs of the Lockhart River. PADI advanced and specialty courses are offered on board. A 3½-day trip fits in up to 12 dives and ranges from A$995 to $1,595 (US$796–$1,276), depending on your cabin choice; budget A$95 (US$76) extra for gear rental. A 7-day, 23-dive trip costs from A$1,345 to $2,395 (US$1,076–$1,916); budget A$135 (US$108) for gear rental. At the end of the 3½-day itinerary, the boat may carry on with its 7-day itinerary, so instead of returning to Cairns aboard the boat, passengers take a low-level 1-hour scenic flight from Cooktown over the Reef back to Cairns; this is included in the price, as are meals and city hotel transfers. On the Far Northern Reef itineraries only, which usually take 7 days, allow an extra A$220 (US$176) for charter flights to this trip's departure gateway of Lockhart River, north of Cairns. Nimrod Explorer's trips depart once or twice weekly. A luggage limit of 20kg (44 lb.), which should be packed in soft bags, applies on the planes.

If you're looking for a laid-back experience, **Down Under Dive's** *Atlantic Clipper* (© **1800/079 099** in Australia, or 07/4052 8300; www.downunderdive.com.au) may be your thing. This 43m (140-ft.), 1890s-style brigantine makes 2-, 3-, and 4-day snorkeling and diving sailing cruises between Hastings, Saxon, and Norman reefs. Built to sleep 44 passengers, it is a nice boat, not glamorous but comfortable, with a Jacuzzi on the foredeck. Below-deck is mostly given over to a big dining room; double, triple, or quad-share air-conditioned cabins; and hot showers. The boat is moored on the Reef; a launch takes you out to it from Cairns. A 2-day/1-night trip costs A$210 (US$168) for snorkelers or A$290 (US$232) for divers in a triple or quad-share cabin. A 3-day/2-night trip costs A$340 (US$272) for snorkelers or A$400 (US$320) for divers in a triple or quad. Add A$20 to $30 (US$16–$24) per person per night for a twin or double cabin. Twin-, triple- and quad-share cabins do not have private showers; doubles do. Prices include all dive and snorkel gear, meals, and a pickup from your Cairns city accommodations.

Other respected companies operating live-aboard vessels to Cod Hole and/or the Coral Sea are **Deep Sea Divers Den** (© **07/4046 7333;** www.divers-den.com), **Taka Dive Australia** (© **07/4051 8722;** www.taka.com.au), and **Mike Ball Dive Expeditions** (© **1888/MIKEBALL** in the U.S. and Canada, or 07/4031 5484; www.mikeball.com). Mike Ball's boats are large and especially well equipped, allowing for an unlimited number of dives and solo dives.

ISLAND RESORTS

For a full discussion of the facilities at the best island resorts off Cairns, see "Where to Stay" later in this chapter and "Which Great Barrier Reef Resort Is Right for You?" in chapter 1. Resorts on **Lizard Island, Green Island,** and **Fitzroy Island** offer diving and learn-to-dive courses. Lizard has some of the most spectacular snorkeling on the Reef, some of it right off the beach. The island is renowned for its abundant giant clams. Green has terrific snorkeling, too, and it's right off the sand. Fitzroy's beachside snorkeling is poor; you will need to take a short boat trip to access better stuff.

LEARNING TO DIVE

Cairns' longest-established dive company, **Deep Sea Divers Den** (© 07/4046 7333; www.divers-den.com), is widely regarded as very professional, and claims to be one of the world's biggest dive schools. Its courses are a good example of what you can expect to pay in Cairns. Its 5-day PADI open-water certification course incorporating nine dives is A$550 (US$440), including a 3-day live-aboard component. They offer a budget 4-day, 5-dive course, including two daytrips to the reef, for A$300 (US$240), or a 4-day, 5-dive course with 2 days live-aboard for A$440 (US$352). A 6-day, 13-dive course that combines beginner and advanced open-water certification costs A$730 (US$584). Free transfers from and to your city hotel are included on days 1 and 2, as are meals on days 3, 4, and 5. Transfers from the northern beaches are A$24 (US$19), round-trip. A new course starts every day. An on-site medical center takes care of your required medical examination. The company runs a range of courses—Deep Diver, Navigator, Search and Recovery, Multi-level Diver, Underwater Naturalist, Boat Diver, and Peak Performance Buoyancy—as well as Rescue, Dive Master and Instructor courses. They also do 2- and 3-day referral courses, either land-based or live-aboard, for folks who have completed their pool and theory training elsewhere.

Other respected dive schools include **Cairns Dive Centre** (© 1800/642 591 in Australia, or 07/4051 0294; www.cairnsdive.com.au); **Down Under Dive** (© 1800/079 099 in Australia, or 07/4052 8300; www.downunderdive.com.au); **Mike Ball Dive Expeditions** (© 1888/MIKEBALL in the U.S. and Canada, or

---

Tips Making Travel Arrangements

Unless you know what Reef trips and other tours you want to take, it often pays to wait until you get to Cairns to book them. Local travel agents, your hotel or B&B host, and other travelers are all good sources of advice. Cairns has some 600 tour operators, so even in peak season, it's rare for a Reef boat or tour to be booked up more than 24 hours in advance.

07/4031 5484; www.mikeball.com), the Cairns branch of the world's biggest dive store chain; **Pro Dive** (✆ **07/4031 5255;** www.prodive-cairns.com.au); **Taka Dive Australia** (✆ **07/4051 8722;** www.taka.com.au); and **TUSA Dive** (✆ **07/4040 6464;** www.tusadive.com). Highly regarded Port Douglas–based company **Quicksilver Diving Services** (✆ **07/4099 5050** for its Port Douglas headquarters; www.quicksilverdive.com.au) conducts a 4-day open-water certification course starting every Tuesday, based at the Novotel Palm Cove Resort at **Palm Cove.** It includes 2 days of pool and theory work, and 2 days of diving the outer Reef.

Taka Dive Australia conducts **underwater photography courses** on its live-aboard trips for an extra A$165 (US$132), plus A$75 (US$60) for camera hire, plus A$25 (US$20) to obtain your official PADI certificate as an underwater photographer.

If you're short on time, consider Pro Dive's 3-day open-water certification course based on **Fitzroy Island.** It includes boat transfers from Cairns and all dive equipment (including prescription mask if you need it) and costs from A$325 (US$260) for 2 nights' bunkhouse accommodations on the island, more if you upgrade your accommodations. Lizard and Green Island also conduct dive courses.

USEFUL DIVE-RELATED BUSINESSES

Loads of companies sell and rent dive gear in Cairns. One of the most conveniently located is **Pro-Dive** at 116 Spence St., (✆ **07/4031 5255**). **Taka Dive Australia,** at 131 Lake St. (✆ **07/4051 8722**), and **Deep Sea Divers Den,** at 319 Draper St. (✆ **07/4046 7333**), are two other major stores.

Cairns Underwater Camera Centre (✆ **07/4051 8722**) sells new and secondhand underwater cameras, plus accessories and film. It is located within Taka Dive Australia's premises.

John Sande of **Scubaquip Services,** 15 Amaroo Close, Smithfield Heights, about a 15-minute drive north of downtown Cairns (✆ **07/4038 1569** or mobile phone 0412/456 046), repairs dive equipment. Deep Sea Divers Den and Pro Dive, above, are service centers for a wide range of dive-equipment brands.

3 Exploring the Islands

GREEN ISLAND 🐠   You can visit Green Island with a snorkel and dive boat such as *Ocean Free* (see "Diving & Snorkeling the Reef," earlier in this chapter), but you can also make a day trip to rent windsurfers and paddle-skis, take glass-bottom boat trips, go parasailing, walk vine-forest trails, or laze on the beach. The island's dive shop rents snorkel gear and offers introductory or certified dives. The beach is coral sand, so it's a little rough underfoot. Day visitors can use one of Green Island Resort's pools, its main bar, its casual or upscale restaurants, and its lockers and showers; and buy basics, ice cream, and beachwear. If you don't snorkel, it's worth the meager admission charge to see the magical display of clown fish, potato cod, and anemones at the little underwater observatory, despite its cloudy old viewing windows. The island has a small attraction called **Marineland Melanesia** (✆ **07/4051 4032**), where you can see old nautical artifacts, primitive art, a turtle and reef aquarium, and live crocodiles. Admission is A$10 (US$8) adults, A$4.50 (US$3.60) kids; croc shows are at 10:30am and 1:45pm.

You can simply take a boat transfer to the island and do your own thing, or you can join an organized trip. Boat transfers with the island's ferry operator, Great Adventures, are A$56 (US$45) adults, A$28 (US$22) kids 4 to 14, or A$120 (US$96) families, round-trip. **Great Adventures** (✆ **07/4044 9944**) and **Big Cat Green Island Reef Cruises** (✆ **07/4051 0444**) both offer day trips to the island. Expect to pay around A$60 (US$48) for a half-day trip that includes snorkel gear or a glass-bottom boat cruise. A full-day trip can be as much as A$98 (US$78), but Big Cat makes a day trip for as little as A$56 (US$45). Big Cat's boat is slower, but you still get 5 hours on the island. Both companies pick up from hotels in Cairns, the northern beaches, and Port Douglas for a little extra; Big Cat also runs to the island direct from Palm Cove.

FITZROY ISLAND It lacks the off-the-beach coral and wide beaches of Green Island, but equally scenic Fitzroy Island is a hilly rainforested national park 45 minutes offshore that offers good diving. You can rent windsurfers, catamarans, and canoes; hike to the mountain-top lighthouse; view coral from a glass-bottom boat or take a short boat trip from the island to snorkel it; take a beginner's or certified dive; and swim in the pool. A day trip is simply the price of the ferry fare at A$36 (US$29) round-trip, A$18 (US$14) for kids 4 to 14. Departures from Cairns are daily at 8:30am, 10:30am, and 4pm, returning at 9:30am, 3pm, and 5pm. Book at ✆ **07/4030 7907,** or through **Raging Thunder Adventures** (✆ **07/4030 7990;** www.ragingthunder.com.au). Raging Thunder also runs guided sea-kayak expeditions around Fitzroy Island. The trips include 3 hours of kayaking, snorkeling gear, lunch on a deserted beach, and a rainforest walk to the lighthouse. The full-day trip costs A$125 (US$100), but you must be age 13 or over. You can also stay on the island for as little as A$31 (US$25) per person per night in multishare bunkhouse accommodations (see "Where to Stay," later in this chapter).

4 Other Things to See & Do In & Around Cairns

If you're staying in Cairns, also check out what there is to see and do in and around Port Douglas (see chapter 4) and Mission Beach (see chapter 5). Many tour operators in Port Douglas, and a few in Mission Beach, offer free or affordable transfers from Cairns.

LEARNING ABOUT ABORIGINAL CULTURE

Tjapukai Aboriginal Cultural Park ★★★   Don't miss this. The Tjapukai (pronounced Jab-*oo*-gai) cultural park is one of the best chances you'll have to discover the history and culture of the Aboriginal people without going to Central Australia. American theater director Don Freeman and his French-Canadian show-dancer wife, Judy, founded the center in 1987. The Freemans worked closely with local Aborigines, including acclaimed dancer and songwriter David Hudson, to establish a small dance theater in Kuranda, which has evolved into the multi–award-winning cultural park you see today. Don and Judy are still heavily involved, but the park is 51% owned by the Aboriginal people who work in it.

Housed in a striking modern building that incorporates Aboriginal themes and colors, the Tjapukai experience needs at least 2 to 3 hours, but you will leave with insight into the history and culture of the traditional people of the Kuranda region.

The Creation Theatre is a mix of culture and technology, where the latest in illusion, theatrics, and technology are used to tell the story of the creation of the world according to the spiritual beliefs of Tjapukai people. Actors work with spectacular special effects and holographic images to illustrate the legends. The production is performed in the Tjapukai language, translated through headsets.

Move on through the Magic Space museum and gallery section to the History Theatre, where a 20-minute film relates the history of the Tjapukai people since the coming of white settlers 120 years ago.

Outside, a suspension bridge links the main building with a cultural village where you can try boomerang and spear throwing, fire-making, and didgeridoo playing, and learn about bush foods and medicines. In the open-sided Dance Theatre, Aboriginal men and women perform dances incorporating ancient and modern steps. Shows and demonstrations are planned so visitors can move

> ## (*Tips* **Croc Alert!**
>
> Crocodiles inhabit all Cairns waterways! Do not swim in, or stand on the bank of, any river, stream, estuary, or mangrove.

from one to another easily, without missing anything. The complex also includes a restaurant and coffee shop, and an arts-and-crafts gallery and shop is stocked with the work of local Aboriginal artists and crafts workers.

"Tjapukai by Night" tours runs daily from 7:30 to 10pm, interactive time in the Magic Space museum, a Creation Show performance, and an outdoor **Serpent Circle**—a new, interactive show featuring tap sticks for each guest to use, a join-in corroboree (an Aboriginal nighttime dance), and a dramatic ceremony involving fire and water. It is followed by a buffet dinner and dance show, and the chance to meet the Tjapukai dancers. The cost is A$96 (US$77) adults, A$48 (US$38) children. Transfers to and from Cairns accommodations are included.

Captain Cook Hwy. (beside the Skyrail terminal), Smithfield. ( ) **07/4042 9900**. Fax 07/4042 9990. www.tjapukai.com.au. Admission A$29 (US$23) adults, A$15 (US$12) children 4–14, A$73 (US$58) family. AE, DC, MC, V. Ask about packages that include transfers, lunch, and a guided Magic Space tour, or Skyrail and/or Scenic Rail travel to and from Kuranda. Daily 9am–5pm. Closed Christmas and New Year's Day. Bus: 1C or 1E. Book shuttle transfers from Cairns and northern beaches hotels (A$9/US$7.20 adults and A$4.50/US$3.60 children, one way) through the park. Park is 15 min. north of Cairns and 15 min. south of Palm Cove. Free parking.

FACE TO FACE WITH AUSSIE WILDLIFE

Cairns Rainforest Dome   For some visitors to Cairns, exploring the rainforest and its wildlife doesn't even involve leaving their hotel, thanks to the city's newest attraction. Here, 100 species—including a huge saltwater crocodile called Goliath—are housed in a 20 meter high glass dome on the rooftop of the Hotel Sofitel Reef Casino (see "Where to Stay" later this chapter). You can get up close with koalas, lizards, kookaburra, pademelons (related to kangaroos), and snakes. There are wildlife presentations and free guided tours throughout the day.

Entry via lifts in the Reef Hotel Casino foyer, 35–41 Wharf St., Cairns, QLD 4870. ( ) **07/4031 7250**; Fax: 07/4031 5265. www.cairnsdome.com.au. Admission A$20 (US$16) adults, A$10 (US$8) children. Daily 7am to 6pm. Closed Christmas.

Cairns Tropical Zoo *(Kids*   Get a dose of your favorite Aussie wildlife here—some kind of talk or show takes place just about every 15 or 30 minutes all day, including koala cuddling (have your photo taken for an extra A$13/US$10), saltwater crocodile and lorikeet feedings, and cane toad racing. Lots of other animals are on show, like kangaroos (which you can hand-feed for A$1/US80¢ a bag), emus, cassowaries, dingoes, and native birds in a walk-through aviary. The park also runs a nocturnal tour, in which you can see many of the more elusive creatures. To take the park's 3-hour Cairns Night Zoo tour, book by 4pm that day, earlier if you want transfers. The evening starts at 7pm and includes a wildlife spotlighting walk, where you can pat a koala and a possum and feed kangaroos; a stargazing interlude; a barbecue dinner with beer and wine, billy tea and damper and supper; and dancing to an Aussie bush band.

Captain Cook Hwy. (22km/14 miles north of the city center), Palm Cove. ℂ 07/4055 3669. Fax 07/4059 1160. www.cairnstropicalzoo.com. Admission A$24 (US$19) adults, A$12 (US$9.60) children 4–15. Cairns Night Zoo experience (daily except Fri and Sun) A$99 (US$79) adults, A$50 (US$40) children 4–15. AE, DC, MC, V. Daily 8:30am–5pm. Closed Christmas. Bus: 1B. Cairns Night Zoo transfers from Cairns through All In A Day Tours (ℂ 07/4032 5050) or from Port Douglas with Night Zoo Tours (ℂ 07/4098 4929). Free parking.

Hartley's Crocodile Adventures 𝒜𝒜 𝐾𝑖𝑑𝑠   Hartley's is the origi-
nal Australian croc show, and after a move to a new location and a multimillion-dollar redevelopment in mid-2002, quite possibly the best. What makes it different from others is the fantastic natural setting—a 2-hectare (5-acre) lagoon surrounded by melaleuca (paper-bark) and bloodwood trees and home to 23 estuarine crocs. The best time to visit is for the 3pm "croc attack" show, when you can witness the saltwater crocodile "death roll" during the 45-minute perform-ance. At 11am you can see these monsters get hand-fed or hear an eye-opening talk on the less aggressive freshwater crocodiles. There are tours of the croc farm at 10am and 1:30pm; at 2pm there is a snake show; and at 4:30pm it's koala-feeding time. This attraction makes a good stop en route to Port Douglas, and also has cassowaries, which are fed at 9:30am and 4:15pm.

Capt. Cook Hwy. (40km/24 miles north of Cairns; 25km/16 miles south of Port Dou-glas). ℂ 07/4055 3576. Fax 07/4059 1017. www.crocodileadventures.com. Admis-sion A$24 (US$19) adults, A$12 (US$9.60) children 4–15, A$60 (US$48) families. Tickets allow return entry for 3 days. Daily 8:30am–5pm. Closed Christmas. Transfers from Cairns available through Hartleys Express (ℂ 07/4038 2992) or All In A Day Tours (ℂ 07/4032 5050), or from Port Douglas through Wildlife Discovery Tours (ℂ 07/4099 6612). Free parking.

EXPLORING THE WET TROPICS RAINFOREST
The dense rainforest that blankets the hills behind Cairns is part of the **Wet Tropics of Queensland World Heritage Area** 𝒜 that

stretches from Cooktown to Townsville. Unchanged by ice ages and other blips on the geological timeline, its animals and plants retain primitive characteristics from the days when Australia belonged to Gondwana, the supercontinent it occupied with Africa, India, South America, and Antarctica. It shelters 65% of Australia's bird species, 60% of its butterfly species, and many of its frogs, reptiles, bats, marsupials, and orchids. The 110-million-year-old World Heritage–listed Daintree Rainforest, 2 hours north of Cairns, gets most of the attention, but tracts of rainforest closer to Cairns are just as pristine. These rainforests and the Daintree are part of the Wet Tropics, a World Heritage area that stretches from Cape Tribulation to Townsville. This dense, lush environment has remained unchanged by Ice Ages and other geological events, and the plants and animals here retain primitive characteristics.

Because so much rainforest wildlife is nocturnal and often difficult to spot, consider joining **Wait-a-While Rainforest Tours** (© 07/4098 2422; www.axioadventures.com.au) on one of their afternoon-into-night trips into Daintree and Cape Tribulation national parks. The tours cost A$265 to A$285 (US$212–US$228) and are designed to maximize your encounters with the wild things.

A RAINFOREST VILLAGE: A SIDE TRIP TO KURANDA

Few travelers visit Cairns without making a day trip to the pretty mountain village of Kuranda, 34km (21 miles) west of the city within the Wet Tropics. Although it's undeniably touristy, the cool mountain air and mist-wrapped, jungly scenery cannot be spoiled, no matter how many visitors clutter the streets. The town is easily negotiated on foot, so pick up a visitors' guide and map at the Skyrail station or train station when you arrive.

GETTING THERE

Getting to Kuranda is part of the fun. Some people drive up on the winding 25km (16-mile) road, but the most popular routes are to

---

Tips Wildlife-Viewing

If you want to spot rainforest wildlife, join a specialist tour. To avoid contact with humans, rainforest animals are retreating to higher altitudes; however, most tour operators in Daintree National Park stick to the lowlands. Rainforest animals are shy, camouflaged, nocturnal, or all three, so evening spotlighting trips offer the most wildlife-viewing bang for your buck.

chuff up the mountainside in a scenic train, or to glide silently over the rainforest canopy on the world's longest cable-car route, with Skyrail Rainforest Cableway. Most people combine the two; they take Skyrail on the way up to Kuranda (mornings are best for photos) and the train back down to Cairns in the afternoon. Both routes traverse the 2,820-hectare (6,965-acre) Barron Gorge National Park.

BY SKYRAIL   The **Skyrail Rainforest Cableway** 👫👫👫 (ℂ **07/ 4038 1555;** www.skyrail.com.au) is a magnificent feat of engineering and one of Australia's top attractions. About 114 six-person gondolas leave every few seconds from the terminal in the northern Cairns suburb of Smithfield for the 7.5km (4½-mile) journey. The view of the coast as you ascend is so breathtaking that even those afraid of heights will find it worth overcoming their nervousness for. As you rise over the foothills, watch the lush green of the rainforest take over beneath you. Looking back, there are spectacular views over Cairns and north towards Trinity Bay. On a clear day, you can see Green Island. There are two stops along the way—at Red Peak and Barron Falls—and about 90 minutes is needed to make the trip. After about 10 minutes, you reach Red Peak. You are now 545m (1,788 ft.) above sea level, and massive kauri pines dominate the view. You must change gondolas at each station, so take the time to stroll around the boardwalks for the ground view of the rainforest. Guided walks are run every 20 minutes.

On to Barron Falls station, built on the site of an old construction camp for workers on the first hydroelectric power station on the Barron River in the 1930s. A rainforest information center has been established here, and there are boardwalks to the lookouts for wonderful views of the Barron Gorge and Falls. From Barron Falls station, the gondola travels over the thickly rainforested range, and it's easy to spot ferns and orchids and the brilliant blue butterflies of the region. As you reach the end of the trip, the gondola passes over the Barron River and across the Kuranda railway line into the station. A one-way ticket is A$34 (US$27) for adults and A$17 (US$14) for children 4 to 14; a round-trip ticket, including transfers from your Cairns or northern beaches hotel, is A$65 (US$52) for adults, A$33 (US$26) for children, or A$163 (US$130) for a family, and A$81 (US$65) for adults, A$41 (US$33) for children, or A$203 (US$162) for a family from Port Douglas. You must make a reservation to travel within a 15-minute time frame. Don't worry if it rains on the day you've chosen to go—one of the best trips I've made on Skyrail was in a misty rain, which added a new dimension to the rainforest.

The cableway operates from 8:30am to 5:30pm, with last boarding at the Cairns end at 4:15pm. Closed Christmas. The Skyrail terminal is on the Captain Cook Highway at Kamerunga Road, Caravonica Lakes, 15km (9½ miles) north of Cairns's city center.

BY SCENIC RAILWAY   The 34km (21-mile) **Kuranda Scenic Railway** (© 07/4036 9249; www.traveltrain.qr.com.au) is rated as one of the top five scenic rail journeys in the world. The train snakes through the magnificent vistas of the Barron Gorge National Park, past gorges and waterfalls on the 90-minute trip from Cairns to Kuranda. It rises 328m (1,076 ft.) and goes through 15 tunnels before emerging at the pretty Kuranda station, which is smothered in ferns. Built by hand over 5 years in the late 1880s, the railway track is today a living monument to the 1,500 men who toiled to link the two towns, and the ride on the historic steam train adds to the atmosphere. It departs Cairns Central at 8:30am daily and 9:30am Sunday through Friday (except Christmas) and leaves Kuranda at 2pm Sunday through Friday and 3:30pm every day. The fare is A$34 (US$27) one-way for adults and A$17 (US$14) for children 4 to 16. A pass for a family of four is A$88 (US$70) one-way.

BY BUS   **White Car Coaches** (© 07/4091 1855) operates several daily bus services to Kuranda departing from 46 Spence St., Cairns. The fare is A$4 (US$3.20) per person.

EXPLORING KURANDA

Kuranda is known for its markets that sell locally made arts and crafts, fresh produce, boomerangs, T-shirts, and jewelry. There are two markets—the "original" markets at 7 Therwine Street, behind Kuranda Market Arcade (open Wed–Fri and Sun, 8am to 3pm), which mainly sell cheap imports; and the 90-stall Heritage markets (open daily 9am–3pm), which offer better quality and a wider variety of goods. Try to visit Kuranda when both markets are open.

Even the Heritage markets have been invaded by commercial imported products, and in response, a group of about 50 local artisans sell their work in the **Kuranda Arts Co-Operative** ♠ (© 07/4093 9026) at Shop 6, "The Settlement," Rob Veivers Drive, next to the Butterfly Sanctuary. It's open from 10am to 4pm daily. You will find quality furniture crafted from recycled Australian hardwoods, jewelry, handicrafts, and all kinds of stuff here.

You can explore the rainforest, the river esplanade, or Barron Falls along a number of easy walking tracks. If you want to learn about the rainforest, explore it with Brian Clarke of **Kuranda Riverboat Tours** (© 07/4093 7476 or 0412 159212), who runs informative

45-minute river cruises. The cruises depart hourly from 10:15am to 2:30pm from the riverside landing across the railway footbridge near the train station. Brian is a former crocodile hunter and has lived in the rainforest for more than 30 years. The cruise costs A$12 (US$9.60) for adults, A$6 (US$4.80) for children 5 to 15, and A$30 (US$24) for families. Buy your tickets on board.

KURANDA'S NATURE PARKS

Kuranda has several small wildlife attractions, including two small but interesting walk-through aviaries. **Birdworld** (𝄢 **07/4093 9188**), located behind the Heritage Markets off Rob Veivers Drive, has eye-catching macaws, a pair of cassowaries and Australia's largest collection of free flying birds. **The Aviary,** 8 Thongon St. (𝄢 **07/4093 7411**), is good if you want to see a bigger range of Australian species. Birdworld is open daily from 9am to 4pm; admission is A$12 (US$9.60) for adults, A$5 (US$4) for children 4 to 14, A$29 (US$23) for families. The Aviary is open from 10am to 3:30pm; admission is A$12 (US$9.60) for adults, $6 (US$4.80) for kids 4 to 16. Both aviaries are closed Christmas.

   Kuranda Koala Gardens (𝄢 **07/4093 9953;** www.koalagardens. com) is a small wildlife park at the Heritage Markets. Here you can cuddle a koala and have your photo taken, and check out other animals including freshwater crocodiles, wombats, lizards, and wallabies. Not for the faint-hearted, take a stroll through the walk-through snake enclosure, while they slither at your feet. A small display about Kuranda's pioneers is made up of photos from the owners' family albums. Kuranda Koala Gardens is open daily from 9am to 4pm, and costs A$14 (US$11) adults and A$7 (US$5.60) children 4–15. It is packaged with Birdworld and the Australian Butterfly Sanctuary (see below) as the Kuranda Wildlife Experience, and a A$33 (US$26) pass to all three can be bought on arrival at any of the three attractions.

Australian Butterfly Sanctuary 𝄐   A rainbow-hued array of 1,500 tropical butterflies—including the electric blue "Ulysses" and Australia's largest species, the Cairns birdwing—is housed in a walk-through enclosure here. Take the free, guided tour and learn about the butterfly's life cycle. The butterflies will land on you if you wear pink, red, and other bright colors, and don't be put off if it's raining–this is an all-weather attraction which is good in any weather.

8 Rob Veivers Dr. 𝄢 **07/4093 7575.** Fax 07/4093 8923. www.australianbutterflies. com. Admission A$13 (US$10) adults, A$12 (US$9.60) seniors, A$6.50 (US$5.20) children 4--15, A$30 (US$24) family pass. AE, DC, MC, V. Daily 9:45am–4pm. Free

---

Tips **Dress Warmly**

Bring some warm clothing to Kuranda in winter (June–Aug). It never gets to freezing, but it does get nippy in the mountains.

---

guided tours every 15 min. from 10am; last tour departs 3:15pm. Closed Christmas. On-street parking. Bus stop 7 min. from sanctuary.

Rainforestation Nature Park   At this 40-hectare (99-acre) nature and cultural complex, you can take a 45-minute ride into the rainforest in a World War II amphibious Army Duck. You'll hear commentary on orchids and other rainforest wildlife along the way. You can also see a performance by Aboriginal dancers; learn about Aboriginal legends and throw a boomerang on the Dreamtime Walk; or have your photo taken cuddling a koala. You can do any of these activities separately, or do them all (except cuddle a koala) in a package that costs A$34 (US$27) for adults, A$17 (US$14) for kids ages 4 to 14, or A$84 (US$67) for a family of five. Koala photos are A$12 (US$9.60). The Duck runs on the hour beginning at 10am; the Aboriginal dancers perform at 10:30am, noon and 2pm; and the 30-minute Dreamtime Walk leaves at 11am, noon, 1:30, and 2:30pm.

On the Kennedy Hwy., a 5-min. drive from the center of Kuranda. ✆ **07/4093 9033.** Fax 07/4093 7578. www.rainforest.com.au. Shuttle from Therwine St., Kuranda every 30 min. from 10:45am–2:45pm costs A$6 (US$4.80) adults, A$3 (US$2.40) children, and A$15 (US$12) families, round-trip. AE, DC, MC, V. Daily 9am–4pm. Closed Christmas. Ample parking.

WHITE-WATER RAFTING & OTHER OUTDOOR ACTIVITIES

RnR Rafting (✆ **07/4051 7777**), and **Raging Thunder Adventures** (✆ **07/4030 7990**) serve as one-stop booking shops for a panoply of action pursuits around Cairns, like hot-air ballooning, skydiving, jet-boating, horse riding, ATV (all-terrain vehicle) safaris, parasailing, and rafting. Ask them about packages.

BIKING   Dan's Mountain Biking (✆ **07/4033 0128**) runs a wide range of full- and half-day guided tours in small groups from A$75 to A$135 (US$60–US$108) per person.

BUNGEE JUMPING   A. J. Hackett Bungy (✆ **1800/622 888** in Australia or 07/4057 7188) launches thrill seekers from a platform in the rainforest, 20 minutes north of town on McGregor Road. A jump costs A$109 (US$87), with free transport from Cairns and northern beaches hotels.

FISHING   Cairns is the giant **black-marlin** capital of the world. Catches weighing in at more than 1,000 pounds hardly raise an eyebrow around here. The **game fishing** season is from September to December; November is peak. Book early, because boats are reserved months ahead. Check out www.fishingcairns.com.au or contact **Destination Cairns Marketing,** 36 Aplin St. (at Sheridan St.; ✆ **1800/807 730** in Australia, or 07/4051 4066), to book a charter. Expect to pay around A$400 (US$320) per person or about A$1,900 (US$1,520) per day for a sole charter for heavy-tackle game fishing, A$250 (US$200) per person for light tackle stuff, from A$155 (US$124) for reef fishing, and A$135 (US$108) for a day or A$75 (US$60) for a half day in the Cairns Inlet estuary.

GOLF   Cairns's best course, the championship **Paradise Palms Golf Course** at Clifton Beach (✆ **07/4059 9900**), abuts the ranges in the northern suburbs. Nine holes are A$70 (US$56), 18 holes are A$120 (US$96), cart included. Greens fees entitle you to use of the clubhouse facilities (including showers) and entry to the recreation club. Club hire is A$30 to $70 (US$24–$56). No public transport operates there.

WHITE-WATER RAFTING   Several companies offer white-water rafting trips from Cairns on the Grade 3 to 4 Tully River, 90 minutes south near Mission Beach; white-water rafting on the Grade 3 Barron River in the hills behind the city; and heli-rafting adventures on the Grade 4 to 5 rapids of the inland Johnstone River. One of the best outfitters is **RnR Rafting** ℛ (✆ **07/4051 7777**).

One-day trips on the **Tully River** are suitable for all ages and abilities and are the most popular. You can do this if you're staying in Cairns or Port Douglas. For details, see chapter 5 "The North Coast: Mission Beach, Townsville & the Islands." The trip costs A$145 (US$116) from Cairns, or A$160 (US$128) from Port Douglas, including transfers.

The gentler **Barron River** is a good choice for the timid. Half-day trips with RnR Rafting featuring 2 hours' rafting depart twice a day and cost about A$88 (US$70) from Cairns or A$99 (US$79) from Port Douglas. There is also a A$6 (US$4.80) National Park fee.

5 Where to Stay

High season in Cairns includes 2 weeks at Easter, the period from early July to early October, and the Christmas holiday through January. Book ahead in those periods. During the low season, from

November to June, always ask about discounted rates, because many hotels will be willing to negotiate.

Cairns has a good supply of affordable accommodations, both in the heart of the city and along the northern beaches. Or you can choose to stay in the village of Kuranda, or at an island resort.

Don't think you have to stay in Cairns if you don't have a car. Most tour and cruise operators will pick you up and drop you off in Cairns, on the northern beaches, or even in Port Douglas (see section 3, earlier in this chapter).

Unless noted otherwise, all accommodations below are within walking distance of shops, restaurants, cinemas, the casino, the tourist office, bus terminals, the train station, and departure terminals for Great Barrier Reef cruises.

IN CAIRNS
VERY EXPENSIVE

Hotel Sofitel Reef Casino   Arguably the most stylish property in Cairns, this six-story hotel is 1 block from the water, with partial water views from some rooms, and nice city/hinterland outlooks from others. All the rooms have lots of natural light, and come with high-quality amenities, Jacuzzis, bathrobes, and small balconies with smart timber furniture. The Cairns casino is attached to the hotel (see "Cairns After Dark," later in this chapter).

35–41 Wharf St., Cairns, QLD 4870. ✆ **1800/808 883** in Australia, 800/221-4542 in the U.S. and Canada, 020/8283 4500 in the U.K., 0800/44 4422 in New Zealand, or 07/4030 8888. Fax 07/4030 8777. www.reefcasino.com.au. 128 units. A$335–A$440 (US$268–US$352) double; A$710–A$2,000 (US$568–US$1,600) suite. Extra person A$33 (US$26). Children under 15 stay free in parent's room with existing bedding. AE, DC, MC, V. Free valet and self-parking. Airport shuttle. **Amenities:** 3 restaurants (Asian, Fusion, grill); bar; small rooftop pool; health club; Jacuzzi; sauna; concierge; tour desk; business center; 24-hr. room service; babysitting; laundry service; dry cleaning. *In room:* A/C, TV/VCR, dataport, minibar, hair dryer, iron, safe.

Shangri-La Hotel, The Marina   Returning guests will not recognize the former Radisson Plaza hotel. After an A$25 million-plus (US$20 million) renovation, the hotel was rebranded in mid-2004 and has a modern new look. Gone is the fake rainforest in the lobby, and an extra 36 contemporary style rooms have been built overlooking the marina, to become part of the exclusive, spacious (more than 50 sq. meters, with 3.3 meters high ceilings) Horizon Club. Bathrooms have ocean views and the rooms have large terraces looking to the moored yachts and the mountains. The five-star hotel adjoins the Pier Shopping Centre, the new Esplanade lagoon and is not far from the Reef Fleet Terminal.

Cairns Accommodations & Dining

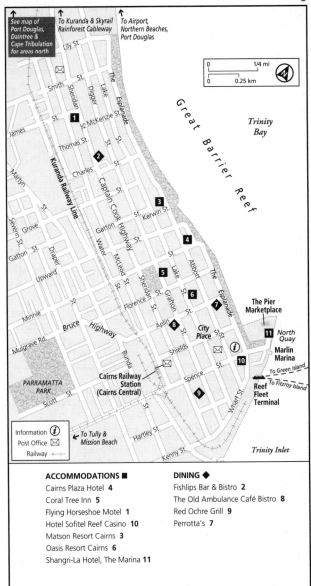

See map of Port Douglas, Daintree & Cape Tribulation for areas north

↑ To Kuranda & Skyrail Rainforest Cableway

↑ To Airport, Northern Beaches, Port Douglas

Lily St.

Smith St.

Sheridan St.

Digger St.

Lake St.

The Esplanade

McKenzie St.

James St.

Kuranda Railway Line

Thomas St.

Charles St.

Captain Cook Highway

Kerwin St.

Gatton St.

Water St.

McLeod St.

Martyn St.

Grove St.

Severin St.

Gatton St.

Draper St.

Upward St.

Sheridan St.

Florence St.

Grafton St.

Abbott St.

Lake St.

The Esplanade

Minnie St.

Bruce Highway

Aplin St.

Mulgrave Rd.

Bunda St.

Shields St.

Spence St.

City Place

The Pier Marketplace

North Quay

Marlin Marina

To Green Island

To Fitzroy Island

PARRAMATTA PARK

Cairns Railway Station (Cairns Central)

Scott St.

Wharf St.

Reef Fleet Terminal

Trinity Bay

Great Barrier Reef

Trinity Inlet

Hartley St.

← To Tully & Mission Beach

Kenny St.

0   1/4 mi
0   0.25 km

Information ℹ
Post Office ✉
Railway ┼┼┼

ACCOMMODATIONS ■

Cairns Plaza Hotel **4**
Coral Tree Inn **5**
Flying Horseshoe Motel **1**
Hotel Sofitel Reef Casino **10**
Matson Resort Cairns **3**
Oasis Resort Cairns **6**
Shangri-La Hotel, The Marina **11**

DINING ◆

Fishlips Bar & Bistro **2**
The Old Ambulance Café Bistro **8**
Red Ochre Grill **9**
Perrotta's **7**

Pierpoint Rd., Cairns, QLD 4870. ℭ **1800/222 448** in Australia, 0800/442 179 in New Zealand, 800/942 5050 in the U.S. and Canada, 020/8747 8485 in the U.K., or 07/4031 1411. Fax 07/4031 3226. www.shangri-la.com. 256 units. A$460 (US$368) double; A$785 (US$628) suite. Children under 18 stay free in parent's room with existing bedding. AE, DC, MC, V. Free outdoor and covered self-parking. Airport shuttle on request. **Amenities:** 2 restaurants (International, Australian); bar; outdoor swimming pool and children's pool; nearby golf course; health club; Jacuzzi; sauna; video arcade; concierge; tour desk; car-rental desk; business center; shopping arcade; salon; 24-hr. room service; in-room massage; babysitting; coin-op laundry; dry cleaning; executive level rooms. *In room:* A/C, TV/VCR w/pay movies, fax, dataport, minibar, coffeemaker, kitchenette (suites and Horizon Club rooms only), hair dryer, iron, safe.

EXPENSIVE

Matson Resort Cairns   Despite its lack of obvious glitz, the 14-story Matson has been the choice of a number of movie stars—most famously Marlon Brando—while on location in Cairns. A 20-minute waterfront walk from downtown, the hotel offers a range of accommodations, from hotel rooms to four-bedroom penthouses (with private rooftop pool), which have been refurbished over the past 5 years. The one- and two-bedroom apartments look out to the sea; hotel rooms have sea or mountain views. The rooms are spacious, but the bathrooms are not, perhaps reflecting the hotel's Japanese market. Out back are studios and apartments, with newly upgraded furnishings, and out front is a pretty pool and sun deck.

The Esplanade (at Kerwin St.), Cairns, QLD 4870. ℭ **1800/079 105** in Australia, or 07/4031 2211. Fax 07/4031 2704. www.matsonresort.com.au. 342 units. A$220–A$260 (US$176–US$208) double; A$160 (US$128) studio; A$165–A$360 (US$132–US$288) tower apt (sleeps 5); A$205 (US$164) 1-bedroom apt (sleeps 4); A$250 (US$200) 2-bedroom apt (sleeps 6); A$950 (US$760) 3-bedroom penthouse; A$1,200 (US$960) 4-bedroom penthouse. Extra person A$28 (US$22). Ask about packages. AE, DC, MC, V. Free covered parking. Courtesy transfers to and from airport, hotel-shuttle service around the city. Bus stop about 100m (328 ft.) from the hotel. **Amenities:** 2 restaurants (Brasserie, Australian); 3 bars; 3 outdoor swimming pools; golf course about 20 min. away; 2 lit tennis courts; health club with facilities including aerobics classes; Jacuzzi; sauna; bike rental; concierge; tour desk; car-rental desk; salon; 24-hr. room service; massage (in-room or at the health club); babysitting; coin-op laundry and laundry service; same-day dry cleaning; nonsmoking rooms. *In room:* A/C, TV w/pay movies, dataport in some rooms, kitchenette in studios and apts only, minibar in hotel rooms and apts, fridge in studios, hair dryer, iron, safe.

Oasis Resort Cairns (Value   The large swimming pool with swim-up bar and a little sandy beach, is the focus of this attractive six-story resort built in 1997. All the colorful, contemporary rooms have balconies with views over the tropical gardens, mountains, or the pool. The suites, with a TV in the bedroom and a large Jacuzzi bathtub, could well be the best-value suites in town.

122 Lake St., Cairns, QLD 4870. ℂ **07/4080 1888.** Fax 07/4080 1889. www.oasis-cairns.com.au. 314 units. A$225–A$255 (US$180–US$204) double; A$395 (US$316) suite. Extra person A$44 (US$35). Children under 16 stay free in parent's room with existing bedding. Free crib. Ask about packages. AE, DC, MC, V. Free valet and self-parking. Airport shuttle. **Amenities:** Restaurant (buffet/Australian); 2 bars; outdoor pool; health club; concierge; tour desk; limited room service; babysitting; coin-op laundry or laundry service; dry cleaning. *In room:* A/C, TV w/pay movies, dataport, coffeemaker, minibar, hair dryer, iron, safe.

MODERATE

Cairns Plaza Hotel   The harbor views at this multistory complex are better than those at most of the more luxurious hotels in Cairns. Two blocks from town, the accommodations are good size, with fresh, appealing furnishings and modern bathrooms. If your balcony does not have a water vista, you overlook a nice aspect of the city or mountains instead. Families can have interconnecting suite and standard room to create more space and privacy.

145 The Esplanade (at Minnie St.), Cairns, QLD 4870. ℂ **1800/117 787** in Australia, or 07/4051 4688. Fax 07/4051 8129. www.cairnsplaza.com.au. 60 units. A$130–A$145 (US$104–US$116) double; A$210 (US$168) interconnecting rooms; A$175 (US$140) suite. Extra person A$15 (US$12). AE, DC, MC, V. Limited free parking. **Amenities:** Restaurant (Australian); bar; small outdoor pool; golf course (1km/ ½ mile away); 4 lit tennis courts nearby; access to nearby health club; Jacuzzi; tour desk; car-rental desk; limited room service; massage; babysitting; coin-op laundry; dry cleaning. *In room:* A/C, TV w/free movies, dataport, minibar, kitchenettes in suites and studios, coffeemaker, hair dryer, iron.

INEXPENSIVE

Coral Tree Inn *(Value*   The focal point of this airy, modern resort-style motel a 5-minute walk from the city center is the clean, friendly communal kitchen that overlooks the palm-lined saltwater pool and sun deck. It's a great spot to cook up a steak or reef fish filet on the free barbecue and join other guests at the communal tables. Local restaurants deliver, free fresh-roasted coffee is on all day, and a vending machine sells wine and beer, so you don't even have to go to the pub for supplies! The smallish, basic but neat motel rooms have painted brick walls, terra-cotta tile or carpeted floors, and clean new bathrooms sporting marble-look laminate countertops. In contrast, the eight suites are huge and stylish enough to do any corporate traveler proud. They are some of the best-value accommodations in town. All rooms have a private balcony or patio; some look out onto the drab commercial buildings next door, but most look out over the pool. Ask about packages that include cruises and other tours.

166–172 Grafton St., Cairns, QLD 4870. ℂ **07/4031 3744.** Fax 07/4031 3064. www.coraltreeinn.com.au. 58 units. A$114 (US$91) double; A$140 (US$112) suite. Additional person A$10 (US$8). AE, DC, MC, V. Limited free parking; ample on-street parking. Airport shuttle. **Amenities:** Bar; outdoor saltwater pool; access to nearby health club; bike rental; tour desk; car-rental desk; babysitting; coin-op laundry and laundry service; same-day dry cleaning; nonsmoking rooms; safe (at reception). *In room:* A/C, TV, dataport, kitchenette in suites, fridge, coffeemaker, hair dryer, iron.

Flying Horseshoe Motel   Well-maintained rooms, each with a desk, await you at this family-run Best Western about 3km (10 blocks) from the city center. In busy times, there's a hearty buffet around the small pool, and guests are encouraged to mingle. The tropical gardens run to a Jacuzzi. The 28 studio apartments, all with kitchenettes, are by the highway, so expect some traffic noise. The bus to the city stops just across the road.

281–289 Sheridan St., Cairns, QLD 4870. ⓒ **1800/814 171** in Australia, or 07/4051 3022. 50 units (all with shower only). A$95–$115 (US$81–$98) double; A$125 (US$100) studio apt. Extra adult A$10 (US$8), extra child A$5 (US$4). Crib A$5 (US$4).AE, DC, MC, V. Free undercover parking. Bus: all "1" series, 7, or N. Call the motel for a free pickup at the airport, train station, or bus terminal. **Amenities:** Restaurant (buffet); bar; outdoor (unheated) pool; nearby tennis courts; access to nearby health club (200m/656 ft. away); Jacuzzi; tour desk; car-rental desk; room service (breakfast and dinner only); babysitting; coin-op laundry; dry cleaning. *In room:* A/C, TV w/free movies, kitchenette (apts only), stocked minibar, coffeemaker, hair dryer, iron.

Lilybank Bed & Breakfast ⽊   This 1870s Queenslander home-stead, originally a mayor's residence, is in a leafy suburb 6km (3¾ miles) from the airport and a 10-minute drive from the city. Guests sleep in large, attractive rooms, all individually decorated with such features as wrought-iron beds and patchwork quilts. Each bathroom is a good size. The largest room has French doors opening onto a "sleep-out," an enclosed veranda with two extra beds. You can also stay in the gardener's cottage, renovated with slate floors, stained-glass windows, a king-size bed, and a bar. The house is set in gardens with an attractive rock-lined saltwater pool. Breakfast is served in the garden room by the fishpond. Your gregarious hosts Mike and Pat Woolford also share their house with three poodles, an irre-pressible galah, and a giant green tree frog. There's a guest TV lounge and kitchen, and phone, fax, and e-mail access. Many tours pick up at the door, and several good restaurants are a stroll away, so you don't need a car to stay here. No smoking indoors.

75 Kamerunga Rd., Stratford, Cairns, QLD 4870. ⓒ **07/4055 1123.** Fax 07/4058 1990. www.lilybank.com.au. 6 units (4 with shower only). A$88–A$110 (US$70–US$88) double. Additional person A$33 (US$26). Rates include full breakfast. AE, MC, V. Free parking. Bus: 1E or 1G. Taxi from airport approx. A$15 (US$12). Bus stop 120m (394 ft.). Children not permitted. **Amenities:** Outdoor pool; tour desk; mas-sage by appointment; coin-op laundry; nonsmoking rooms. *In room:* A/C, hair dryer, no phone.

ON THE NORTHERN BEACHES

Cairns has a string of white sandy beaches starting 15 minutes north of the city center. **Trinity Beach,** 15 minutes from the airport, is secluded, elegant, and scenic. The most upscale is **Palm Cove,** 20 minutes from the airport. Here cute, rainbow-hued shops and apartment blocks nestle among giant paperbarks and palms fronting a postcard-perfect beach. It has several advantages over other beach suburbs: A nine-hole resort golf course and a gym are within walking distance; a few Great Barrier Reef and Green Island cruise companies including Quicksilver, Sunlover Cruises, and Big Cat pick up passengers here; and it has the greatest choice of places to eat. Add 5 to 10 minutes to the traveling times above to reach the city.

VERY EXPENSIVE

The Sebel Reef House & Spa Palm Cove 🐨🐨🐨   Picture yourself inside a Somerset Maugham novel—but substitute the Queensland tropics for Singapore—and you've almost got it right. This must be one of the most romantic hotels in Queensland, or all of Australia. The white walls are swathed in bougainvillea, and the beds with mosquito netting. Airy interiors are furnished with rustic handmade artifacts and white wicker furniture. The Veranda Spa rooms, which have a Jacuzzi on the balcony, overlook the pool, waterfalls, and lush gardens and there are extra touches such as bathrobes and CD player, as well as generous balconies within earshot of the ocean. In mid-2003, the hotel opened a health spa operated by Daintree Spa. Built in 1958, the Reef House's guest list has read like an excerpt from Who's Who—the most recent addition being Bob Dylan and his band. But no matter who you are, you will never want to leave.

99 Williams Esplanade, Palm Cove, Cairns, QLD 4879. ✆ **1800/079 052** in Australia, or 07/4055 3633. Fax 07/4055 3305. www.reefhouse.com.au. 69 units (14 with shower only). A$280–$480 (US$224–$384) double; A$480–$595 (US$384–$476) suite. Extra person A$40 (US$32). Children under 14 stay free in parents' room using existing bedding. AE, DC, MC, V. Free undercover parking (for limited number of cars); ample on-street parking. Courtesy airport shuttle. Bus: 1, 1B, 1X, 2X, or N. **Amenities:** Restaurant (Modern Australian); bar; cafe; honor bar; 3 small outdoor pools; nearby golf course; access to nearby health club; spa; concierge; tour desk; room service (6:30am–9:30pm); babysitting; coin-op laundry or laundry service; same-day dry cleaning. *In room:* A/C, TV/DVD, CD player, kitchenette, minibar, coffeemaker, hair dryer, iron, safe.

EXPENSIVE

Outrigger Beach Club & Spa 🐨   A "resort within the resort," with 42 suites and a private rainforest pool, is the final touch to this

new complex on the beachfront. Opened in late 2002, the main hotel has rooms and apartments overlooking the water, with touches of Queensland colonial style about it. Hotel rooms are small, but have Jacuzzis and timber outdoor furniture on the decks. The two penthouses (three floors up) have private rooftop terraces and pools, but there's no elevator. There's a large lagoon-style swimming pool with a sandy beach and swim-up pool bar. Coconut palms, with their trunks painted white, have been planted around the lagoon, which is lit by flaming torches at night. Suites are more secluded, with gas barbecues and entertainment areas, and state-of-the-art entertainment units, including DVDs and flat-screen televisions. Pampering awaits you at the Sanctum Spa, which has seven wet and dry treatment rooms and also offers yoga classes as well as beauty and massage treatments for both men and women. To arrive in style, order the Rolls Royce transfers from Cairns to Palm Cove.

123 Williams Esplanade, Palm Cove, Cairns, QLD 4879. ℰ 800/688-7444 in the U.S., 1800/134 444 in Australia, or 07/4059 9200. Fax 07/4059 9222. www.outrigger.com. 220 units. A$270–A$360 (US$216–US$288) double rooms with Jacuzzi; A$330–A$440 (US$264–US$352) double 1-bedroom suite; A$360–A$390 (US$288–US$312) double 1-bedroom suite with Jacuzzi; A$420–A$540 (US$336–US$432) 2-bedroom suite with Jacuzzi (sleeps 4); A$550–A$700 (US$440–US$560) 2-bedroom penthouse suite (sleeps 4). Extra person A$35 (US$28). Minimum 3 night stay at Easter and Christmas to mid-January. AE, DC, MC, V. Security car parking. **Amenities:** Restaurant (Thai); coffee shop; heated outdoor pool; golf course nearby; spa; gymnasium; concierge; tour desk; nonsmoking rooms; tennis court. In room: A/C, TV w/pay movies, dataport, kitchen (suites only), fridge, coffeemaker, hair dryer, iron, safe, Jacuzzi, washing machine and dryer (suites only).

MODERATE

Ellis Beach Oceanfront Bungalows ✿ (Finds) On what is arguably the loveliest of the northern beaches, about 30 minutes from Cairns, these bungalows and cabins are set under palm trees between the Coral Sea and a backdrop of mountainous rainforest. Lifeguards patrol the beach, and there are stinger nets in season as well as a shady swimming pool and toddlers' wading pool. There's plenty of privacy, and the accommodations are basic but pleasant. You can sit on the veranda and gaze at the ocean. Keep an eye out for dolphins. Each bungalow and cabin sleeps four and has full

---

Safe Swimming

All of the northern beaches have small, netted enclosures for safe swimming from October to May, when deadly box jellyfish (stingers) make mainland beaches off-limits.

kitchen facilities (with microwave, fridge, and freezer), but cabins have no en-suite bathroom. There are coin-op barbecues and phone and fax facilities.

Captain Cook Hwy., Ellis Beach, QLD 4879. ✆ **1800/637 036** in Australia, or 07/4055 3538. Fax 07/4055 3077. www.ellisbeachbungalows.com. 15 units (all with shower only). A$68 (US$54) double cabins; A$155 (US$124) double bungalows. Extra person A$15 (US$12) cabins, A$24 (US$19) bungalows. AE, MC, V. **Amenities:** Restaurant; 2 outdoor pools; golf course nearby; tour desk; car-rental desk; coin-op laundry. *In room:* A/C and ceiling fans, TV, kitchen, iron, no phone.

The Reef Retreat 🏆🏆 Tucked back one row of buildings from the beach is this gem—a low-rise collection of contemporary studios and suites built around a swimming pool in a peaceful grove of palms and silver paperbarks. All the rooms in the newer or extensively renovated wings have cool tile floors and smart teak and cane furniture. The studios are a terrific value and much larger than the average hotel room. In the oceanview suites, you can even lie in bed and see the sea. The extra-private honeymoon suites (and some oceanview suites) have a Jacuzzi and a kitchenette outside on the balcony. There's a barbecue on the grounds and a Jacuzzi. There's no elevator. Units are cleaned twice weekly; one free cleaning for stays of 5 days or longer. Extra cleanings A$20 (US$16).

10–14 Harpa St., Palm Cove, Cairns, QLD 4879. ✆ 07/4059 1744. Fax 07/4059 1745. www.reefretreat.com.au. 36 units (16 with shower only, 20 with shower and Jacuzzi). A$140 (US$112) studio double; A$150 (US$120) suite with Jacuzzi; A$160 (US$128) oceanview suite; A$260 (US$208) 2-bedroom apt (sleeps 4). Additional person A$25 (US$20). Children under 3 stay free in parent's room with existing bedding; crib A$25 (US$20). AE, MC, V. Free parking. Bus: 1, 1B 1X, 2X, or N. Airport shuttle A$15 (US$12) per person one-way. **Amenities:** Outdoor saltwater pool; nearby golf course; nearby tennis courts; Jacuzzi; tour desk; car-rental desk; coin-op laundry; laundry service; dry cleaning. *In room:* A/C, TV, dataport, kitchenette, fridge, coffeemaker, hair dryer, iron.

ON AN ISLAND

Several island resorts are within the Great Barrier Reef Marine Park off Cairns. They afford you safe swimming, because the October-to-May infestations of marine stingers don't make it to the islands. They also offer snorkeling and diving opportunities every day.

VERY EXPENSIVE

Green Island Resort 🏆 Step off the beach at this Great Barrier Reef national-park island, and you are surrounded by acres of coral. The resort is a high-class cluster of rooms tucked away in a dense vine forest. Each room is private, roomy, and elegantly outfitted, with polished wooden floors and a balcony looking into the forest.

Windsurfing, surfskiing, canoeing, diving and snorkeling (both on the island and on day trips to the outer Reef), glass-bottom-boat trips, guided rainforest walks, parasailing, and beach volleyball are among the activities available, or you can simply laze on the coarse white-coral sand or by the guests-only pool. Helicopter and seaplane flights and cruises are available. Many activities and equipment are free for guests, such as non-motorized sports, snorkel gear, and glass-bottom-boat trips, while there's a charge for scuba diving and other activities using fuel. Both the resort and the island are small (you can walk around it in 45 minutes), so you may feel a bit cramped when the day-trippers from Cairns descend; but after they leave at 4:30pm, the place is blissfully peaceful.

27km (17 miles) east of Cairns (P.O. Box 898, Cairns, QLD 4870). © **1800/67 3366** in Australia, or 07/4031 3300. Fax 07/4052 1511. www.greenislandresort.com.au. 46 units. A$475 (US$380) double; A$575 (US$460) suite. Extra person A$90 (US$72). Ask about packages. AE, DC, MC, V. Launch transfers are included in the room rate. Helicopter and seaplane transfers are available through the resort. **Amenities:** 2 restaurants (Australian); 2 bars; 2 outdoor saltwater pools; Spa; wide array of watersports equipment available; concierge; tour desk; laundry service and coin-op guest laundry. *In room:* A/C, TV, free cable TV, minibar, hair dryer, safe.

Lizard Island ★★★ Luxury lodges, huge potato cod so tame divers can pet them, snorkeling off the beach, and isolation—that's what lures the well-heeled to this small, exclusive resort. Lizard is a rugged 1,000-hectare (2,470-acre) national-park island on the Great Barrier Reef, sparsely vegetated but stunningly beautiful, ringed by 24 white sandy beaches, with fringing reefs that support a multitude of marine life including giant clams. No day-trippers are allowed. Many activities are free: snorkeling and glass-bottom-boat trips, catamarans, paddle-skis, fishing tackle, tennis, and hiking trails, such as the muscle-straining 545m (½-mile) climb to Cook's Look, where Captain Cook spied his way out of the reefs in 1770. You pay for fishing and diving trips to nearby Reef sites, including Cod Hole. Introductory dive lessons and night dives are available.

The 40 villas, elegant freestanding lodges tucked under palms along the beach or on cliff tops overlooking the bay, were renovated in 2000. They are built of timber and stone, in a tropical style, with earth and sea tone finishes. A guest lounge has Internet facilities, TV and video, bar facilities, and a book and games library. The Azure Spa has been expanded, now offering a Vichy shower, double-massage room and steam-room and a new range of therapies.

In mid-2003, an even more exclusive accommodation option, **The Pavilion,** opened offering complete privacy, sheer luxury and spectacular panoramic views. It has private decks leading down to its own plunge pool, and comes with extras such as a laptop, binoculars and Bollinger on arrival.

240km (149 miles) north of Cairns; 27km (16¾ miles) offshore (P&O Australian Resorts, G.P.O. Box 478, Sydney, NSW 2001). ℭ **1800/737 678** in Australia, 800/225-9849 in the U.S. and Canada, 020/7805 3875 in the U.K., or 02/9277 5050 (Sydney reservations office). Fax 02/9299 2477 (Sydney reservations office). www. poresorts.com. 40 units (all with shower only). A$1,480 (US$1,184) double room; A$1,800 (US$1,440) double suites and villas; A$3,200 (US$2,560) double The Pavilion. Extra person A$440 (US$352). Rates include all meals and many activities. Ask about packages; some combine stays at Silky Oaks Lodge (Port Douglas) and Bedarra Island (off Mission Beach). AE, DC, MC, V. Transfers are by twice-daily 1-hr. flight from Cairns (book through Qantas); round-trip advance purchase fare is about A$480 (US$384) per person. Aircraft luggage limit 15kg (33 lb.) per person. Air-charter transfers also available. No children under 10. **Amenities:** Restaurant (seafood/Australian); freshwater pool; night/day tennis court; gymnasium; spa; laundry service. *In room:* A/C and fans, dataport, minibar, coffeemaker, hair dryer, iron.

MODERATE/INEXPENSIVE

Fitzroy Island Resort This is probably the most affordable island resort on the Great Barrier Reef. It's targeted at a young crowd looking for action and ecofun in a pristine, beautiful location. It's no glamour-puss palace, but was revamped in 2000 to include a Hard Rock Cafe–style restaurant and spruced-up interiors. Fitzroy is a continental island offering little in the way of fringing coral and only a few narrow strips of coral sand. What it does have are catamarans, outrigger canoes, and surf skis; glass-bottom-boat rides; and hiking trails through dense national park forest to a lighthouse. Divers can make drift dives over the reefs dotted around the island to see manta rays, reef sharks, turtles, and coral. There is good snorkeling at two points around the island that you can reach twice a day on the dive boat, at an extra fee. You can also catch the Sunlover Cruises day trip to the outer Great Barrier Reef. The dive shop runs introductory and certified dives and certification courses. Each of the comfortable beach cabins has a queen-size bed and two bunks in the back, and the rooms have ceiling fans and a balcony with views through the trees to the sea. The bunkhouse accommodations are basic fan-cooled carpeted rooms with bunks and/or beds. Bunkhouse guests can use the communal kitchen, but must bring their own supplies.

The restaurant is moderately priced, a kiosk sells takeout food, and the poolside grill and bar offers casual meals. The **Raging Thunder Beach Bar,** billed as "the only nightclub on the Reef," gets going on Saturday nights.

35km (22 miles) southeast of Cairns (P.O. Box 1109, Cairns, QLD 4870). ☎ **07/4051 9588.** Fax 07/4052 1335. www.ozhorizons.com.au/qld/cairns/fitzroy/fi.htm. 8 cabins (all with shower only); 32 bunkhouses, none with private bathroom. Cabins A$220 (US$176) double. Extra person A$35 (US$28). Bunkhouses A$31 (US$25) per person per bed (sharing with up to 3 other people); A$116 (US$93) double (sole use); A$124 (US$99) family bunkhouse (sleeps 4). Ask about packages. AE, DC, MC, V. Round-trip transfers 3 times daily from Cairns (approx. 45 min.) cost A$36 (US$29) adults, A$18 (US$14) children 4–14. **Amenities:** 2 restaurants; bar; outdoor pool; watersports equipment; tour desk; dive shop. *In room* (cabins only): TV, minifridge, coffeemaker, hair dryer, iron.

6 Where to Dine

IN CAIRNS

The Esplanade is great for eating; it's lined with cafes, pizzerias, fish-and-chips shops, food courts, ice-cream parlors and bars.

EXPENSIVE

Fishlips Bar & Bistro 😊😊 MODERN AUSTRALIAN/SEAFOOD Ask locals where they go for seafood—as opposed to where they send tourists—and they direct you to this 1920s bluebird-blue shack about 2km (1¼ miles) from town. Chef Ian Candy is renowned for his flair and innovation with seafood. All dishes come in small or large servings, and the local barramundi, or "barra," shows up in several incarnations, maybe beer-battered with rough-cut chips (fries) and fresh tartar sauce, simply grilled, or served with eggplant pickle and rocket pesto on chargrilled zucchini and onion with charred polenta. There are plenty of non-seafood options as well. Be daring—try the crocodile, pan-fried with pine nuts, coriander, and cumin. For dessert, have the homemade ice cream with flavors that change each week. How nice to see that almost every choice on the wine list comes by the glass. Dine inside (air-conditioned for those humid nights) or on the front deck, with its bright blue pots and palm trees. Licensed Sunday through Thursday, and BYO wine only (no BYO beer or spirits).

228 Sheridan St. (between Charles and McKenzie sts.) ☎ **07/4041 1700.** www.fishlips.com.au. Reservations recommended. Main courses A$12–A$19 (US$9.60–US$15) small sizes, A$20–A$41 (US$16–US$33) large sizes. AE, DC, MC, V. Fri noon–2:30pm; daily 6pm–late.

Red Ochre Grill 😊 🄺 GOURMET BUSH TUCKER You could accuse this restaurant/bar of using weird and wonderful Aussie ingredients as a gimmick, but the diners who have flocked here for the past 10 years know good food when they taste it. Daily specials are big on fresh local seafood, and the regular menu—which changes often—lets you devour the Aussie coat of arms in several different ways. Try the emu pâté with bush tomato chile sauce, or kangaroo filets done over a mallee wood-fired grill. A renovation in 2004 has given the restaurant a fresh look; it's slick enough for a big night out but informal enough for a casual meal. There's also a kids' menu.

43 Shields St. ☎ 07/4051 0100. www.redochregrill.com.au. Reservations recommended. Main courses A$5–A$27 (US$4–US$22) at lunch, A$27–A$32 (US$22–US$26) at dinner. Australian game platter A$44 (US$35) per person; seafood platter A$58 (US$46) per person. Tastes of Australia 4 course set menu A$58 (US$46) (minimum 2 people). AE, DC, MC, V. Daily noon–midnight; 6pm–midnight public holidays. Closed Christmas.

MODERATE

Perrotta's MODERN AUSTRALIAN   The locals flock here for brunch and lunch, particularly on the weekends, and you can team it with a visit to the Cairns Regional Art Gallery, as the cafe is just outside. Breakfast differs from the usual bacon and eggs or pancakes fare, offering delights such as smoked salmon and Klimera hash browns with roasted Roma tomatoes, sour cream, and avocado. Sweettooths may go for the French toast with star anise–scented pineapple and lime mascarpone. For lunch there's a choice of bruschettas, focaccia, or panini, pasta dishes, or more individual dishes such as Thai style calamari with roasted peanuts, lemon grass, and chile. At dinner, try the barramundi, local swordfish, or Tasmanian salmon. Remember to check out the specials board.

Abbott and Shields sts. ☎ 074031 5899. Reservations recommended. Breakfast A$4–A$10 (US$3.20–US$8). Main courses (at dinner) all A$25 (US$20). MC, V. Daily 8am–late.

ON THE NORTHERN BEACHES

Colonies MODERN AUSTRALIAN   It may not have the ocean frontage of the grander restaurants along Williams Esplanade, but you are still within earshot of the waves from the veranda of this cheery little aerie upstairs behind a seafront building. The atmosphere is simple and the menu includes loads of inexpensive choices such as pastas, soups, green chicken curry, and seafood. Licensed and BYO.

Upstairs in Paradise Village shopping center, Williams Esplanade, Palm Cove. ☎ 07/4055 3058. Fax 07/4059 1559. www.palmcoveonline.com/colonies. Reservations recommended. Main courses A$16–A$29 (US$13–US$23). AE, DC, MC, V. Daily 10am–10:30pm. Closed mid-Jan to mid-Mar. Bus: 1, 1B, 1X, 2X, or N.

Far Horizons MODERN AUSTRALIAN   You can't quite sink your toes into the sand, but you are just yards from the beach at this pleasant restaurant within the Angsana Resort. The laid-back fine-dining fare includes plenty of fresh seafood—the catch of the day comes with chunky homemade fries and tartar sauce, and there are interesting choices like Vietnamese salad with chargrilled reef fish. The restaurant sometimes sets up dining on the lawn among the palm trees beside the beach. The service is relaxed and friendly and the crowd is a mix of hotel guests from this and other nearby resorts. On Friday and Saturday nights a guitarist plays in the cocktail bar.

Angsana resort, 1 Veivers Rd. (southern end of Williams Esplanade), Palm Cove. (C) 07/4055 3000. Reservations recommended. Main courses A\$24–A\$29 (US\$19–US\$23). AE, DC, MC, V. Daily 6:30pm–midnight (last orders at 9:30pm). Bus: 1, 1B, 1X, 2X, or N.

7 Cairns After Dark

Pick up a copy of the free entertainment newspaper *Barfly,* published every Thursday, for a guide to the week's after-hours action. Top spots recommended by the locals include **Metropolis,** upstairs at 15 Spence St. ((C) **07/4041 0258**), which is popular with the 25-to-45 market and features a sophisticated chocolate decor and a cigar lounge. The **Hotel Sofitel Reef Casino,** 35–41 Wharf St. ((C) **07/4030 8888**), has two levels of blackjack, baccarat, reef routine, roulette, sic-bo, money wheel, paradise pontoon, Keno, and slot machines. It's open from 10am to 4am Monday through Thursday, and 24 hours from 10am Friday until 4am Monday (closed Good Friday, Anzac Day, and Christmas). No entry for children under 18.

If you're over 18, but under 35 or so, and it's Saturday night, you may want to take the boat to the DJs or live bands at the **Raging Thunder Beach Bar** on Fitzroy Island (see "Where to Stay," above). The Fitzroy Flyer leaves Cairns' Reef Fleet terminal at 4pm and 7pm, and returns at 1am Sunday for A\$15 (US\$12). You must book ahead, through Raging Thunder Adventures ((C) **07/4030 7907**).

4

Port Douglas, Daintree National Park & the Cape Tribulation Area

The tiny fishing village of Port Douglas is the actual place where two World Heritage areas—the Daintree Rainforest and the Great Barrier Reef—lie side by side (as noted in the previous chapter, this is the only region in the world that can make that claim). This is truly where "the rainforest meets the reef." Just over an hour's drive from Cairns, through rainforest and along the sea, Port Douglas may be a one-horse town, but its main street is lined with stylish shops and trendy restaurants; and its beautiful 4 Mile Beach is not to be missed.

People often base themselves in "Port," as the locals call it, rather than in Cairns, because they like the peaceful rural surroundings, the uncrowded beach, and the charming absence of tacky development (so far, anyway). Don't think you will be isolated if you stay here—many reef and rainforest tours originate in Port Douglas and many tours from Cairns (see chapter 3) pick up from here.

The Great Barrier Reef is just as accessible from Port Douglas as it is from Cairns. The town is the departure point for several snorkel and dive vessels to the Reef, including the large catamarans, medium-size boats, and a good 30-passenger vessel catering just to snorkelers, including first-time snorkelers.

Daintree National Park lies just north of Port Douglas; and just north of there is Cape Tribulation National Park, another wild tract of rainforest and hilly headlands sweeping down to the sea. Both are part of the vast Wet Tropics World Heritage Area that stretches from Cooktown in the north to Townsville in the south. While ice ages came and went, the rainforest here has not changed much in the past 110 million years. It's home to rare plants that are key links in the story of evolution. In the 76,000-hectare (187,720-acre) Daintree National Park, you'll find cycads, dinosaur trees, fan palms, giant strangler figs, basket ferns, staghorns, and elkhorns. Exploring the park is easy on one of the many 4WD day safaris operating from Port Douglas. Nighttime crocodile-spotting tours on the Daintree River vie for popularity with early-morning cruises to see the incredibly rich bird life, while pythons, lizards, frogs, and electric blue Ulysses butterflies attract photographers.

1 Essentials

Port Douglas: 67km (42 miles) N of Cairns; Mossman: 19km (12 miles) N of Port Douglas; Daintree: 49km (30 miles) N of Port Douglas; Cape Tribulation: 34km (21 miles) N of Daintree

GETTING THERE   Port Douglas is a 65-minute drive from Cairns, in parts through rainforest and on a narrow winding road that skirts the sea. Take Sheridan Street north out of the city when it becomes the Captain Cook Highway; follow the signs to Mossman and Mareeba until you reach the Port Douglas turnoff on your right.

One of the most pleasant ways to get to Port Douglas is to take one of the giant **Quicksilver Wavepiercer** 🏄 (© **07/4087 2100**) catamarans along the coast. They depart Reef Fleet Terminal in Cairns at 8am, Palm Cove jetty at 8:30am, and arrive in Port Douglas at 9:30am. You can stay onboard and go straight to the Great Barrier Reef for the day for an extra charge. The cost of the trip from Cairns is A$26 (US $21) one-way, A$39 (US$31) round-trip, half price for kids 4 to 14.

A one-way ticket aboard **Sun Palm Express Coaches** (© **07/4031 7577**) to Port Douglas hotels is A$30 (US$24) from the Cairns airport. Fares for children aged 4 to 14 are half price.

There is no train to Port Douglas, and no scheduled air service. A small airport handles light aircraft and helicopter charters. A **taxi** from Cairns would run around A$100 (US$80); call **Black & White Taxis** (© **13 10 08** in Cairns).

VISITOR INFORMATION   For information before you go, contact the **Port Douglas Daintree Tourism Association,** P.O. Box 511, Port Douglas, QLD 4877 (© **07/4099 4588;** www.pddt.com.au). It has no visitor information office in Port Douglas itself. Instead, drop by one of the several private tour booking centers in town. One of the biggest and most centrally located is the **Port Douglas Tourist Information Centre,** 23 Macrossan St. (© **07/4099 5599**), open from 7:30am to 6pm daily.

GETTING AROUND   Avis (© **07/4099 4331**) and **Thrifty** (© **07/4099 5555**) have car rental offices in Port Douglas. Check

Port Douglas, Daintree & Cape Tribulation

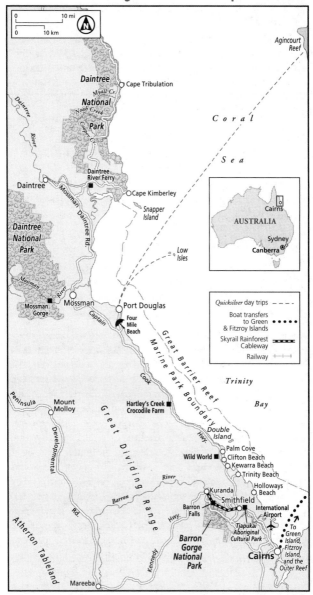

(Tips Staying Safe

Deadly marine **stingers** (box jellyfish) infest the waters offshore from October to May; swim in the stinger nets on 4 Mile Beach during those months. **Crocodiles** inhabit this region, so never swim in, or stand on the bank of, any stream, river, or estuary.

---

out the local companies, including **Port Douglas Car Rental** (© 07/4099 4988). All rent regular vehicles as well as four-wheel-drives, which are needed if you plan to drive to Cape Tribulation. If you need a taxi, call **Port Douglas Taxis** (© 07/4099 5345).

A good way to get around the town's flat streets is by bike. **Bike 'n' Hike** (© 07/4099 4000; www.bikenhike.com.au), 40 Macrossan St, is open daily from 8am to 6pm or later and has a large range of good mountain bikes from A$17 (US$14) a day or A$11 (US$8.80) a half day. **Port Douglas Bike Hire** (© 07/4099 5799), corner Warner and Wharf streets, rents bikes for A$14 (US$11) a day or A$10 (US$8) for a half day. They're open 9am to 5pm daily.

Cruise and fishing boats depart **Marina Mirage,** an upscale retail/marina complex on Dickson Inlet in Wharf Street, a 10-minute walk from the main street, Macrossan Street.

2 Diving & Snorkeling the Reef
MAJOR REEF SITES

The waters off Port Douglas boast just as many wonderful reefs and marine life forms as the waters around Cairns; the reefs are equally close to shore and equally colorful and varied. Some of the most visited reefs are **Tongue, Opal,** and **St. Crispin Reefs.** The **Agincourt** complex of reefs also has many excellent dive sites; the dive team aboard *Quicksmart* (see below) recommends the double figure-eight swim-through at the **Three Sisters,** where baby gray whaler sharks gather, and the wonderful coral walls of **Castle Rock,** where stingrays often hide in the sand. Among the 15-plus dive sites visited by *Poseidon* (see below) are **Turtle Bay,** where you may meet "Killer," a friendly Maori wrasse; **The Cathedrals,** a collection of coral pinnacles and swim-throughs; and **Barracuda Pass,** home to coral gardens, giant clams, and schooling barracudas. Other popular sites to ask your chosen dive vessel about include **Nursery Bommie** (a "bommie" is a coral outcrop), a 24m (79-ft.) pinnacle that is a popular haunt with big fish like barracuda, rays, sharks, and moray eels; the big plate corals of **Light Reef** under which giant grouper hide out; the staghorn coral garden (so named because the coral looks like a stag's antlers) at the **Playground;** one of the region's biggest swim-throughs at **The Maze,** where parrotfish and an enormous Maori wrasse hang out; the **Stepping Stones,** home of the exquisitely pretty clownfish (brightly colored little striped things); **Turtle Bommie,** where hawksbill turtles are frequently sighted; and **Harry's Bommie,** where divers see the occasional manta ray.

If you're staying in Port Douglas, refer to chapter 3 for descriptions of Reef sites farther north and farther east in Queensland, such as the **Ribbon Reefs** and the **Coral Sea,** usually accessed from Cairns aboard a live-aboard vessel, but which can also be accessed from Port Douglas.

The closest Reef site off Port Douglas, the **Low Isles,** lies only 15km (9 miles) northeast. Coral sand and 55 acres of coral surround these two tiny coral cays, which are covered in lush vegetation and are home to many seabirds. The coral is not quite as dazzling as the outer Reef's, so head to the outer Reef if you have only 1 day to spend on the Great Barrier Reef; but the fish life here is rich, and you may spot sea turtles. Because you can wade out to the coral right from the beach, the Low Isles are a good choice for nervous snorkelers. A half-day or day trip to the Low Isles makes for a more relaxing day than a visit to outer Reef sites, because in addition to exploring the coral, you can walk or sunbathe on the sand or laze under palm-thatched beach umbrellas. *Note:* If you visit the Low Isles, wear old shoes, as the coral sand can be rough underfoot.

DAY-TRIP DIVE & SNORKEL BOATS

Remember to add the A$4.50 (US$3.60) Environmental Management Charge (EMC), or "reef tax," to the prices below for every traveler over 4 years of age, unless otherwise noted. Remember, too, that if you stay in Port Douglas, you can join many Great Barrier Reef cruises that leave from Cairns, because some cruise operators arrange transfers between the two towns. This can be handy if you want to make an evening flight from Cairns airport after your day on the Reef. See chapter 3.

Departure times below are the time the boat heads out to sea; boarding begins 15 to 30 minutes earlier.

LOW ISLES Several sailing boats make full-day outings to the Low Isles, taking about an hour or 90 minutes to get there. One of the nicest is the 30m (98-ft.) luxury sailing catamaran *Wavedancer*

(© 07/4087 2100; www.quicksilver-cruises.com) run by Port Douglas's biggest operator of Reef boats, Quicksilver. The 150-passenger *Wavedancer* is big, gleaming, and white, and has ample room to sit down. As well as plenty of deck space and a bar, it has an air-conditioned lounge. You'll hear a Reef ecology briefing from a marine biologist during the 1-hour sail to the isles, where the boat moors at its own 24m (80-ft.) pontoon with shaded seating. Boats ferry you back and forth to the cay throughout the day. You can snorkel or take a glass-bottom boat ride to see giant clams, take an educational walk along the beach led by a marine biologist, or take a free snorkel safari. Safety officers watch over snorkelers. The cost is A$124 (US$99) adults, A$65 (US$52) kids 4 to 14, and A$313 (US$250) families. You have the option of making an introductory scuba dive for an extra A$106 (US$85) per person. The Wavepiercer departs Reef Fleet Terminal in Cairns at 8am and Palm Cove Jetty on the northern beaches at 8:30am to connect with *Wavedancer* departures from Port Douglas at 10am. The company picks you up free of charge from your hotel.

OUTER REEF   By far the biggest diving and snorkeling boats in Port Douglas are the ***Quicksilver Wavepiercer*** (© 07/4087 2100; www.quicksilver-cruises.com) catamarans. These two big, high-speed vessels each carry 300 or 440 passengers daily to Agincourt Reef, a ribbon reef 72km (45 miles) offshore. They moor about 8km (5 miles) apart. Both boats have a bar and plenty of indoor and outdoor seating space. After the 90-minute trip, during which you hear a talk from a marine biologist, you tie up at a large two-story pontoon, where you spend 3½ hours snorkeling, taking semisubmersible rides over the coral, or diving. The pontoons have a dry underwater viewing chamber and freshwater showers. If you visit the Reef between June and August and you're prone to feeling the cold, you will want a wet suit; the Wavepiercers provide these for divers, but may not have enough for every snorkeler, so try to reserve one in advance. The cost for the day is A$180 (US$144) for adults and A$95 (US$76) for kids 4 to 14. Coach transfers from your Port Douglas hotel are an extra A$5 (US$4) adults, A$2.50 (US$2) children. Guided snorkel safaris cost A$55 (US$44) per person, and introductory dives cost A$125 (US$100) per person. Qualified divers can make one dive for A$87 (US$70) or two for A$129 (US$103) per person, all gear included.

Because Quicksilver carries so many passengers, booking snorkel safaris and dives in advance is a good idea. With prior notice, the boat can cater to divers with disabilities, though this may cost extra.

Ten-minute helicopter flights over the Reef from the pontoon are A$125 (US$100) per person. You can fly by helicopter one-way to the pontoon, and cruise the other way with Quicksilver, for a total A$350 (US$280) per person. You can fly one-way from Cairns and cruise back to shore with Quicksilver for A$425 (US$340) per person. All Quicksilver prices above include the reef tax. Quicksilver Wavepiercers depart Marina Mirage at 10am, returning at 4:30pm. Passengers joining the boat in Cairns need to make an 8am departure time, or 8:30am if you board at Palm Cove. Quicksilver departs Marina Mirage at 10am daily except Christmas Day.

Several smaller Reef dive/snorkel boats operate out of Port Douglas, and their ranks are growing every year as tourism booms in this town. They lack Quicksilver's comfortable pontoon, but tend to visit two or three dive sites, compared to Quicksilver's single site.

Two of the best are **Quicksmart** (see below) and **Poseidon III** (**℡ 07/4099 4772;** www.poseidon-cruises.com.au), which are both medium-size motorized catamarans. Both offer a similar experience. Both are recently built, with indoor air-conditioned seating, outside seating, and a bar. *Poseidon III* visits three Reef sites compared to *Quicksmart's* two, carries fewer passengers (65 compared to *Quicksmart's* 80), and, being family operated, its service is a touch more personal. Both take about 90 minutes to get to the Reef (which gives you 5 hr. on the coral), sell videos of your day trip, are very professionally run, give thorough snorkel and dive briefings, and are safety-conscious. You will have a great day on either boat.

The **Poseidon III,** a 24m (72-ft.) high-speed catamaran, was custom-built in 2001 for Great Barrier Reef excursions. The day includes an ecological Reef talk and a free snorkel safari led by a marine biologist. The day costs A$140 (US$112) for adults, and A$105 (US$84) for kids 3 to 12. The day with an introductory dive is A$190 (US$152), plus A$40 (US$32) for each extra dive. *Poseidon* is unusual among Queensland dive boats for letting first-time divers make up to three dives during the day; most boats allow only one, or sometimes two. Certified divers pay A$180 (US$144) for the day including two guided dives, or A$195 (US$156) with three dives. Divers can rent underwater cameras for A$55 (US$44) including film. The boat departs Marina Mirage daily at 8:30am and returns to shore around 4pm. Wet suits are A$5 (US$4) extra. Round-trip pickups from Port Douglas hotels are free; round-trip transfers from Cairns and the northern beaches are A$15 (US$12) adults, A$10 (US$8) for a child.

The 24m (79-ft.) *Quicksmart* (© **07/4087 2100;** www.quick silver-cruises.com.au) is operated by the same company that operates the giant Wavepiercer catamarans. It was built new in 2000, and its dive equipment was bought new then. It moors at two sites on Agincourt Reef (away from the crowds, not at the Quicksilver pontoon). You get 5 hours on the Reef. A day trip is A$136 (US$109) for adults, and A$103 (US$82) for kids 4 to 14, including the reef tax. The day, including a single introductory dive, costs A$198 (US$158), or A$240 (US$192) with two introductory dives. The cost of the day for certified divers ranges from A$188 to $223 (US$150–$178), depending on whether you make one, two, or three dives. All gear is provided and all divers are equipped with a computer. Round-trip transfers are free from your Port Douglas hotel, or A$10 (US$8) per person from Cairns or the northern beaches. The boat departs Marina Mirage daily at 8:30am and gets back at 4:30pm.

One of the best boat operators in Port Douglas is **Wavelength** (© **07/4099 5031;** www.wavelength.com.au), an eco-oriented company that carries a maximum 30 snorkelers, and no divers. Satisfied customers enjoy the friendly service and small-scale ambience. A marine biologist gives reef education talks and answers your questions during the day. During a free snorkel safari with the biologist, you can even help the crew gather data as part of its Reef monitoring program for the Great Barrier Reef Marine Park Authority. Wavelength is the best choice for **nervous or first-time snorkelers,** as the helpful crew get right down there in the water with you. The company's two 16m (50-ft.) monohulls are not flashy and don't have air-conditioned areas; but they zip along as fast as the bigger boats in town, and they're pretty comfortable. The trip visits three Reef sites in a day, taking 90 minutes to get to the Reef, which gives you about 5 hours on the coral. A$135 (US$108) for adults, A$95 (US$76) for children 2 to 12, or A$430 (US$344) for a family of 4. Wet suits are A$5 (US$4) extra. Round-trip transfers are A$25 (US$20) from Cairns or A$20 (US$16) from the northern beaches. The trip departs the Wavelength Jetty daily in Wharf Street at 8:15am, getting back to shore at 4:30pm.

LIVE-ABOARD EXCURSIONS

Port has only two live-aboard vessels, the *Undersea Explorer* (© **1800/648 877** in Australia, or 07/4099 5911; www.undersea. com.au) and *Diversity* (© **07/4087 2100;** www.quicksilver-cruises. com.au). *Undersea Explorer* runs 6-day live-aboard dive trips for certified divers from Port Douglas to Cod Hole, Osprey Reef in the Coral Sea, and some of the many ribbon and patch reefs off Port Douglas. The 25m (82-ft.) purpose-built dive vessel, built in 1990 and refitted in 1998, specializes in marine research, in which you are encouraged to participate, both on deck and under water. It's not luxurious, but it's large and comfortable, with twin or queen-size beds in air-conditioned cabins, and shared bathrooms. This boat has all the gear: digital underwater video, electronic animal tracking equipment, a hydrophone to listen to whale and other animal noises, and a microscope linked to a television on board to encourage passengers to learn more about the Reef's ecology. The boat usually carries two scientists along with 20 passengers and 5 crew. It also encourages you to get adventurous, so the crew conducts advanced PADI courses on board for A$190 (US$152), as well as on-board refresher courses for out-of-practice divers. From mid-June to late July, you can join **dwarf minke whale** expeditions to snorkel with, watch, and help scientists photograph and record these majestic mammals.

The *Undersea Explorer* departs weekly on Saturday evenings and returns Friday evenings; the trip costs A$2,450 (US$1,960) plus approximately A$200 (US$160) extra for gear rental. They will also arrange transfers from Cairns.

Quicksilver's 12-passenger dedicated dive boat, *Diversity,* is—at the time of writing—only available for charters. It takes in Agincourt, Ribbon and Northern Ribbon reefs, and the Cod Hole. The boat has three twin or double cabins, two with ensuite bathrooms.

USEFUL DIVE-RELATED BUSINESSES
Quicksilver Dive at Marina Mirage (© **07/4099 5050**) sells dive gear. *Poseidon,* Shop 2, 34 Macrossan St. (© **07/4099 4772**), sells gear and can service some kinds of equipment.

3 Exploring the Rainforest & Other Things to See & Do

DAINTREE NATIONAL PARK ✿✿
Just about everyone who comes to Port Douglas takes a guided 4WD day trip into the beautiful Daintree National Park. The park is in several sections. You should make time to visit the southern inland part containing Mossman Gorge, and the rugged northern Cape Tribulation section, which sweeps down to sandy beaches and fringing coral reefs.

Any tour desk in town can book you on a 4WD safari to the Daintree, but at the **Daintree Discovery Centre** (℗ **07/4098 9171;** www.daintree-rec.com.au), at Cow Bay, across the Daintree River, you can obtain information on the ecology of North Queensland's World Heritage–listed Wet Tropics rainforests, of which Daintree National Park is part. The center is a font of information, has details on camping, walking tracks, and road conditions, and is worth visiting even if you go no further into the Daintree. It is open daily (except Christmas) from 8:30am to 5pm and is accessible with a conventional vehicle. There is another **Wet Tropics Information Centre** located within the Rainforest Habitat (see below).

You can rent a 4WD and explore on your own, but you may not see much except palm fronds and ferns without a guide to interpret it all. Most companies cover pretty much the same territory and sights, including a 1-hour Daintree River cruise to spot crocs, a visit to the short but interesting Marrdja Botanical Walk in the mangroves, an isolated beach stroll, lunch at a pretty spot somewhere in the forest, and a visit to Mossman Gorge. Some also go to the Bloomfield Falls deeper north in Cape Tribulation National Park. Expect to pay about A$130 (US$104) per adult and about A$90 (US$72) per child. Trips that include Bloomfield Falls cost more. You may not see much wildlife on these trips, because rainforest animals are shy, camouflaged, nocturnal, or all three! Keep your eyes peeled for a cassowary, though, large flightless birds with a striking red-and-blue neck and a bony crown on their heads. Floods and swollen creeks can quash your trip in the Wet Season, especially January through April, so keep your plans flexible then.

Pete Baxendell's **Heritage & Interpretive Tours** ℞ (℗ **07/4098 7897;** www.nqhit.com.au) is one of the best ways of getting to see this area. On a day-long bushwalk into a tract of privately owned rainforest with Pete, a naturalist and professional tour guide, you taste green ants (be brave, it's quite an experience) and other native "bush tucker," discover how to rustle up a toothbrush from a shrub if you forgot to pack yours, learn about bush medicine and the wildlife around you, and clamber up a stream to a waterfall. He takes a maximum six people at a time. Lunch and Port Douglas pickups are included in the price of A$110 (US$88) adults and A$85 (US$68) child. Walks run Tuesday and Saturday, leaving Port at 8:30am. You can also charter Pete and his 4WD on other days for day bushwalks for A$160 (US$128) per person (minimum of two) or for a "go anywhere" adventure for A$540 (US$432) per day.

Pickups from the northern beaches cost A$30 (US$24) extra for bushwalks, but are included in the price for "go anywhere" charters.

The charter prices compare favorably to a regular Daintree four-wheel-drive tour if there's three or more of you—and you get a tailored itinerary, Pete's knowledge, and the vehicle all to yourself. He often takes charter customers inland to Outback gold mining ghost towns, or north to tiny Cooktown, which boasts an excellent museum devoted to Australia's "discoverer," Captain James Cook. If you have 2 days, he can take you farther west to see Aboriginal rock art and stay at an upscale tented camp, or to the amazing Undara Lava Tubes. Other established operators are **Trek North Safaris** (✆ 07/4051 4328) and **BTS Tours** (✆ 07/4099 5665). As is the case in most tourist hot spots, some tour operators battle each other fiercely to pay tour desks the highest commission to recommend their tours, even though those tours may not necessarily be the best ones for your needs. Take tour desks' recommendations with a grain of salt, and ask other travelers for their recommendations.

If your chosen safari does not visit Mossman Gorge, 21km (13 miles) northwest of Port Douglas near the sugar town of Mossman, try to get there on your own. The gushing river tumbling over boulders, and the network of short forest walks are magical. But don't climb on the rocks or enter the river, as strong currents are extremely dangerous and have claimed at least one life in recent years.

A 1-hour **croc-spotting cruise** on the Daintree River is high on the list of most visitors. You are not guaranteed to see crocodiles, but chances are you will. To see the Daintree's bird life, take an early-morning cruise when birds are active. To see the most wildlife, it is best to go at night. Most Daintree rainforest 4WD safaris include a river cruise, but if yours does not, a variety of boats from open-sided "river trains" to small fishing boats run short cruises. Most leave from the Daintree River ferry crossing (see below).

One of the best is offered by **Dan Irby's Mangrove Adventures** 🐊 (✆ 07/4090 7017; www.mangroveadventures.com.au), whose small

---

Tips **Drat Those Aussie Mozzies!**

Mozzies, as Aussies call mosquitoes, love the rainforest as much as people do, so throw some insect repellent in your day pack when touring the Daintree and Cape Tribulation. Aerogard and RID are two effective brands. Another tip: Wear light-colored clothing, as mosquitoes are attracted to dark clothing.

Finds   **Spotting Birds of a Feather**

More than half of Australia's bird species have been recorded within a 200km (124-mile) radius of the Daintree rainforest. Ornithologist Del Richards of **Fine Feather Tours** *(€ 07/4094 1199;* www.finefeathertours.com.au) leads a range of tours including a full-day bird-watching safari in the Wet Tropics and to dryer inland grasslands on the edge of the Outback for A$195 (US$156), and an afternoon cruise on the bird-rich Daintree River for A$145 (US$116).

---

open boat can get up side creeks the bigger boats can't. Originally from Oklahoma, Dan has been in Australia for 30 years, and is extremely knowledgeable about the wildlife and habitat. He takes no more than 10 people at a time on 2-, 3-, and 4-hour cruises. It is *very* important to make advance reservations with Dan (at least 24 hr. if possible) to ensure seats are available and to determine departure times. Chances are you will spot lots of wildlife on his 2-hour night cruise, and even if you don't, it's worth it just to see the stars! A 2-hour trip costs A$45 (US$36). Night trips depart from Daintree Eco Lodge, 20 Mossman Daintree Rd., 4km (2½ miles) south of Daintree village; day trips leave from the public jetty next to the Daintree River ferry crossing. You can combine both, taking an afternoon tour, followed by a 45-minute break for a snack at Daintree Eco Lodge, then heading off on the night tour. Take the Captain Cook Highway north to Mossman, where it becomes the Mossman Daintree Road, and follow it for 24km (15 miles) to the signposted turnoff for the ferry on your right. The ferry is 5km (3 miles) from the turnoff. You'll need a car to get there. Bring a sweater in winter.

Rainforest Habitat wildlife sanctuary (*€ 07/4099 3235;* www.rainforesthabitat.com.au) is a great place to get to see the animals that are too shy to be spotted in the wild. Here, there are 180 animal species from the Wet Tropics for you to see up close. You can see saltwater and freshwater crocodiles, hand-feed kangaroos, and have your photo taken beside (but not holding) a koala (from 10–11am and 3–4pm for the cost of a donation). The highlight is the walk-through aviary, which houses 70 Wet Tropics bird species including cassowaries. You'll get the most out of your visit if you take one of the excellent free guided tours that leave every hour on the hour between 9am and 3pm. Rainforest Habitat is located on Port Douglas Road at the turnoff from the Captain Cook Highway.

Open daily (except Christmas) from 8am to 5:30pm (last entry at 4:30pm). Admission is A$28 (US$22) for adults, A$14 (US$11) for kids 4 to 14. Between 8am and 11am, the park serves a champagne buffet breakfast for A$39 (US$31) for adults and A$19 (US$15) for kids, including admission. From July to October, you can see Habitat After Dark, an evening tour which includes dinner and costs A$85 (US$68) adults and A$43 (US$34) kids. Allow 2 hours here.

DISCOVERING ABORIGINAL CULTURE

Hazel Douglas of **Native Guide Safari Tours** *(© 07/4098 2206;* www.nativeguidesafaritours.com.au) runs four-wheel-drive tours of the rainforest from an Aboriginal perspective. Hazel is a full-blooded Aborigine who grew up in a tribal lifestyle in the Daintree. She imparts her traditional knowledge of the plants, animals, Dreamtime myths, and Aboriginal history on a full-day tour departing at 9:15am from your Port Douglas hotel. Passengers from Cairns transfer up on the Quicksilver catamaran and return either by coach (northern beaches) or catamaran (Cairns city). The trip costs A$130 (US$104) for adults and A$80 (US$64) for children ages 3 to 14 from Port Douglas, and A$10 (US$8) extra from Cairns or the northern beaches. Charter and half-day tours are also available.

KuKu-Yalanji Dreamtime Tours *(© 07/4098 1305)* offers a guided walk through the rainforest to see cave paintings and visit "special sites"; the tour is followed by a Dreamtime story over billy tea and damper in a bark *warun* (a kind of shelter). The KuKu-Yalanji people have called this area home for tens of thousands of years and guides will talk about bush medicines and foods, Dreamtime legends, and sites sacred to their people. You can buy artifacts from the tribe's information center, gift shop, and art gallery. The tours depart Monday through Friday at 10am, noon, and 2pm from the Kuku-Yalanji community on the road to Mossman Gorge (1km/½ mile before you reach the Gorge parking lot). Tours cost A$17 (US$14) for adults and A$8.25 (US$6.60) for children. Allow 2 hours.

MORE TO SEE & DO

Remember that in addition to the companies below, some outdoor-activity companies in Cairns provide inexpensive or free pickups from Port Douglas hotels. See "White-Water Rafting & Other Outdoor Activities," in chapter 3.

The best outdoor activity in Port Douglas, however, is to do nothing but laze on spectacular **4 Mile Beach** *. May through September the water is stinger-free. October through April, swim in the stinger safety net. **Extra Action Water Sports** (© **07/4099 3175**) offers parasailing, jet-skiing, and half day trips to the Low Isles. A half-hour jet ski or parafly is A$70 (US$56) solo or A$90 (US$72) tandem. Low Isles trips leave at 8:30am and 1:30pm and cost A$125 (US$100) per person or A$450 (US$360) for a family of four, including snorkeling equipment. For an extra A$50 (US$40) you can parafly on the way; for an extra A$100 (US$80) you can follow the boat to the island on a jet ski. The booking office is at the end of the jetty on the Port Douglas slipway.

Visitor greens fees at the championship Sheraton Mirage golf course on Port Douglas Road are A$145 (US$116) for 18 holes or A$85 (US$68) for 9 holes, including a buggy. Club rentals range from A$38 to $60 (US$30–$48). Whacking a ball on the hotel's aquatic driving range costs A$6.50 (US$5.20) for a bucket of 25 balls, A$13 (US$10) for 50 balls, plus A$2.15 (US$1.70) for club rental. Contact the **Pro Shop** (© **07/4099 5537**).

Fishing Port Douglas (© **07/4098 5354**; www.fishingport douglas.com.au) is a booking service for a range of reef, estuary, and big game fishing boats based in Port Douglas and the Daintree. Expect to pay between A$155 and A$180 (US$124 and US$144) per person for a full day's reef fishing.

Mowbray Valley Trail Rides (© **07/4099 3268**), located 13km (8 miles) inland from Port Douglas, offers 2-hour horseback rides for A$88 (US$70) or half-day rides through rainforest and sugar cane fields to Collards Falls, or to a swimming hole in the Hidden Valley, for A$95 (US$76), including a barbecue lunch. It also runs full-day trips along the mountainous Bump Track (weather permitting), followed by a dip in a rainforest pool and barbecue lunch at Mowbray Falls for A$130 (US$104). Transfers from your Port Douglas accommodations are included. Transfers from Cairns are A$25 (US$20) per person. **Wonga Beach Equestrian Centre** (© **07/4098 7583**) does 3-hour rides through the rainforest and along Wonga Beach, 35 minutes north of Port Douglas, for A$89 (US$71) adults and A$79 (US$63) children, plus A$9 (US$7.20) for insurance. Transfers from Port Douglas are included. Rides start at 8:30am and 3pm.

Bike 'n' Hike (© **07/4099 4000**; www.bikenhike.com.au) takes small groups biking, hiking, and swimming in natural lagoons in the Mowbray Valley in the rainforest near Port Douglas. You don't need to be a strong cyclist to take part but you must be aged 12 or over. A half-day tour costs A$88 (US$70), including pickups from your Port Douglas hotel, a 27-speed mountain bike, helmet, gloves and backpack, a snack and drinks.

Every Sunday, a colorful **handicrafts and fresh food market** sets up on the lawns under the mango trees beside Dickson Inlet at the end of Macrossan Street. Stalls sell everything from foot massages to fresh coconut milk. It runs from 7:30am to 1pm. While you're here, take a peek, or attend a nondenominational service, inside the pretty timber church, St. Mary's By The Sea.

4 Where to Stay

Port Douglas Accommodation Holiday Rentals (© 1800/645 566 in Australia, or 07/4099 4488; www.portdouglasaccom.com.au) has a wide range of apartments and homes for rent.

High season in Port Douglas is from about June 1 to October 31.

VERY EXPENSIVE

Sheraton Mirage Port Douglas əəə   One of Australia's most luxurious properties, this low-rise Sheraton has 2 hectares (5 acres) of saltwater pools, and a championship Peter Thomson–designed 18-hole golf course. It is a bit too far from Port's main street by foot, but a free shuttle runs from 9am to 6pm to the golf course's country club/health center, to Marina Mirage shopping center, and into town. All the rooms are large and light-filled, and the resort has undergone an extensive refurbishment in the past year, with new color schemes, furniture and artworks, and extras like mini stereo systems. All rooms have Sony Playstations and Internet access. You might fancy upgrading to a Mirage room with a corner Jacuzzi and king beds, but I thought the standard rooms just fine. The 101 privately owned two-, three-, and four-bedroom luxury villas with golf course, garden, or sea views are rented out by Sheraton; the decor varies, but each has a Jacuzzi and two bathrooms.

Davidson St. (off Port Douglas Rd.), Port Douglas, QLD 4877. © **1800/07 3535** in Australia; 800/325-3535 in the U.S. and Canada; 00800/325 353535 in the U.K., Ireland, and New Zealand; or 07/4099 5888. Fax 07/4099 4424, or Starwood Hotels reservation fax 07/4099 5398. www.sheraton-mirage.com.au. 394 units (including 101 villas). A$619–A$830 (US$495–US$664) double; A$2,895 (US$2,316) 1- or 2-bedroom suite; A$950–A$1,250 (US$760–US$1,000) 2-, 3-, or 4-bedroom villa. Extra person A$70 (US$56). Children under 17 stay free in parent's room with existing bedding. Discounted rates available. AE, DC, MC, V. Free valet and self-parking. Helicopter transfers available. **Amenities:** 3 restaurants (seafood, Mediterranean, Japanese); 2 bars; 25m (82-ft.) outdoor lap pool; 18-hole championship golf course with country club and pro shop, aquatic driving range (with targets in a lake), putting green, and golf clinics; 9 day/night tennis courts; health club; spa; Jacuzzi; bike rental; daily day care for kids under 5, kids' club for children 5–15 during school vacations (for additional fee); concierge; tour desk; car-rental desk; business center (with extra charge for Internet access); salon; 24-hr. room service; massage; babysitting; dry cleaning;

nonsmoking rooms. *In room:* A/C, TV, kitchenette (villas only), minibar (hotel rooms only), coffeemaker, dataport, hair dryer, iron, safe.

EXPENSIVE

Port Douglas Peninsula Boutique Hotel 🐙🐙   Built in 1999 over three levels, this intimate studio apartment hotel fronting Four Mile Beach is one of the nicest places to stay in town. Every apartment features an open-plan living room/bedroom, a contemporary kitchenette (with microwave and dishwasher), and a groovy bathroom boasting a giant double tub (or Jacuzzi, in some units). Corner apartments are a little bigger. The decor is a stylish mélange of terra cotta, mosaic tiles, granite, and wicker, with classy extra touches like a CD player and boxed Twining's teas. Most have beach views from the roomy balcony or patio, while a few look onto the green and mauve complex of petite Art Deco-ish pools, waterfalls, hot and cold Jacuzzis, and sun deck rising and falling on several levels. A 2-minute walk brings you to the main street. No children under 15.

9–13 The Esplanade, Port Douglas, QLD 4877. ☎ **1800/676 674** in Australia, or 07/4099 9100. Fax 07/4099 5440. www.peninsulahotel.com.au. 34 units. A$320–A$420 (US$256–US$336) double. Rates include full breakfast. Ask about packages. AE, DC, MC, V. Complimentary round-trip transfers from Cairns airport. Covered parking. **Amenities:** Restaurant (Australian); small bar; large outdoor pool; hot and cold Jacuzzis; bike rental; tour desk; guest laundry; dry cleaning. *In room:* A/C, TV/VCR, dataport, kitchenette, coffeemaker, hair dryer, iron, safe.

MODERATE

Archipelago Studio Apartments 🐙   You won't find a friendlier or more convenient place in Port Douglas than these apartments, seconds from the beach and less than 10 minutes' walk from town. Your hosts Wolfgang Klein and Christel Bader are eager to help with tour bookings and to give useful advice—and they also speak fluent German, conversational French, and some Spanish. The apartments are on the small side (most suit only three people, at the most), but all are well cared for and were refurbished in 2001. You can opt for a tiny Garden apartment with a patio; or upgrade to a Balcony or Seaview apartment, both a bit larger and with private balconies. Seaview apartments are roomy, and have side views of Four Mile Beach. Towels are changed daily and linen weekly, but general servicing will cost A$20 (US$16) extra. There's no elevator and no porter, so be prepared to carry your luggage upstairs. No children under 6 permitted.

72 Macrossan St., Port Douglas, QLD 4877. ☎ **07/4099 5387.** Fax 07/4099 4847. www.archipelago.com.au. 21 units (all with shower only). High season (June–Oct) A$120–A$205 (US$96–A$164) double; low season A$105–A$175 (US$84–US$140)

double. Additional person A$20 (US$16). 3-night minimum stay applies. MC, V. Free undercover parking. **Amenities:** Outdoor saltwater pool; nearby golf course; 6 nearby day/night tennis courts; access to nearby health club; Jacuzzi; tour desk; coin-op laundry; laundry service; same-day dry cleaning can be arranged; nonsmoking rooms. *In room:* A/C, TV, kitchenette, fridge, coffeemaker, hair dryer.

Port Douglas Retreat   This well-kept two-story studio apartment complex on a quiet street, featuring the white-battened balconies of the Queenslander architectural style, is a good value, because even some of the ritzier places in town can't boast its lagoonlike saltwater pool surrounded by dense jungle and wrapped by an ample shady sun deck that cries out to be lounged on with a good book and a cool drink. The apartments are not enormous, but are fashionably furnished with terra-cotta tile floors, wrought-iron beds, cane seating, and colorful bedcovers. All have large furnished balconies or patios looking into tropical gardens (some on the ground floor open onto the common-area boardwalk, so maybe ask for a first-floor unit). The town and beach are 5 minutes walk away. No smoking indoors. The newer **Cayman Villas** (www.caymanvillas.com.au) next door are run by the same management but are more expensive.

31–33 Mowbray St. (at Mudlo St.), Port Douglas, QLD 4877. ℭ 07/4099 5053. Fax 07/4099 5033. www.portdouglasretreat.com.au. 36 units (all with shower only). High season A$143 (US$114) double; low season A$107 (US$86) double. Crib A$5.50 (US$4.40) per night. AE, MC, V. Security covered parking. **Amenities:** Outdoor saltwater pool; tour desk; car-rental desk; coin-op laundry. *In room:* A/C, TV w/free movies, kitchenette, iron.

INEXPENSIVE

Port O'Call Lodge   There's a nice communal feeling to this modest motel on a suburban street a 10-minute walk from town. Backpackers, families, and anyone on a budget seem to treat it like a second home, swapping travel stories as they cook up a meal in the communal kitchen and dining room. The rooms are light, cool, and fresh with tile floors, loads of luggage and bench space, and small patios. The compact bathrooms are efficiently laid out with old but neat fixtures (bring your own hair dryer). Only the deluxe rooms have a TV, clock radio, self-serve tea and coffee facilities, and a minifridge. The hostel rooms have private bathrooms and no more than five beds and/or bunks in each. A 24-bed bunkhouse opened in 2001, and includes facilities for travelers with disabilities. New double and four-share rooms have been added in the past year. At night the lively poolside bistro, **Port O' Call Bistro** (p. 110) is the place to be. Other facilities include free board games, a pay phone, Internet access, and a kiosk selling refreshments.

Port St. at Craven Close, Port Douglas, QLD 4877. ☎ **1800/892 800** in Australia, or 07/4099 5422. Fax 07/4099 5495. www.portocall.com.au. 28 units (all with shower only). High season (May–Oct, Christmas, and Easter) A$59–A$99 (US$47–US$79) double; low season (Nov–Apr) A$59–A$89 (US$47–US$71) double. Additional person A$15 (US$12). Hostel rooms A$24 (US$19) or A$25 (US$20) YHA/Hostelling International members; bunkhouse A$21 (US$17) or A$20 (US$16) YHA/Hostelling International members. Children under 3 stay free. MC, V. Free once-daily shuttle to and from Cairns and the airport Mon–Sat. Free on-site parking. Bus stop at front door. **Amenities:** Restaurant (Bistro); outdoor pool; 3 golf courses nearby; access to nearby health club; bike rental; tour desk; coin-op laundry; nonsmoking rooms. *In room:* A/C, TV, fridge (double motel rooms only), safe.

5 Where to Dine

Nautilus ⭑⭑ TROPICAL/SEAFOOD   Bill and Hillary Clinton dined here during a visit Down Under, and by all accounts loved it. So did I. The restaurant, which has been keeping the locals happy since 1953, is set under the palm trees and stars, with a clever seating plan and unusual high-backed chairs which give a wonderfully intimate atmosphere. Local produce and seafood is the mainstay of the menu, which serves such delights as deep fried whole coral trout, served with green paw paw, mint, coriander, chilli and lime salsa or Gulf mud crab, wok-steamed in a spicy coconut cream laksa with chilli and lemongrass. Or you may prefer to go for crispy skin duck or one of the many other choices for non-seafood eaters.

17 Murphy St. (entry also from Macrossan St.), Port Douglas. ☎ **07/4099 5330.** www.nautilus-restaurant.com.au. Reservations recommended. Main courses A$26–A$38 (US$21–US$30). AE, DC, MC, V. Daily 6:30–10:30pm or until the last diners leave. Closed Feb. No children under 8.

Port O' Call Bistro *(Kids)* CAFE/BISTRO   Locals patronize this poolside bistro and bar at the Port O' Call Lodge (p. 109) almost as often as guests do, because it offers good, honest food like lamb shanks and steaks in hearty portions at painless prices. The atmosphere is fun and friendly. There are pasta, curry and roast nights, and every night you can try one of the "chef's blackboard surprises," including local beef and seafood. Kids' meals are all A$6 (US$4.80), and there are burgers, nachos, and pastas as well.

Port St. at Craven Close. ☎ **07/4099 5422.** Main courses A$9–A$17 (US$7.20–US$14). MC, V. Daily 6pm–midnight.

Salsa Bar & Grill ⭑⭑ *(Kids)* MODERN/TROPICAL   This trendy restaurant, in its lovely timber Queenslander with wrap-around verandas, has terrific food, great value prices, and lively, fun service. Here you can choose between the simplest of fare such as gnocchi,

Caesar salad, or fantastic spring rolls, or such mouth-watering delights as whitebait and crab fritters with wasabi aioli, wakame and beetroot salad, or pan-fried barramundi with tagliatelle, tomato vinaigrette, corn and prosciutto salsa. Even if you usually resist dessert, don't. The buttermilk and almond nougat panna cotta is to-die-for, and the chocolate Cointreau soufflé is a must. On Sundays there's a salsa band and the place really gets jumping.

26 Wharf St. (at Warner St.). ℂ **07/4099 4922.** www.salsa-port-douglas.com.au. Reservations essential. Main courses A$20–A$25 (US$16–US$20). AE, DC, MC, V. Mon–Sat 10am–midnight; Sun 8am–midnight.

5

The North Coast: Mission Beach, Townsville & the Islands

For years the lovely town of **Mission Beach** was a well-kept secret. Farmers retired here; then those who liked to drop out and chill out discovered it; today, it's a small, prosperous, and stunningly pretty rainforest town. The beach is one of the most beautiful in Australia, a long white strip fringed with dense tangled vine forests, the only surviving lowlands rainforest in the Australian tropics. It is also one of the least crowded and least spoiled, so clever has **Mission Beach** been at staying out of sight, out of mind, and off the tourist trail.

From Mission Beach it's a short ferry ride to **Dunk Island,** a large resort island that welcomes day-trippers. You can even sea kayak there from the mainland. Mission Beach is closer to the Great Barrier Reef than any other point along the coast—just an hour—and cruise boats depart daily from the jetty, stopping en route at Dunk Island. Just south of Dunk Island is one of Australia's most exclusive island resorts, **Bedarra Island,** which hosts just 30 lucky guests at a time, who get to soak up its glorious rainforest and unspoiled beaches.

The nearby **Tully River** is white-water–rafting heaven for thrill-seekers. You can also bungee jump and tandem skydive when you're not rushing down the rapids, flanked by lush rainforest.

A few hours' drive south brings you to the city of **Townsville,** also a gateway to the Great Barrier Reef. It has more to offer divers than Mission Beach, not least because its waters are the last resting place of the **SS *Yongala*** ✷, now an excellent wreck dive. More dive boats are based at Townsville than at Mission Beach, offering a small array of good live-aboard trips, a couple of day excursions, and a choice of dive courses. Townsville is the gateway to **Magnetic Island,** a picturesque, laid-back haven for divers and snorkelers, watersports enthusiasts, and hikers.

The drive from Cairns to Townsville through sugar cane fields, cloud-topped hills, and lush bushland is a pretty one—one of the most picturesque stretches in Queensland.

The North Coast

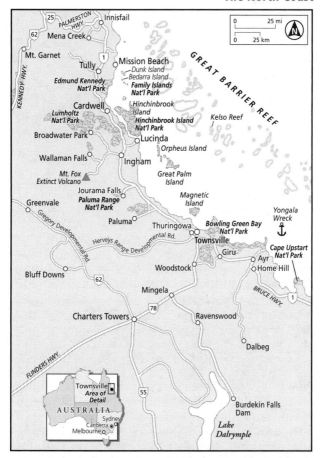

1 Mission Beach: The Cassowary Coast

140km (86 miles) S of Cairns; 240km (149 miles) N of Townsville

Tucked away off the Bruce Highway, the township of Mission Beach has managed to duck the tourist hordes. It's actually a conglomeration of four beachfront towns: South Mission Beach, Wongaling Beach, Mission Beach proper, and Bingil Bay. Most commercial activity centers on the small nucleus of shops and businesses at Mission Beach proper. It's so isolated that signs on the way into town warn you to watch out for ultra-shy cassowaries emerging from the jungle to cross the road. Dense rainforest hides the town from view, until you round the corner to Mission Beach proper and discover appealing hotels, neat shops, and smart little restaurants. Just through the trees is the fabulous beach. A mile or so north of the main settlement of Mission Beach is Clump Point Jetty.

The jungle around the town is **cassowary** country. Cassowaries, an endangered species, are flightless birds about the size of an emu; they have black plumage, red and blue necks, and bony cones on their heads that give them a definite Jurassic Park look. Watch out for them crossing the road when you're driving.

For a **map** of this area, see the Great Barrier Reef map in chapter 1, p. 2.

ESSENTIALS

GETTING THERE   From Cairns, follow the Bruce Highway south. The Mission Beach turnoff is at the tiny town of El Arish, about 15km (9 miles) north of Tully. Mission Beach is 25km (16 miles) off the highway. It's a 90-minute trip from Cairns. If you're coming from Townsville, there is an earlier turnoff just north of Tully that leads 18km (11 miles) to South Mission Beach.

Airport Connections (© 07/4099 5950) operates door-to-door shuttles twice a day from Cairns for A$35 (US$28) adults and A$18 (US$14) children, and from the northern beaches for A$44 (US$35) adults and A$25 (US$20) children. **McCafferty's** (© **13 14 99** in Australia) and **Greyhound Pioneer** (© **13 20 30** in Australia) coaches both stop in Mission Beach proper (not South Mission Beach) several times daily on their Cairns-Brisbane-Cairns runs. The fare is A$15 (US$12) from Cairns, or A$181 (US$145) for the 26-hours-plus trip from Brisbane.

Five trains a week on the Cairns-Brisbane-Cairns route call at the nearest train station, Tully, about 20km (12½ miles) away. One-way travel from Cairns on the Tilt Train costs A$43 (US$34) for the 2-hour 50-minute journey. From Brisbane, fares range from A$183 (US$146) in an economy seat to A$345 (US$276) for a first-class sleeper on *The Sunlander*. For more information, call Queensland Rail's long-distance division, **Traveltrain** (© **13 22 32** in Australia, or 07/3235 1122). A taxi from Tully to Mission Beach with **Supreme Taxis** (© 07/4068 3937) is about A$40 (US$32).

VISITOR INFORMATION   The **Mission Beach Visitor Centre,** Porters Promenade, Mission Beach, QLD 4852 (© **07/4068 7099;** www.missionbeachtourism.com), is at the northern end of

> ## *Tips* Staying Safe
>
> Crocodiles inhabit the waterways around Mission Beach. Do not swim in, or stand on the bank of, any river, stream, or estuary.
>
> It's frustrating, but the area's 14km (8¾ miles) of beaches are all but off-limits in the deadly marine stinger season October through April or May. Swim only in the stinger nets at Mission Beach and South Mission Beach then. Stingers do not make it as far offshore as the Reef, so the waters are safe there year-round.
>
> Cassowaries can kill with their powerful claws. If you run across one, back away slowly and hide behind a tree.

Mission Beach proper. It's open Monday through Saturday from 9am to 5pm, until 4pm Sunday.

GETTING AROUND   Trans North Bus & Coach (© **07/4068 7400**) provides a bus service linking the beach communities from Bingil Bay to South Mission Beach. Just flag the bus down outside your accommodations or wherever you see it. **Sugarland Car Rentals** (© **07/4068 8272**) is the only rental-car company in town. For Mission Beach taxi service, call © **07/4068 8155.**

DIVING & SNORKELING THE REEF
MAJOR REEF SITES
Mission Beach is the closest point on the mainland to the Reef, 1 hour by boat. The main site visited is **Beaver Cay,** a sandy coral cay surrounded by marine life. The waters are shallow there, making it ideal for both snorkelers eager to see the coral's vibrant colors and novice divers still getting a feel for the sport. The cay is a perfect spot for an introduction dive.

DAY-TRIP DIVE & SNORKEL BOATS
The modern, air-conditioned high-speed **Quick Cat Cruises** catamaran (© **1800/654 242** in Australia, or 07/4068 7289; fax 07/4068 7185) makes a day trip to Beaver Cay on the Outer Reef. The trip starts with an hour at Dunk Island 20 minutes offshore, where you can walk rainforest trails, play on the beach, or parasail or jet ski for an extra fee. Then it's a 1-hour trip to the sandy cay, where you have 3 hours to snorkel or check out the coral from a glass-bottom boat. There's no shade on the cay, so come prepared with a hat and sunscreen. The trip departs daily from Clump Point Jetty at 9:30am.

It costs A$140 (US$112) for adults, A$70 (US$56) for children ages 4 to 14 and A$350 (US$280) for a family of 4. An introductory scuba dive costs A$80 (US$64) for the first dive and A$35 (US$28) for the second. You should pre-book your introductory scuba dive to ensure a place. Qualified divers pay A$60 (US$48) for the first dive, A$35 (US$28) for the second, all gear included. Free pickups from Mission Beach are included, as are reef tax, buoyancy vests, and a lavish lunch. You can also join this trip from Cairns; coach connections from your Cairns or northern beaches hotel will cost extra. On Sundays and Wednesdays, the trip costs as little as A$88 (US$70), with a 10:30am start and traveling direct to the reef.

ISLAND RESORTS

Neither Dunk nor Bedarra Islands offers the Reef's best snorkeling, and neither has a dive shop of its own. If you stay on the islands, you can still visit the outer Reef by taking a day trip aboard the *Quick Cat* (see above). It picks up passengers at Dunk at 11am, returning to the island at 4:30pm. Guests at Bedarra will need to pay for a transfer to Dunk Island to join the trip.

LEARNING TO DIVE

Mission Beach Dive Charters (© 07/4068 7277) operates openwater certification courses.

USEFUL DIVE-RELATED BUSINESSES

Contrary to its name, **Mission Beach Dive and Tackle,** on Porter's Promenade in Mission Beach proper (© 07/4068 7294), doesn't sell much dive gear, but it will sell you snorkel gear, plus a few dive accessories like weight belts and dive knives.

OTHER THINGS TO SEE & DO
WHITE-WATER RAFTING ON THE TULLY

A day's rafting through the rainforest on the Grade 3 to 4 Tully River is an adventure you won't soon forget. In raft-speak, Grade 4 means "exciting rafting on moderate rapids with a continuous need to maneuver rafts." On the Tully, that translates to regular hair-raising but manageable rapids punctuated by calmer stretches that let you just float downstream. You don't need experience, just a decent level of agility and an enthusiastic attitude. **RnR Rafting** (© 07/4051 7777) runs a trip that includes 5 hours on the river with expert guides, a barbecue lunch in the rainforest, and a video screening of your adventure. With transfers, the day costs A$135 (US$108) from Mission Beach, A$145 (US$116) from Cairns, Palm Cove or Townsville, and A$160 (US$128) from Port Douglas, plus a A$10 (US$8) national park fee. The trip runs daily; you must be 13 years or older.

EXPLORING THE RAINFOREST & COAST

Several companies offer sea kayaking along the unspoiled island-dotted shoreline and guided nature walks in the rainforest. Ingrid Marker of **Sunbird Adventures** (© 07/4068 8229; sunbird.adventures@ bigpond.com) offers a range of sea-kayaking and trekking expeditions that interpret the rich environment around you. No more than eight people are allowed on each trip, so you get personal attention and time to ask questions. Her half-day sea-kayak expedition (A$55/ US$44 per person) journeys around Bingil Bay. Night walks, starting at 7pm and returning around 9:30pm, are held on Bicton Hill and are great for kids because they spot glow-in-the-dark fungi, and frogs and shrimps in the streams (A$30/US$24 per person). Ingrid also runs 3-day sea kayak/camping trips, and a 3-day Misty Mountain Trails hike in the Tully River Gorge. They can be combined to make a 6-day trip, and prices for both can be worked out with Ingrid according to your needs. All trips include pickup from your accommodations, and all food is locally grown organic produce. Not all tours depart every day, so check with her first.

Ask the Mission Beach Visitor Centre (see "Visitor Information," above) for a free map of the town's **walking trails.**

A DAY TRIP TO DUNK ISLAND

Day-trippers can pop over to Dunk Island to swim, snorkel (the coral isn't great; the best spot is off Muggy Muggy Beach and Naturist Beach), hike, and pay to use the watersports equipment. **Dunk Island Ferry & Cruises** (© **07/4068 7211**) runs day trips for A$69 (US$55) for adults and A$25 (US$20) for kids ages 4 to 14 (free for younger kids). The cruise includes lunch, boom-netting, a swing around Bedarra Island, and free snorkeling gear (with a A$20/US$16 refundable deposit). Daily departures from Clump Point Jetty are at 8:45 and 10:30am. You can also get to Dunk by the **water taxi** (© **07/4068 8310**), which runs five times a day from Wongaling Beach. The round-trip fare is A$29 (US$23) for adults and A$15

Tips **Bring Money to Mission Beach!**

There is no bank in Mission Beach, and only one ATM, located within Mission Beach Resort at Wongaling Beach. That's a drive from Mission Beach proper or South Mission Beach.

(US$12) for kids ages 4 to 14. Ask at your accommodations about transfers between Clump Point and South Mission Beach.

Once on Dunk, you pay as you go for activities and equipment rental on the island. Everything from water-skiing to catamaran sailing is available, and Dunk has lovely beaches and half a dozen rainforest walking trails, ranging in duration from 15 minutes to 4 hours. On Monday and Thursday mornings, you can visit an artist's gallery reached via a 40-minute trail through the rainforest; admission is A$4 (US$3.20).

Ingrid Marker of Sunbird Adventures (see above) runs unusual full-day guided **sea-kayak expeditions** $\mathcal{R}$ to Dunk Island. Ingrid says if you can pedal a bike for an hour, you can sea kayak for the hour it takes to get to the island. You glide over reefs, looking for sea turtles; spend the morning snorkeling in Coconut Bay; have a picnic lunch of oysters, mussels, and fresh produce (all organic) in Hidden Palm Valley; then hike the rainforest. At morning and afternoon tea you get a choice of no less than nine organic teas and coffees. The trip costs A$95 (US$76) per person.

WHERE TO STAY IN MISSION BEACH

The Horizon $\mathcal{R}$ With its beguiling views across the pool to Dunk Island, its rainforest setting, and its impressive rooms, this resort on a steep hillside is one of the most comfortable and beautiful you will find. Even the least expensive rooms are spacious and have luxurious bathrooms. All but a handful have some kind of sea view; a half dozen retain the older-style bathrooms from a previous resort development, but the sea views from these rooms are the best. It's just a minute or two down the rainforest track to the beach.

Explorer Dr., South Mission Beach, QLD 4852. ✆ **1800/079 090** in Australia, or 07/4068 8154. Fax 07/4068 8596. www.thehorizon.com.au. 55 units. A$220–A$420 (US$176–US$336) double. Children A$20 (US$16) extra. Ask about packages and specials. Rates are higher Dec 22–Jan 2. AE, DC, MC, V. **Amenities:** 3 restaurants (International); bar; large saltwater pool; day/night tennis courts; tour desk. *In room:* A/C, TV w/cable, minibar, coffeemaker, hair dryer, iron.

Mackays *(Value*   This delightfully well-kept motel is one of the best-value places to stay in town. It's just 80m (262 ft.) from the beach and 400m (¼ mile) from the heart of Mission Beach. The friendly Mackay family repaints the rooms annually, so the place always looks brand new. All the rooms are pleasant and spacious with white-tiled floors, cane sofas, colorful bedcovers, and very clean bathrooms. Those in the newer section are air-conditioned, and some have views of the attractive granite-lined pool and gardens. Rooms in the older painted-brick wing have garden views from a communal patio and no air-conditioning. Ask about special packages; they can be extremely good deals and may include extras like rafting on the Tully River and day trips to the Reef and Dunk Island.

7 Porter Promenade, Mission Beach, QLD 4852. (✆ 07/4068 7212. Fax 07/4068 7095. www.mackaysmissionbeach.com. 22 units, 12 with bathroom (10 with shower only). A$85–A$105 (US$68–US$84) double; A$120 (US$96) 1- and 2-bedroom apt. Higher rates apply at Easter. Additional person A$20 (US$16) extra; children under 14 A$10 (US$8) extra. Crib A$6.50 (US$5.20) extra. Ask about packages. AE, DC, MC, V. Free covered off-street parking. **Amenities:** Outdoor pool; access to nearby tennis courts; access to bike rental; tour desk; car-rental desk; room service at breakfast; in-room massage; babysitting; coin-op laundry; nonsmoking rooms. *In room:* A/C (in 12 units only), TV, fax, kitchenettes (4 units only), fridge, safe.

WHERE TO STAY ON DUNK ISLAND

Dunk Island *(Kids)* Families love Dunk Island because there's so much to do, but it also has appeal for honeymooners or retired couples. For those who are more inclined to relaxation, Dunk has beautiful beaches and gentle pastimes like champagne sunset cruises. Just 5km (3 miles) offshore from Mission Beach, Dunk is a thickly rain-forested 12-sq.-km (7½-sq.-mile) island that attracts everyone. The island is renowned for bird life and neon-blue Ulysses butterflies, which you will see everywhere.

Among the free activities are windsurfing, catamaran sailing, paddle skiing, tennis and squash courts, fitness classes and aqua-aerobics, beach and pool volleyball, badminton, bocce, and archery, to name just a few. You pay for a range of other activities, including guided jet-ski tours, parasailing, water-skiing, tube rides, tandem skydiving, game-fishing trips, motorboats, sunset wine-and-cheese cruises, and horse riding. The 18-hole golf course is Australia's only island resort course. A yacht calls to make trips around nearby islands, and a game-fishing boat picks up here regularly. The kids will love the playground and a visit to Coonanglebah (the island farm), as well as the kids' club. A private artists' colony in the rainforest sells works Monday and Thursday, from 10am to 1pm.

All four kinds of low-rise accommodations were refurbished and restyled in 2003. To truly relax, visit the **Spa of Peace and Plenty,** two tropical-style buildings connected by a floating boardwalk on a man-made lake, for a facial, massage, body wrap or other pampering.

Off Mission Beach. C/o P&O Australian Resorts, G.P.O. Box 478, Sydney, NSW 2001. (✆ 1800/737 678 in Australia, 800/225-9849 in the U.S. and Canada, 020/7805 3875 in the U.K., or 02/9277 5050 (Sydney reservations office). Fax 02/9299 2477 (Sydney reservations office). www.poresorts.com. 146 units (72 with shower only). A$500–A$780 (US$400–US$624) double. Rates include full breakfast and dinner daily. Extra adult A$140 (US$112), extra child 3–14 A$80 (US$64). Ask about packages; some combine stays at Bedarra Island and Silky Oaks Lodge. AE, DC, MC, V. Daily 45-min. flights operate from Cairns (book through Qantas or the resort). Aircraft luggage limit 16kg (35 lb.) per person. Dunk Island Ferry & Cruises (© 07/ 4068 7211) makes round-trip ferry transfers from Mission Beach for A$32 (US$26) adults. Including the ferry fare, the company does daily door-to-door coach connections from Port Douglas for A$150 (US$120), Cairns for A$96 (US$77), and Cairns northern beaches for A$116 (US$128) adult. Fares for children 4–14 are half price. Disembarkation from the ferry is sometimes into shallow water—be prepared to get your feet wet! Airport pickups must be booked. Transfers also available by air charter and "Quick Cat" Great Barrier Reef cruise boat (see earlier in this chapter). **Amenities:** 3 restaurants (tropical, modern Australian); bar; 2 large outdoor pools; 18-hole golf course; 3 day/night tennis courts (1 indoor); exercise room; spa; extensive watersports equipment rental; bike rental; daily kids' club for ages 3–14 (an additional fee); babysitting; coin-op laundry. *In room:* A/C and ceiling fans, TV, minibar (beachfront units and suites only), fridge, coffeemaker, hair dryer, iron.

BEDARRA ISLAND: THE ULTIMATE LUXURY GETAWAY

Only a mile long, Bedarra is home to an exclusive 16-room resort favored by the rich, the famous, and anyone who treasures privacy. The staff is discreet, and day-trippers are banned. Rainforested and fringed by beaches, Bedarra is a few miles south of Dunk Island.

Bedarra Island 🐟🐟🐟   Bedarra is one of those rare and fabulous places that throws not just meals, but vintage French champagnes, fine cognacs and wines, and other potable treats into the price, shocking though that price may be. If you feel like Louis Roederer champagne at 3am, help yourself. The private villas have large verandas, and there's a sense of light and space in the public areas. The lobby, restaurant, and 24-hour bar are open, with ironbark and recycled timber beams, and feature panels of volcanic stone. Each villa is tucked into the rainforest with a balcony and sea views. All come with generous living areas, king beds, CD players, bathrobes, and the important things in life, like double hammocks on the veranda, big double bathtubs, and aromatherapy oil-burners. Bathrooms offer divine pampering treats including signature Bedarra aromatherapy oils.

Two premium villas, The Pavilions at Bedarra, are set away from the main resort, perched on cliff tops overlooking Wedgerock Bay, and offer superior facilities including separate living and sleeping areas and large decks and outdoor area with a private plunge pool. In 2003, one of the villas was converted into a similarly exclusive retreat, The Point, and a second was added in 2004, with many of the same features as the Pavilions, and the additional luxury of a gorgeous outdoor living area.

The emphasis here is on relaxation. Walk along rainforest trails, fish off the beach, snorkel, or take a catamaran, paddle-ski, or windsurf out on the water. These activities are free; chartering a yacht or game-fishing boat costs extra. To visit the Great Barrier Reef, you will need to transfer to Dunk Island to join the Quick Cat catamaran (see earlier in this section). The Beachclub offers watersports facilities and a gym and massage therapy room as well as a lounge area with Internet access. Many guests do nothing more strenuous than have the chef pack a gourmet picnic with a bottle of bubbly and set off in search of a deserted beach. Dress at night is smart casual.

Off Mission Beach (c/o P&O Australian Resorts, G.P.O. Box 478, Sydney, NSW 2001). ℂ 1800/737 678 in Australia, 800/225-9849 in the U.S. and Canada, 020/7805 3875 in the U.K., or 02/9277 5050 (Sydney reservations office). Fax 02/9299 2477 (Sydney reservations office). www.poresorts.com.au. 16 villas. A$1,980–A$3,200 (US$1,584–US$2,560) double. Rates include all meals, 24-hr. open bar and transfers from Dunk Island. Ask about packages; some combine stays at Dunk Island (see above), Silky Oaks Lodge, and Lizard Island. AE, DC, MC, V. Air or coach/ferry transfer to Dunk Island from Cairns (see above), then 15-min. boat transfer. Water transfers can be arranged from Mission Beach. No children under 16. **Amenities:** Restaurant; bar; secluded outdoor pool with timber decking and private Jacuzzi area; day/night tennis court; watersports (see above); gym; massage; laundry service. *In room:* A/C and ceiling fan, TV/VCR, free minibar, hair dryer, iron.

WHERE TO DINE IN MISSION BEACH

Friends MEDITERRANEAN/SEAFOOD   The cozy interior and a hearty menu favoring local seafood make this place a long-standing favorite with locals. Appetizers include mussels Normandy, oysters done three ways, and garlic prawns; main courses feature lamb shanks; steak with mushrooms or green peppercorn sauce; and chicken hot pot. Settle in with a homemade dessert and liqueur coffee after dinner. Licensed.

Porters Promenade (opposite Campbell St.), Mission Beach. ℂ 07/4068 7107. Reservations recommended. Main courses A$15–A$25 (US$12–US$20). AE, MC, V. Tues–Sat 6:30–10:30pm or until the last diners leave. Open Sun on long weekends. Closed for 1 month during Feb–Mar.

2 Townsville & Magnetic Island

346km (215 miles) S of Cairns; 1,371km (850 miles) N of Brisbane

With a population of 140,000, Townsville claims to be Australia's largest tropical city. Because of its size, and an economy based on mining, manufacturing, education, and tourism, it is sometimes overlooked as a holiday destination. Unjustly so, I think. The people are friendly, the city pleasant, and there's plenty to do. The town is nestled by the sea below the pink face of Castle Rock, which looms 300m (about 1,000 ft.) directly above, and the beachfront has recently undergone a A$29-million (US$23 million) revamp.

The Great Barrier Reef is roughly 2½ hours by boat from Townsville, about an hour longer than it takes to reach the Reef from elsewhere in Queensland. As a result, the dive industry is not the boomtown business it is in Cairns. Townsville's diving is generally suited to the more experienced diver, although it is certainly possible to learn to dive here, or to simply make an introductory dive if you don't want to gain certification. Divers come to visit the excellent SS *Yongala* wreck and assorted other remote Coral Sea reefs that are much less visited than the Cairns Great Barrier Reef sites farther north. Townsville is also the headquarters of the **Great Barrier Reef Marine Park Authority,** where you can visit a marvelous man-made living reef in a giant tank at **Reef HQ.** Day cruises depart to the real thing most days from the harbor.

Townsville's major new attraction is the world-class **Museum of Tropical Queensland,** where a full size replica of the HMS *Pandora* is the stunning centerpiece. The museum is next door to Reef HQ.

Just 8km (5 miles) offshore is Magnetic Island—"Maggie" to the locals—a popular place for watersports, hiking, and spotting koalas in the wild.

Although Townsville can be hot and humid in the summer—and sometimes in the path of cyclones—it is generally spared the worst of the wet season rains.

ESSENTIALS

GETTING THERE   Townsville is on the Bruce Highway, a 3-hour drive north of Airlie Beach and 4½ hours south of Cairns. The Bruce Highway breaks temporarily in the city. From the south, take Bruce Highway Alt. 1 route into the city. From the north, the highway leads into the city.

Qantas (© **13 13 13** in Australia; www.qantas.com) and subsidiary **QantasLink** have many flights a day from Cairns, and several from Brisbane. QantasLink also flies from Sydney, Hamilton Island in the Whitsundays and Mackay. **Virgin Blue** (© **13 67 89** in Australia) flies direct to Townsville from Brisbane and Sydney daily, and newcomer **Alliance Airlines** (© **1300/130 092;** www. allianceairlines.com.au) flies between Brisbane and Townsville.

Abacus Charters & Tours (© **07/4775 5544**) runs a door-to-door airport shuttle. It meets all flights from Brisbane, and from Cairns or elsewhere if you book in advance. A trip into town is A$7

(US$5.60) one-way or A$11 (US$8.80) return. A taxi from the airport to most central hotels costs about A$12 (US$9.60).

Seven **Queensland Rail** (☎ **13 22 32** in Queensland, or 07/3235 1122) long-distance trains stop at Townsville each week. The 19-hour **Tilt-Train** journey from Brisbane costs A$244 (US$195). The 24-hour *Sunlander* journey costs from A$163 (US$130) for an economy seat to A$339 (US$271) for a first-class sleeper.

Greyhound Pioneer (☎ **13 20 30** in Australia) and **McCafferty's** (☎ **13 14 99** in Australia) coaches stop at Townsville many times a day on their Cairns-Brisbane-Cairns routes. The fare from Cairns is A$49 (US$39); trip time is 6 hours. The fare from Brisbane is A$169 (US$135); trip time is 23 hours.

VISITOR INFORMATION   For an information packet, contact **Townsville Enterprise Limited,** P.O. Box 1043, Townsville, QLD 4810 (☎ **07/4726 2728;** www.townsville.com). It has two Information Centers. One is in the heart of town on Flinders Mall (☎ **1800/ 801 902** in Australia, or 07/4721 3660); it's open Monday through Friday from 9am to 5pm, and weekends from 9am to 1pm. The other is on the Bruce Highway 10km (6 miles) south of the city (℡ **07/4778 3555**); it is open daily from 9am to 5pm. Townsville Enterprise supplies information on Magnetic Island, but also check www.magnetic-island.com.au.

GETTING AROUND   Local **Sunbus** (℡ 07/4725 8482) buses depart from Flinders Street Mall. Car-rental chains include **Avis** (℡ 07/4721 2688), **Budget** (℡ 07/4725 2344), **Hertz** (℡ 07/4775 5950), and **Thrifty** (℡ 07/4725 4600).

Detours Coaches (℡ **07/4728 5311**) runs tours to most attractions in and around Townsville. For a taxi, ℡ **131 008.**

DIVING & SNORKELING THE REEF

The prices quoted below include all snorkel and dive gear, unless otherwise specified, and lunch. Departure times given are the time the boat heads out to sea; plan to board about 30 minutes earlier.

Remember to add the A$4.50 (US$3.60) Environmental Management Charge, or "reef tax," to the fare of every passenger over 4 years old.

MAJOR REEF SITES

Townsville's waters boast hundreds of large patch reefs, some miles long, and many virtually never visited by humans. Here you can find excellent coral and fish life, including mantas, rays, turtles, and sharks, and sometimes canyons and swim-throughs in generally good visibility. One of the best reef complexes is **Flinders Reef.** Actually in the Coral Sea, beyond the Great Barrier Reef Marine Park boundaries, we include it because many dive trips incorporate it into their Great Barrier Reef itineraries. At 240km (149 miles) offshore, it has 30m (100-ft.) visibility, plenty of coral, and big walls and pinnacles with big fish to match, like whale shark and barracuda.

What draws most divers to Townsville, though, is one of Australia's best wreck dives, the **SS *Yongala*** ✿. Still largely intact, the sunken remains of this steamer lie 90km (56 miles) from Townsville, 16km (10 miles) off the coast, in 15 to 30m (50–100 ft.) with visibility of 9 to 18m (approximately 30–60 ft.). A cyclone sent the *Yongala* and its 49 passengers and 72-member crew to the bottom of the sea in 1911. Today it's surrounded by a mass of coral and rich marine life, including barracuda, enormous grouper, rays, sea snakes, turtles, moray eels, shark, cod, and reef fish. You can even enter the ship and swim its length, with care.

The *Yongala* is not for beginners, as the boat is deep and there is a strong current. Most dive companies require their customers to have advanced certification, or to have logged a minimum of 15 dives with open-water certification. The boat is usually visited on a live-aboard trip of at least 2 days, but **Adrenalin Dive** (see below) runs day trips. Some companies run open-water certification dive courses that finish with a dive on the *Yongala,* but freshly certified scuba hounds might be wise to skip this advanced dive.

DAY-TRIP DIVE & SNORKEL BOATS

Most boats visiting the Reef from Townsville are live-aboard vessels that make trips of 2 or more days, designed for serious divers. **Barrier Reef Dive, Cruise & Travel** (② 1800/636 778 in Australia, or 07/ 4772 5800; www.divecruisetravel.com) has day trips to Keeper Reef and John Brewer Reef. It takes only 1½ hours to reach John Brewer Reef, where you can make introductory dives for A$60 (US$48) for the first and A$30 (US$24) for the second, while certified divers can make two dives for A$90 (US$72); all gear is included. The cruise costs A$129 (US$103) for adults, A$94 (US$75) for seniors, A$64 (US$51) for children 5 to 15, and A$319 (US$255) for a family of 4. The price includes lunch and morning and afternoon tea. There are fresh water showers on board. Cruises depart Townsville at 8:30am, with a pickup at Magnetic Island en route, and returns by about 5pm. Several other operators have trips to the *Yongala* wreck, the Coral Sea, and the Reef.

   Adrenalin Dive (② **1300/664 600** in Australia or **07/4724 0600;** www.adrenalindive.com.au) runs daily diving trips to the *Yongala* in a 14m (49-ft.) flybridge cruiser. The trip leaves Townsville at 7am and Magnetic Island at 7:15am, giving you time for two dives. The company recommends you make at least the first dive with their guide if you hold only open-water certification; if you have fewer than 15 dives logged, you must dive with their guide. The day's cost is A$179 (US$143), plus $35 (US$28) extra for gear rental. It costs A$30 (US$24) extra for 2 guided dives and A$10 (US$8) extra for a guided wreck tour (experienced divers only). Reef tax is A$6 (US$4.80) extra.

LIVE-ABOARD EXCURSIONS

The best live-aboard vessel departing Townsville is the 30m (100-ft.) *Spoilsport* catamaran, operated by Cairns-based **Mike Ball Dive Expeditions** (② **1888/MIKEBALL** in the U.S. and Canada, or 07/4031 5484; www.mikeball.com). Mike began his business in Townsville, so the company knows the reefs in these parts very well. The company does two 6- and 7-day itineraries from Townsville, which show you a shark feed with 30-plus sharks, gorgonian fans including a beauty with a 5m (16-ft.) span, big walls and pinnacles, Flinders Reef, and the *Yongala*. The trips depart every Tuesday at 8pm, returning Monday at 4pm (the 6-day version) or Tuesday at 3:30pm (the 7-day version). Some of these trips tie in with Mike Ball's Cairns-based trips to popular sites off Cairns (see chapter 3), such as Cod Hole and the Ribbon Reefs, and sometimes even include extras like white-water rafting. Costs are between A$2,467 and A$4,010 (US$1,974–US$3,208).

The *Spoilsport* is a three-level, stable cat and one of the best live-aboards in Australia. It's outfitted with air-conditioned double, twin, and bunk cabins (some with en suite bathrooms and windows), a big comfy lounge, a sun deck, photo processing and underwater video rental, waveskis, and fishing tackle. Specialty dive courses like Underwater Naturalist or Nitrox are available on board. Unlimited diving and, for divers with the right experience, solo diving are allowed on all Mike Ball trips.

Pro Dive Townsville (© 07/4721 1760; www.prodivetownsville. com.au) also runs 3-day, 3-night trips from Townsville featuring both the *Yongala* and various reefs, for A$525 (US$420), plus A$95 (US$76) gear hire.

ISLAND RESORTS

Two Great Barrier Reef islands with resorts are located off Townsville, the cheap and easily accessible **Magnetic Island,** and the lovely, expensive **Orpheus Island** (see section 3, later in this chapter). The section below titled "A Side Trip to Magnetic Island" contains more detail about "Maggie." Also see "Which Great Barrier Reef Resort Is Right for You?" in chapter 1. Both islands offer diving day trips, dive courses, and good snorkeling.

LEARNING TO DIVE

The local arm of the world's biggest international dive store chain, **Pro Dive Townsville** (© 07/4721 1760; www.prodivetownsville. com.au) incorporates a 3-day, 3-night live-aboard trip to the *Yongala* and local reefs into a 5-day open-water certification course starting every Monday and Thursday. Including up to nine dives, the course costs A$615 (US$521). Certified divers can attain advanced certification during the 3-day trip for A$570 (US$456), plus A$90 (US$72) for gear. The company also runs rescue, dive master, and instructor courses.

Adrenalin Dive (© 1800/242 600 in Australia or 07/4724 0600; www.adrenalindive.com.au) also conducts diving courses.

Local dive club **Diving Dreams** (© 07/4721 2500; www.diving dreams.com) runs courses in its special training pool, which has a horizontal tube for practicing swim-throughs, and a deep well to train you in buoyancy and equalization. It offers open-water certification and other specialty courses.

Pleasure Divers (© 07/4778 5788) conducts a choice of two open-water certification courses on Magnetic Island. The company offers a cost-conscious 3-day course, featuring six dives around the island for A$219 (US$175). It also organizes a 4-day, six-dive course for A$339 (US$271), featuring a day diving the outer Reef, and a 4-day live-aboard course for A$550 (US$440). All courses run three times a week and prices include gear. Pleasure Divers also teaches two advanced courses, one of which features a dive on the *Yongala*.

USEFUL DIVE-RELATED BUSINESSES

Pro Dive Townsville (© 07/4721 1760), 14 Plume St., South Townsville (opposite the Transit Centre); **Adrenalin Dive** (© 07/4724 0600), 121 Flinders St.; and **Diving Dreams** (© 07/4721 2500), 252 Walker St., all sell, rent, and service dive equipment.

THE TOP ATTRACTIONS IN TOWN

Museum of Tropical Queensland ☆☆   A stunning 2002 addition to Townsville's skyline is this A$22 million (US$17.6 million) museum, with its curved roof reminiscent of a ship in full sail. In pride of place is the amazing exhibition of relics salvaged from the wreck of HMS *Pandora*, which lies 33m (108 ft.) underwater on the edge of the Great Barrier Reef, 120km (74 miles) east of Cape York. The *Pandora* exhibit includes a built-to-scale replica of a section of the ship's bow and its 17m (56-ft.) high foremast. Standing three stories high, the replica and its copper-clad keel were crafted by local shipwrights for the museum. *Pandora* sank in 1791, and the wreck was discovered in 1977. The exhibition traces the ship's voyage and the retrieval of the sunken treasure. The museum has six galleries, including a hands-on science center, and a natural history display that looks at life in tropical Queensland—above and below the water. Another is dedicated to north Queensland's indigenous heritage, with items from Torres Strait and the South Sea Islands as well as stories from people of different cultures about the settlement and labor of north Queensland. Touring exhibitions change every 3 months. Allow 2 to 3 hours.

70–102 Flinders St. (next to Reef HQ). © **07/4726 0600**, or 07/4726 0606 info line. www.mtq.qld.gov.au. Admission A$9 (US$7.20) adults, A$6.50 (US$5.20) seniors and students, A$5 (US$4) children 4–16, A$24 (US$19) families of 5. MC, V. Daily 9am–5pm. Closed Christmas, Good Friday, and until 1pm on Anzac Day (Apr 25).

Reef HQ 🐠 *Kids*   Reef HQ is the education center for the Great Barrier Reef Marine Park Authority's headquarters and is the largest living coral reef aquarium in the world. It underwent a A$6.4 million (US$5.1 million) upgrade in 2002, but the highlight is still walking through a 20m-long (66-ft.) see-through acrylic tunnel, gazing right into a giant predator tank where sharks cruise silently. The wreck of the SS *Yongala* provides an eerie backdrop for blacktip and whitetip reef sharks, leopard sharks, and nurse sharks, sharing their 750,000-liter (195,000-gal.) home with stingrays, giant trevally, and a green turtle. Watching them feed is quite a spectacle. The tunnel also reveals the 2.5-million-liter (650,000-gal.) coral reef exhibit, with its hard and soft corals providing a home for thousands of colorful fish, giant clams, sea cucumbers, sea stars, and other creatures. There's a regular scuba dive show where the divers speak to you via intercom while they swim with the sharks and feed the fish. Other highlights include a marine creature touch-tank, a wild sea-turtle rehabilitation center, plus great interactive activities for children. Reef HQ is an easy walk from the city center.

2–68 Flinders St. ℭ **07/4750 0800**. www.reefHQ.org.au. Admission A$20 (US$16) adults, A$15 (US$12) seniors and students, A$9.50 (US$7.60) children 4–16. AE, DC, MC, V. Daily 9am–5pm. Closed Christmas. Public parking lot opposite Reef HQ. Bus stop 3-min. walk away.

WHERE TO STAY

Holiday Inn Townsville   The "Sugar Shaker" (you'll know why when you see it) has been Townsville's favorite hotel for years, especially with the corporate set. Right on Flinders Mall, it's a stroll from Reef HQ, Museum of Tropical Queensland, and Magnetic Island ferries. The rooms are fitted out in sleek blonde-wood decor, and because the 20-story building is circular, every one faces the city, the bay, or Castle Hill. The star attractions are the rooftop pool and sun deck with barbecues.

334 Flinders Mall, Townsville, QLD 4810. ℭ **1800/079 903** in Australia, 800/835-7742 in the U.S. and Canada, 0345/581 666 in the U.K. or 020/8335 1304 in London, 0800/801 111 in New Zealand, or 07/4729 2000. Fax 07/4721 1263. www.sixcontinentshotels.com. 197 units. A$280–A$315 (US$224–US$252) double; A$375–A$450 (US$300–US$360) suite. Extra person A$33 (US$26). Children under 20 stay free in parent's room with existing bedding. Free crib. Ask about weekend rates, advance-purchase rates, and packages. AE, DC, MC, V. Free undercover valet parking. **Amenities:** Restaurant (Australian); 2 bars; rooftop pool; free access to nearby gym; bike rental; secretarial services; 24-hr. room service; massage; babysitting; coin-op laundry; laundry service; dry cleaning. *In room:* A/C, TV w/pay movies, kitchenette (in suites only), dataport, minibar, coffeemaker, hair dryer, iron.

The Rocks ✿ *(Finds)* If you have a weakness for Victoriana, you will sigh with delight when you enter this exquisitely renovated old Queenslander home. The owners have fitted it with 19th-century antiques, from the velvet settee to the grandfather clock in the drawing room. Even your meals are served on collectible dinnerware. Every room is decorated with lovely linens, old trunks, and in a few, original washbasins tastefully wrapped in muslin "gowns." Four have en-suite bathrooms; the others share a historically decorated bathroom with a cast-iron claw-foot bath. Complimentary sherry is served at 6pm on the veranda, where you have views of Magnetic Island and Cleveland Bay. Despite the old-world ambience, the house has telephone, fax, Internet, and e-mail access for guests (although not in your room). Free tea and coffee are available. There's also an outdoor Jacuzzi, a billiards table (antique, of course), and a guest laundry. The Strand is a minute's stroll away, and you are a 5-minute walk from town and the Magnetic Island ferries.

20 Cleveland Terrace, Townsville, QLD 4810. ℃ 07/4771 5700, or 0416/044 409 mobile phone. Fax 07/4771 5711. www.therocksguesthouse.com. 7 units, 4 with private bathroom (shower only). A$85–A$99 (US$68–US$79) single; A$105–A$119 (US$84–US$95) double. Rates include continental breakfast. AE, DC, MC, V. Airport shuttle. Limited free on-street parking. **Amenities:** Outdoor Jacuzzi; tour desk; business center; laundry service. *In room:* A/C.

Seagulls Resort This popular low-key resort, a 5-minute drive from the city, is built around an inviting free-form saltwater pool in 1.2 hectares (3 acres) of tropical gardens. Despite its Esplanade location, the motel-style rooms do not boast waterfront views, but they are comfortable and a good size. The larger deluxe rooms have painted brick walls, a sofa, dining furniture, and a kitchen sink. Apartments have a main bedroom and a bunk bedroom, a kitchenette, dining furniture, and a balcony. The whole resort is wheelchair-friendly, with bathroom facilities for people with disabilities. The accommodations wings surround the pool and its pretty open-sided restaurant, which is popular with locals. It's a 10-minute walk to The Strand; the resort makes free transfers to the city and Magnetic Island ferry terminals, and most tour companies pick up at the door.

74 The Esplanade, Belgian Gardens, QLD 4810. ℃ **1800/079 929** in Australia, or 07/4721 3111. Fax 07/4721 3133. www.seagulls.com.au. 70 units (all with shower only). A$103–A$114 (US$82–US$91) double; A$139 (US$111) 2-bedroom apt; A$150 (US$120) executive suite (with Jacuzzi). Additional person A$15 (US$12), extra children under 14 A$9 (US$7.20); crib A$9 (US$7.20). AE, DC, MC, V. Airport shuttle A$3 (US$2.40) one-way. Bus: 7. Free parking. **Amenities:** Restaurant (Seafood/Australian); bar; 2 large outdoor saltwater pools; children's wading pool; access to nearby golf course; small tennis court; access to nearby health club; children's playground;

business center; tour desk; room service (dinner only); coin-op laundry; laundry service (Mon–Fri only); dry cleaning. *In room:* A/C, TV w/free movies, dataport, kitchenette (Reef rooms and suites), fridge, coffeemaker, hair dryer, iron.

WHERE TO DINE

Apart from the suggestions below, you will find more restaurants and cafes on Palmer Street, an easy stroll across the river from Flinders Mall, Flinders Street East, and The Strand. Try the courtyard restaurant of the beautifully restored **Australian Hotel,** 11 Palmer St. (© **07/4771 4339**). Errol Flynn is said to have stayed here.

Michel's Cafe and Bar MODERN AUSTRALIAN   This big contemporary space is popular with Townsville's "in" crowd. Choose a table on the sidewalk, or opt for air-conditioning inside. Owner/chef Michel Flores works in the open kitchen where he can keep an eye on the excellent service. You might choose a Louisiana blackened rib filet, or kangaroo, or something more casual like the stylish pizzas, pastas, seafood, or warm salads.

7 Palmer St. © **07/4724 1460.** Reservations recommended. Main courses A$11–A$23 (US$8.80–US$18). AE, DC, MC, V. Tues–Fri 11:30am–3pm; Tues–Sun 5:30–10pm.

Zouí Alto ⋒⋒ MODERN AUSTRALIAN   This is not just one of the best restaurants in Townsville, it's one of the best in the country. Chef Mark Edwards, who has cooked for the king of Norway, turns out terrific food, while his effusive wife Eleni runs the front of the house, which is idiosyncratically decked out in primary color splashes and Greek urns. Main courses include ravioli with choice of filling—pumpkin and blue vein cheese, sweet potato and ginger, or sun-dried tomato and goat's cheese. Arrive before sunset, to make the most of the spectacular views of Castle Hill on one side and the bay on the other.

On 14th floor at Aquarius on the Beach, 75 The Strand. © **07/4721 4700.** Reservations recommended. Main courses A$18–A$22 (US$14–US$18). AE, MC, V. Tues–Sat 6:30–9:30pm. Bus: 1B.

A SIDE TRIP TO MAGNETIC ISLAND ⋒
8km (5 miles) E of Townsville

"Maggie" is a delightful 51-sq.-km (20-sq.-mile) national-park island 20 minutes from Townsville by ferry. About 2,500 people live here, but it's also popular with Aussies, who love its holiday atmosphere. It is a busy little place as visitors and locals zip about between the small settlements dotted around its coast; in fact, the island has a good range of restaurants; laid-back cafes, and take-out joints. But peace-seeking visitors will find plenty of unspoiled nature to restore their souls. Most people come for the 20 or so pristine (and amazingly uncrowded) bays and white beaches that rim the island, but hikers, botanists, and bird-watchers may want to explore the eucalyptus woods, patches of gully rainforest, and granite tors. (The island got its name when Captain Cook thought the "magnetic" rocks were interfering with his compass readings.) The place is famous for wild koalas that are easily spotted up in the gum trees by the side of the road; ask a local to point you to the nearest colony. Rock wallabies are often spotted in the early morning. Maggie, off the tourist trail by and large, is definitely a flip-flops kind of place; leave the Prada stilettos in your suitcase.

GETTING THERE & GETTING AROUND   A taxi from Townsville Airport to the ferry will cost about A$15 (US$12), or you can get a shuttle bus for A$8 (US$6.40) single or A$12 (US$9.60) double. If you're flying with **Virgin Blue** (© 13 67 89 in Australia), ask about fares that include airport and ferry transfers. **Sunferries** (© 07/4771 3855 or 1800/447 333 in Australia) runs 14 return services a day from the 168–192 Flinders Street East terminal and the Breakwater terminal on Sir Leslie Thiess Drive throughout the day. Round-trip tickets are A$20 (US$16) for adults, A$10 (US$8) for children 5 to 15, and A$42 (US$34) for a family of 5. The trip takes about 25 minutes.

You can take your car across on the ferry, but most people get around by renting an open-sided minimoke (similar to a golf cart) from the many moke-rental outfits on the island. Minimokes are unlikely to send your speedometer much over 60kmph (36 mph). **Moke Magnetic** (© 07/4778 5377) rents them for around A$65 (US$52) a day. The **Magnetic Island Bus Service** (© 07/4778 5130) runs a 3-hour guided tour of the island for A$35 (US$28) for adults, A$15 (US$12) for kids aged five to 15.

OUT & ABOUT ON THE ISLAND

There is no end to the things you can do on Maggie—snorkeling, swimming in one of a dozen or more bays, catamaran sailing, waterskiing, paraflying, horseback riding on the beach, biking, tennis or golf, scuba diving, sea kayaking, sailing or cruising around the island, taking a Harley-Davidson tour, fishing, and more. Equipment for all these activities is for rent on the island. There is a catch, though: deadly marine stingers (box jellyfish) inhabit Maggie's waters from October to May (in summer)! Outside the safe swimming enclosures at Picnic Bay and Horseshoe Bay, you can enter the water only with a full-length Lycra stinger-suit that most watersports companies provide.

Most activities are spread out around Nelly Bay (where the ferry pulls in), the island's other two settlements, Arcadia and Horseshoe Bay, and Picnic Bay.

The island is not on the Great Barrier Reef, but surrounding waters are part of the Great Barrier Reef Marine Park. There is good reef snorkeling at Florence Bay, Arthur Bay, and Geoffrey Bay, where you can reef-walk at low-tide (wear sturdy shoes). First-time snorkelers will have an easy time of it in Maggie's weak currents and softly sloping beaches. Alma Bay is a good choice for families as it is reef free and has shady lawns and a playground; Rocky Bay is a small, secluded cove. The island has a good diversity of **dive sites,** including the many pockets of reef fringing pretty bays, rocky headlands with lots of tropical reef fish and the odd turtle, swim-throughs, and a couple of wrecks. Visibility is not always as good here as it is on the outer Reef. **Pleasure Divers** (© **07/4778 5788**) leads day trips to dive sites around the island for a reasonable A$39 (US$27) for one dive, or A$65 (US$52) for two, including gear rental. It also conducts diving courses (see "Learning to Dive," earlier in this chapter). Its store at 10 Marine Parade, Arcadia, rents snorkeling and dive gear, including stinger suits.

One of the most popular activities is a jet-ski circumnavigation of the island offered by **Adrenalin Jet Ski Tours & Hire** (© **07/4778 5533**). The half-day tour is conducted on two-seat jet skis and costs A$135 (US$108) per person, which includes your wet suit, life jacket, and stinger suits in season. Tours depart from Horseshoe Bay morning and afternoon. Keep your eyes peeled for dolphins, dugongs (manatees), and sea turtles.

One of the best of the island's 20km (12 miles) of hiking trails is from Nelly Bay to Arcadia, a one-way trip of 5km (3 miles) that takes 2½ hours. The first 45 minutes, starting in rainforest and climbing gradually to a saddle between Nelly Bay and Horseshoe, are the most interesting. Another excellent walk is the 2km (1¼-mile) trail to the Forts, remnants of World War II defenses, which, not surprisingly, have great 360 degree sea views. The best koala spotting is on the track up to the Forts off Horseshoe Bay Road. Carry water when walking, as some bays and hiking trails are not near shops.

WHERE TO STAY & DINE

Magnetic Island has oodles of accommodations, including hotels, motels, luxury resorts, serviced self-contained holiday units, bed and breakfasts, holiday apartments, backpacker hostels, camping

> **Tips** **Magnetic Island Travel Tips**
>
> If you're going to Magnetic Island for the day, pick up a copy of the free "Magnetic Island Guide" from any tourist information center or hotel lobby or at the ferry terminal in Townsville before you go. Because there are so many choices of activities and tours, it will help if you plan your day before you arrive. Also, there is no bank on the island, so carry cash (not every business will cash traveler's checks) and a credit card.

grounds and holiday homes. Check out www.magnetic-island.com. au for some ideas. In peak season (June–Sept), some apartments rent by the week only.

The island also has a good supply of reasonably priced restaurants, cafes, and take-out joints.

Magnetic International Resort   This is a pleasant, convenient place to stay. It's a short drive or bus ride from the ferry, and a long but level walk of about half a dozen blocks from the beach. The resort runs a courtesy coach for your transfers to the ferry. The rooms, set in motel-style blocks among the gardens and around the pool, are on the small side but nicely decorated in summery colors. In the 4 hectares (10 acres) of tropical palm-studded gardens, you can hand-feed wild kookaburras and lorikeets every evening, and may spot a rare rock wallaby.

Mandalay Ave., Nelly Bay, Magnetic Island, QLD 4819. © **1800/079 902** in Australia, or 07/4778 5200. www.magneticresort.com. 96 units (all with shower only). A$136–$196 (US$109–$157) double; A$196 (US$157) family room (sleeps 4). Extra person A$25 (US$20). Children under 14 stay free in parents' room using existing bedding. AE, DC, MC, V. **Amenities:** Restaurant (seafood/Australian); bar; swimming pool; 2 day/night tennis courts; gymnasium; children's playground; tour desk; game room; babysitting; coin-operated laundry. *In room:* A/C and ceiling fan, TV with free movies, dataport, minibar, kitchenette, fridge, hair dryer, iron.

3 Orpheus Island

80km (50 miles) N of Townsville; 190km (119 miles) S of Cairns

In the 1930s, actress Vivien Leigh and novelist Zane Grey were among the stars who sought seclusion at this beautiful island. More recently, rock star Elton John vacationed here. One of the Great Barrier Reef's most exclusive retreats, Orpheus Island Resort is a popular getaway for executives, politicians, and any savvy traveler eager for peace and beauty. The surrounding waters are home to 340 of the 350 or so coral species found on the Great Barrier Reef, 1,100 species of fish, green and loggerhead turtles, dolphins, manta rays, and, from June through September, humpback whales. With a maximum of 42 guests and no day-trippers allowed, the only other people you will see are attentive but unobtrusive resort staff, and the occasional scientist from the James Cook University marine research station in the next bay.

GETTING THERE   Transfers are by eight-seater Cessna seaplane from Townsville daily or from Cairns twice a week. Fares are A$450 (US$360) from Townsville, A$780 (US$624) from Cairns or A$640 (US$512) mixed ports, per person round-trip. Book through the resort. Luggage limit is 15 kilograms (55 lb.) per person.

Orpheus Island Resort 🛱   The resort is a cluster of rooms lining one of the prettiest turquoise bays you'll find anywhere. Most guests spend their time snorkeling over coral reefs, chilling with a good book or magazine in the Quiet Lounge, or lazing in a hammock. Free activities include tennis, snorkeling, catamaran sailing, canoeing, paddle-skiing, fishing, and taking a motorized dinghy around the shore to explore some of the island's 1,300 national-park hectares (3,211 acres). You can pay to go game fishing, charter a boat or seaplane to the outer Reef, or do a dive course.

All the rooms and suites on Orpheus are absolute beachfront. The 17 Orpheus Retreats are set in blocks of three, and each has a personal patio and a Jacuzzi. Four Nautilus Suites are more spacious, with separate lounge and bedroom areas, large private patios and large Jacuzzi. Two have enclosed garden courtyards. The whole resort was refurbished in late 2002, and if seclusion and tranquillity is what you are looking for, this is the place to find it.

Orpheus Island, Great Barrier Reef via Townsville (PMB 15, Townsville, QLD 4810). 🕾 07/4777 7377. Fax 07/4777 7533. www.orpheus.com.au. 21 units. A$1,450 (US$1,160) double Orpheus Retreat, A$1,700 (US$1,360) double Nautilus Suite. Rates include all meals; drinks cost extra. Ask about packages. AE, DC, MC, V. No children under 15. **Amenities:** Restaurant (seafood/Australian); 2 bars; 2 small outdoor pools, 1 with swim-up bar; day/night tennis court; exercise room; Jacuzzi; watersports rentals; concierge; business center; in-room massage. *In room:* A/C, CD player, minibar, coffeemaker, hair dryer, iron, no phone.

6

The Whitsunday Coast & Islands

A day's drive or a 1-hour flight south of Cairns brings you to the dazzling collection of 74 Whitsunday Islands. No more than 3 nautical miles separates most of the islands, and altogether they represent countless bays, beaches, dazzling coral reefs, and fishing spots that comprise one fabulous Great Barrier Reef playground. Sharing the same latitude as Rio de Janeiro and Hawaii, the water is at least 72°F (22°C) year-round, the sun shines most of the year, and winter requires only a light jacket at night.

This is Australia's premier sailing territory. Whether you take a day trip aboard one of the many yachts based on the mainland, book one of the popular 3-day/2-night sailing jaunts, or charter your very own sailboat—known as "bareboat" (unskippered) charter—from the region's plethora of charter outfits, sailing is easy in these calm blue waters. And it's not all that expensive.

All the islands are composed of densely rainforested national-park land, mostly uninhabited, and the surrounding waters belong to the Great Barrier Reef Marine Park. Don't expect palm trees and coconuts—these islands are covered with dry-looking pine and eucalyptus forests full of dense undergrowth, and rocky coral coves far outnumber the few sandy beaches. More than half a dozen islands have resorts that offer just about all the activities you could ever want—snorkeling, scuba diving, sailing trips, reef fishing, water-skiing, jet-skiing, parasailing, sea kayaking, hiking, rides over the coral in semisubmersibles, fish feeding, putt-putting around in dinghies to secluded beaches, tennis, squash, and aqua-aerobics classes. Accommodations range from small, low-key wilderness retreats to mid-range family havens to Australia's most luxurious resort, Hayman.

The village of Airlie Beach is the center of the action on the mainland. The Whitsundays are just as good a stepping-stone to the outer Great Barrier Reef as Cairns—some people think they are better because you don't have to make the 90-minute trip to the Reef before you hit coral. Just about any Whitsunday island has fringing reef around its shores, and there are good snorkeling reefs between the islands, a quick boat ride away from your island or mainland accommodations.

April through October is the best time to visit. November ain't bad; but December through March is hot and humid, and that's when most rain falls.

1 Whitsunday Essentials

GETTING THERE   By Car   The Bruce Highway leads south from Cairns or north from Brisbane to Proserpine, 26km (16 miles) inland from Airlie Beach. Take the "Whitsunday" turnoff to reach Airlie Beach and Shute Harbour. Allow a good 8 hours to drive from Cairns. There are several car-storage facilities at Shute Harbour. **Whitsunday Car Security** (© **07/4946 9955** or 0419/729 605) will collect your car anywhere in the Whitsunday area and store it in locked undercover parking for around A$15 (US$12) per 24 hours.

By Plane   There are two air routes into the Whitsundays: Hamilton Island airport, and Whitsunday Coast Airport at Proserpine on the mainland. **Qantas** (© **13 13 13** in Australia) flies direct to Hamilton Island from Melbourne. **QantasLink** flies from Sydney, Brisbane, Cairns, and Townsville. **Virgin Blue** (© **13 67 89** in Australia) flies to Proserpine direct from Brisbane and Sydney, and with connections from Canberra, Adelaide, Melbourne, Hobart, and Launceston in Tasmania. **Jetstar** (© **13 15 38** in Australia) flies from Brisbane to Proserpine and from Brisbane, Melbourne, and Sydney to Hamilton Island daily.

If you stay on an island, the resort may book your launch transfers automatically. These may appear on your airline ticket, in which case your luggage will be checked through to the island.

Air Whitsunday seaplanes (© **07/4946 9111;** www.airwhitsunday. com.au) and **Hamilton Island Aviation** (© **07/4946 8249;** www. avta.com.au) do charter mainland-island and interisland transfers from the small Whitsunday airport near Shute Harbour, Proserpine airport, or Hamilton Island airport. Hayman, Hamilton, Daydream, South Molle, and Long islands all have landing strips. Hamilton Island Aviation uses helicopter, seaplane, or fixed-wing aircraft. Both companies fly charter to the Whitsundays from Cairns, Townsville, and other northern Queensland cities.

By Train   Several **Queensland Rail** (© **13 22 32** in Queensland, or 07/3235 1122) long-distance trains stop at Proserpine every week.

The Whitsunday Region

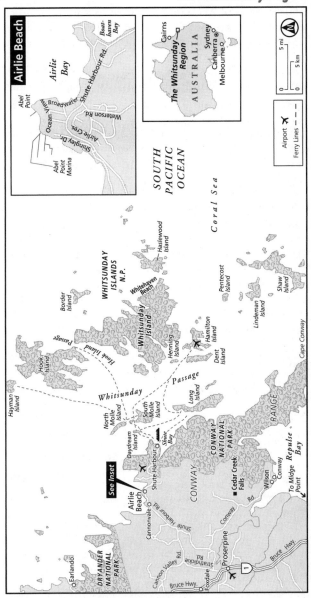

Airlie Beach

Boathaven Bay

Airlie Bay

Shute Harbour Rd.

Abel Point

Broadwater

Ocean View

Waterson Rd.

Airlie Crek.

Shingley Dr.

Abel Point Marina

Cairns

The Whitsunday Region

AUSTRALIA

Sydney

Canberra

Melbourne

Airport ✈

Ferry Lines ---

SOUTH PACIFIC OCEAN

Coral Sea

Haslewood Island

Border Island

WHITSUNDAY ISLANDS N.P.

Whitehaven Beach

Pentecost Island

Shaw Island

Whitsunday Island

Lindeman Island

Hook Island

Hook Passage

Hayman Island

Henning Island

Hamilton Island

Dent Island

Whitsunday Passage

Long Island

North Molle Island

South Molle Island

Daydream Island

Shute Bay

Cape Conway

RANGE

See Inset

Shute Harbour

Airlie Beach

CONWAY NATIONAL PARK

Cedar Creek Falls

Conway Rd.

Wilson

Conway

To Midge Point

Repulse Bay

Cannonvale Rd.

CONWAY

Shute Harbour Rd.

Proserpine

Cannon Valley Rd.

Sturdiddie Rd.

Bruce Hwy.

1

Bruce Hwy.

Foxdale

Earlando

DRYANDER NATIONAL PARK

137

The one-way fare is A$134 (US$107) from Cairns on the Tilt Train. Brisbane fares range from A$217 (US$174) on the Tilt Train to A$309 (US$247) for a first-class sleeper on *The Sunlander.*

By Bus   Greyhound Pioneer (📞 **13 20 30** in Australia) and **McCafferty's** (📞 **13 14 99** in Australia) operate plentiful daily services to Airlie Beach from Brisbane (trip time: around 18½ hr.) and Cairns (trip time: 10 hr.). The fare is A$132 (US$106) from Brisbane and A$82 (US$66) from Cairns.

Whitsunday Transit (📞 **07/4946 1800**) meets all flights and trains at Proserpine to provide door-to-door transfers to Airlie Beach hotels, or to Shute Harbour. The fare from the airport is A$30 (US$24) to Airlie Beach or A$32 (US$26) to Shute Harbour, or from the train station it is A$15 (US$12) to Airlie Beach or A$18 (US$14) to Shute Harbour.

VISITOR INFORMATION   For information before you travel, contact **Tourism Whitsundays,** P.O. Box 83, Whitsunday, QLD 4802 (www.whitsundaytourism.com). The **Whitsundays Information Center** (📞 **1800/801 252** in Australia, or 07/4945 3711; fax 07/4945 3182) is in Proserpine, on the Bruce Highway in the town's south. It's open Monday to Saturday from 9am to 5pm and Sundays and public holidays (except Christmas) from 8:30am to 1:30pm. Another useful website is www.whitsunday.net.au.

If you're staying in Airlie Beach, it's easier to pick up information from the private booking agents lining the main street, which all stock a vast range of cruise, tour, and hotel information, and which make bookings free of charge. They all have pretty much the same

---

The Secret of the Seasons

High season is school vacations (mid-Apr, late June to early July, late Sept to early Oct, and mid- to late Dec through Jan). The Aussie winter from June to August is popular, too. During school holidays, book accommodations months in advance. The rest of the year, though, expect tour operators to compete fiercely for your dollars; blackboards outside tour agencies in Airlie Beach will shout about specials and discounted deals.

If you are prepared to book accommodations with just 24 or 48 hours' notice, you can snare some incredibly cheap standby rates at hotels and island resorts in off-peak season, even the swanky ones like Hayman.

---

stuff; but because some manifest certain boats exclusively, and prices can vary a little from one to the next, shop around.

GETTING AROUND   Island ferries and Great Barrier Reef cruises leave from **Shute Harbour,** a 10-minute drive south of Airlie Beach on Shute Harbour Road. Most other tour-boat operators and bareboat charters anchor at **Abel Point Marina,** a 15-minute walk west from Airlie Beach. Also, many tour-boat operators pick up guests free from Airlie Beach hotels and call at some or all island resorts.

Avis (℘ **07/4946 6318**), **Hertz** (℘ **07/4946 4687**), and **Thrifty** (℘ **07/4946 7727**) have outlets in Airlie Beach and Proserpine Airport (telephone numbers serve both locations). Budget has no Whitsundays office.

Local bus company **Whitsunday Transit** (℘ **07/4946 1800**) runs a half-hourly service between Airlie Beach and Shute Harbour to meet all ferries. The fare is A$4.55 (US$3.65). An **Explorer Pass** for unlimited travel between Shute Harbour, Airlie Beach, Cannonvale and Proserpine between 6am and 10:30pm on the date of issue, costs A$8 (US$6.40) adults and A$4 (US$3.20) children

FantaSea Cruises' Blue Ferries (℘ **1800/650 851** in Australia, or 07/4946 5111) makes ferry transfers from Shute Harbour to the islands and between the islands. One-way transfers from the mainland cost A$18 (US$14) to South Molle, Long, and Daydream islands, and A$29 (US$23) to Hamilton Island. Children 4 to 14 pay A$11 (US$8.80) and A$14 (US$11). It is not necessary to book, but do book your arrival and departure ferry so that you don't miss your connections. Most islands receive a boat only every 2 to 4 hours, so it's a long wait if you miss your boat.

CHOOSING A WHITSUNDAY BASE

The advantages of staying on the mainland are cheaper accommodations, a choice of restaurants, and freedom to visit a different island each day. There is jet-skiing, kayaking, parasailing, catamaran rental, and windsurfing on the mainland.

The main advantage of staying on an island is that swimming, snorkeling, bushwalking, and a huge range of watersports, many of them free, are right outside your door. The deadly stingers that can infest Airlie's shores do not make it to the islands, so swimming in the islands is safe year-round. You won't be isolated if you stay on an island, as most Great Barrier Reef cruise boats, "sail and snorkel" yacht excursions, Whitehaven Beach cruises, dive boats, fishing tour

Tips Gorgeous Spots Not to Miss

The 6km (3¾-mile) stretch of white silica sand on **Whitehaven Beach** 🗗 on uninhabited Whitsunday Island will leave you in raptures. It doesn't have coral; but the swimming is good, and the forested shore is beautiful for strolling. Take a book and chill out. There are several options for getting there. **Whitehaven Xpress** (© **07/4946 7172;** www.whitehavenxpress.com. au) runs trips from Shute Harbour leaving at 9am daily and returning about 5pm. The cost is A$99 (US$79) adults, A$55 (US$44) children aged 4 to 14 or A$295 (US236) for a family of 4, including lunch and snorkel equipment. **FantaSea Cruises** (© **07/4946 5111**) has a day trip there from Hamilton Island, which costs A$77 (US$62) adults, A$42 (US$34) children aged 4 to 14, or A$203 (US$162) for a family of four. The sailing boat *Ragamuffin* (© **1800/454 777;** www.maxiaction.com.au) does day cruises to both Whitehaven Beach and **Blue Pearl Bay,** which is renowned for spectacular coral and fish life.

vessels, and so on stop at the island resorts every day or on a frequent basis. Be warned, however, that once you're "captive" on an island, you may be slugged with high food and drink prices. Bear in mind, too, that although most island resorts offer non-motorized watersports, such as windsurfers and catamarans, free of charge, you will pay for activities that use fuel, such as parasailing, water-skiing, and dinghy rental.

In some places in the Whitsundays, extreme low tides may reveal rocky mud flats below the sand line. Watersports can be limited at low tide because of the low water level.

2 Diving & Snorkeling the Reef
MAJOR REEF SITES

Visitors to the Whitsundays get to have their cake and eat it too; they can visit the outer Reef, as well as enjoy some good dive and snorkel sites in and around the islands. Many islands have rarely visited fringing reefs, which you can explore in a rented dinghy. The reef here is just as good as off Cairns, with many drop-offs and drift dives, a dazzling range of corals, and a rich array of marine life including whales, mantas, sharks, reef fish, morays, turtles, and pelagics. Visibility is usually around 15 to 23m (49–75 ft.).

The Stepping Stones on 800-hectare (1,976-acre) **Bait Reef** is one of the most popular sites on the outer Reef. It is made up of a series of pinnacles that abound with fish life and offer caverns, swim-throughs, and channels. A family of grouper often greets divers at Groupers Grotto on **Net Reef,** and a pod of dolphins hang around Net Reef's southeast wall. **Oublier Reef** has plate corals over 2m (7-ft.) wide in its lovely coral gardens.

Among the island sites, most folks' favorite is **Blue Pearl Bay** ⊛ off Hayman Island, whether they're snorkeling or diving. It has loads of corals and some gorgonian fans in its gullies, and heaps of reef fish including Maori wrasse and sometimes even manta rays. It's a good place to make an introductory dive, walking right in off the beach. **Mantaray Bay** on Hook Island is renowned for its range of marine life, from small reef fish and nudibranchs to bigger pelagics further out. Mantas hang around here in November. Another good snorkel and dive spot is **Black Reef** ⊛, commonly called **Bali Hai Island,** between Hayman and Hook Islands. You'll see marvelous soft shelf and wall coral, tame Maori wrasse, octopus, turtles, reef shark, various kinds of rays including mantas, eagles, and cow-tails, plus loads of fish. Divers may even see hammerhead sharks.

DAY-TRIP DIVE & SNORKEL BOATS

The prices quoted below include all snorkel and dive gear, unless otherwise specified, and lunch. Departure times given here are the time the boat heads out to sea; plan to board about 30 minutes earlier. Most boat operators depart Airlie Beach; some pick up at the islands. In addition to the operators listed below, you can also snorkel and dive off many sailing boats. See "Exploring the Islands," below.

Remember to add the A$4.50 (US$3.60) Environmental Management Charge, or "reef tax," to the fare of every passenger over 4 years old.

The vast majority of snorkelers, and many divers, visiting the Reef from the Whitsundays travel with **FantaSea Cruises (☏ 07/ 4946 5111;** www.fantasea.com.au), which makes a daily trip to **Hardy Reef** from Shute Harbour in a 350-passenger, air-conditioned catamaran. Travel time takes about 2 hours, and you can hear a Reef talk by a marine biologist en route. You anchor at the company's massive Reefworld pontoon, which takes 600 people and boasts an underwater observatory, a semisubmersible for coral viewing, freshwater showers, kids' swimming pools, and a choice of seating in shade or sun. The trip allows about 3½ hours on the large

Hardy Reef, where there is a good variety of coral and fish life. The trip costs A$161 (US$129) for adults, A$138 (US$110) for seniors and students, A$87 (US$70) for kids 4 to 14, and A$379 (US$303) for a family of four. Guided snorkel safaris cost A$20 (US$16) extra. The day with an introductory or certified dive is A$243 (US$194). An extra dive is A$99 (US$79) for certified divers and A$89 (US$71) for an extra introductory dive; two is the maximum number of dives allowed. Passengers over 55 must have a diving medical certificate issued by a qualified dive physician.

Free coach transfers run from Airlie Beach hotels to the wharf at Shute Harbour, and the FantaSea boat picks up passengers free at South Molle and Hamilton island resorts en route to the Reef. It departs the mainland at 8am, picks up at Daydream, South Molle, and Hamilton islands on the way and returns between 5:15pm and about 6pm. If you're staying on Long Island, you can connect with transfers to Airlie Beach or South Molle Island respectively. Unlike most other Reef boats, this one runs Christmas Day; Santa Claus even makes an appearance in a red wet suit.

Scenic helicopter flights from FantaSea's pontoon, and fly/cruise packages to it incorporating FantaSea day on the Reef, are available

Nighttime on the Reef

Snorkeling at night is a different experience from snorkeling in the day, because the coral is luminescent in the dark. Although you don't really think of fish needing to sleep, they actually do, so at night you see them tucked up among the coral. Parrotfish, for example, weave a cocoon of mucus around themselves at night to sleep in. At the same time, nocturnal creatures you wouldn't see in the day come out to play. **FantaSea Cruises** (℃ 07/4946 5111; www.fantasea.com.au) offers a 2-day, 1-night **ReefSleep** experience overnighting on the company's large pontoon. The trip includes a slide presentation from a marine biologist, two scuba dives, night snorkeling, two buffet lunches, dinner under the stars with wine, breakfast, and more snorkeling on the second day. You sleep in the quad-share bunkhouse for A$343 (US$274) per person, or in a room with a king-size bed and French champagne for A$404 (US$323) per person. No children under 12.

through **Hamilton Island Aviation** (© **07/4946 8249**). A 10-minute flight from the pontoon over Hardy and the perfectly heart-shaped **Heart Reef** is A$98 (US$78) per person. The fly-cruise trip is A$389 (US$311) per person from Hamilton Island.

If you're looking for smaller crowds, you might enjoy a day trip with **Whitsunday Dive Charters** (© **07/4946 5366;** www.reefjet. com.au). Its modern 24m (79-ft.), 68-passenger *Reefjet* gets you to **Bait Reef** in just 75 minutes. The boat is smart and comfortable with seating in the air-conditioned indoors or on the sunny top deck. The trip runs daily from Abel Point Marina and costs A$120 (US$96) for adults, A$70 (US$56) for kids ages 4 to 14, or A$320 (US$256) for a family of four. That includes snorkel gear, lunch, and round-trip hotel shuttles in Airlie Beach. A snorkel safari is A$15 (US$12) extra. An introductory dive is A$70 (US$56) or A$110 (US$88) for two, and an unguided certified dive is A$60 (US$48) extra, or A$90 (US$72) for two.

If you have only 1 day, visit the outer Reef. If you have a second day up your sleeve, however, you could do worse than spend it on a day out on **Black Reef** (Bali Hai Island) offered by **FantaSea Cruises** (© 07/4946 5111). After a cruise to this little sandy islet, you can snorkel over lovely reef or view the coral from the large Yellow Sub semisubmersible, sunbathe and enjoy lunch on the sub. The boat then takes you to lovely **Whitehaven Beach** on the way home. The cruise departs Shute Harbour at 8:15am and picks up at Long, Hamilton, Daydream, and South Molle islands, getting back at 5pm. The day costs A$99 (US$79) adults, A$59 (US$47) for children ages 4 to 14, A$89 (US$71) for a student or senior, or A$257 (US$206) for a family of four. An optional snorkel safari is A$20 (US$16) extra.

LIVE-ABOARD EXCURSIONS

Among the best live-aboards in the Whitsundays are those operated by **Oceania Dive** (© **1800/075 035** in Australia, or 07/4948 1888; www.oceaniadive.com.au). Oceania Dive's *Oceania,* is a big, upscale 27m (88½-ft.) catamaran, purpose-built for diving in 1999. It incorporates 10 dives (including an optional night dive) in its 3-day, 3-night voyages to the outer Reef on the edge of the continental shelf, where visibility hits 30 to 40m (100–130 ft.) and the marine life is rich. The boat carries 30 passengers in air-conditioned twin, double, triple, and quad cabins, some with en-suite bathrooms. The entire top deck is given over to sunbathing. Trips depart Airlie Beach every Tuesday and Friday evening. The cost is A$445

(US$356) for snorkelers or A$525 (US$420) for divers, all gear included, plus A$18 (US$14) per person reef tax.

Also see "Exploring the Islands," below, for details of crewed sailing vacations. Although these are laid-back vacations not expressly designed for divers, some give you the opportunity to make certified and introductory dives.

ISLAND RESORTS

Most Whitsunday island resorts have dive shops that offer diving day trips, introductory dives, and diving courses. Most islands have at least some fringing coral, which you can snorkel either from the beach or by taking a dinghy around the shore. See "The Whitsunday Island Resorts," later in this chapter, for details of what each island offers in the way of diving and snorkeling.

LEARNING TO DIVE

A look at the courses offered by established Whitsunday dive company, **Reef Dive & Sail Whitsundays** (℃ **07/4946 6508;** www.reef dive.com.au), is a good example of what a dive course includes and costs in this area. Its 5-day open-water certification course includes 2 days of pool training and theory, then a 3-night live-aboard journey on the Reef. The course, including eight dives, costs A$580 (US$464). A shorter 4-day course costs A$430 (US$344), which includes four dives. These prices include transfers to and from your Airlie Beach hotel. The company also does referral courses, a range of specialty courses such as underwater photography and dive courses right up to Instructor level. Open-water courses start four times every week. If you have dive certification but think your skills are a little rusty, join a scuba "tune-up" session.

Another reputable dive company offering a range of courses from open-water to Instructor level is **Oceania Dive** (℃ **1800/075 035** in Australia or 07/4948 1888; www.oceaniadive.com.au). Its 5-day open-water certification costs A$575 (US$460), with the final 3 days spent aboard the *Oceania*. See "Live-Aboard Excursions," above.

USEFUL DIVE-RELATED BUSINESSES

Reef Dive & Sail Whitsundays, Commerce Close, Cannonvale, (℃ **07/4946 6508**), sells, rents, and services dive gear. **Oceania Dive** (℃ **1800/075 035** in Australia, or 07/4946 6032) sells and services gear from its premises on Shute Harbour Road.

The **Whitsunday Scuba Centre** (℃ **07/4946 1067;** www.scuba centre.com.au) is a booking agency that books diving holidays and courses in the Whitsundays.

3 Exploring the Islands

SAILING & SEA KAYAKING   Many yachts in the Whitsunday region offer **island sailing adventures,** usually of 3 days' duration. Take a hand in sailing, if you want to, snorkel over reefs, call into secluded bays, swim, sunbathe, hike, and have a laid-back good time. A few boats offer introductory and qualified scuba diving at extra cost. Most carry a maximum 12 passengers, although some take more. You typically sleep in comfortable but small berths off the galley, sometimes there are twin or double cabins available. The food is generally good, and the showers are hot.

In peak season, expect to pay around A$600 (US$480) per person. Prices usually include all meals, any Marine Park entrance fees, snorkel gear, and courtesy transfers to the departure point (Abel Point Marina or Shute Harbour). In the off-season, the boats compete fiercely for passengers; you'll see signboards on the main street in Airlie Beach advertising standby deals. **ProSail** (© **1800/810 116** or 07/4946 5433; www.prosail.com.au) has a fleet of 18 yachts running 3- and 6-day crewed sailing package holidays. The company's boats include some of Australia's best-known and fastest racing yachts, plus a selection of luxury vessels, and it has a reputation for good food and on-board service. **Barefoot Cruises** (© **07/4946 1777;** www.barefootcruises.com.au) is another good choice; it conducts upmarket sailing vacations on a small fleet of lovely boats, which are all personally owned by the company's proprietors. Tourism Whitsundays can supply you with brochures on other charters. See "Visitor Information," earlier in this chapter.

Myriad yachts will pick you up from Airlie Beach or the islands to take you out for a day trip to snorkel over reefs, swim, sail, and dive, and feast on a buffet lunch on a beach or on the boat. Among the best known is *Maxi Ragamuffin* (© **1800 454 777** in Australia or 07/4946 7777; www.maxiaction.com.au), whose day trips cost A$99 (US$65) for adults, A$89 (US$58) for seniors and students, A$50 (US$33) for kids 4 to 14, or A$248 (US$160) for a family of four. The day costs A$140 (US$98) for a prebooked first-time or regular scuba dive.

ProSail (© **07/4946 5433;** www.prosail.com.au) offers 3-hour "day sails" on America's Cup yachts *Australia* and *Steak 'N Kidney,* giving you the chance to "race" in a mock challenge between the two boats. You can get involved in the racing, calling tactics, grinding, and even protesting an offending yacht, or just sit back and watch the action. Day sails start at 9am and 1pm, and cost A$79 (US$63) adults, A$75 (US$60) student/YHA member or A$59 (US$47) children 10-15, including pick-up from your accommodations.

Sea kayaking is a great way to soak up the islands' natural beauty and even spot dolphins and turtles along the way. Daydream Island and North, Mid, and South Molle islands are all within paddling distance of the mainland. **Salty Dog Sea Kayaking (℡ 07/4946 1388;** www.saltydog.com.au) takes escorted trips through the islands. Half-day trips run on Tuesday, Wednesday, and Saturday and full-day trips on Monday, Thursday, and Friday, departing Airlie Beach at 8:30am. A half-day trip is A$58 (US$47) per person, and a day trip is A$95 (US$76). Two- and 6-day trips, where you camp out, are A$265 (US$212) and A$1,120 (US$896); rates include snorkel gear, meals, hotel pickup, and, on overnight trips, camping gear. They also deliver sea kayaks to you anywhere in the Whitsundays. A full day's rental is from A$50 (US$40) for a single kayak, A$80 (US$64) for a double, including delivery and pickup and all safety equipment. A security deposit of A$200 (US$160) is required for rentals. On Hamilton Island, **Sea Kayaking Whitsundays (℡ 07/4948 9711;** www.seakayakingwhitsundays.com.au) offers a range of guided tours. The Sunset Paddle (A$35/US$28) includes champagne while you bob on the water watching the day draw to a close, or you might choose a half day Adventure Paddle for A$60 (US$48), the amazing five-hour Turtle and Sea Eagle Tour for A$110 (US$88) or the unique Full Moon Tour at A$40 (US$32). No kayaking experience is necessary.

ISLAND HOPPING Day-trippers to Hamilton, Daydream, South Molle, Long Island, and Hook Island resorts can rent the hotels' watersports equipment, laze by the beaches and pools, scuba dive, join the resorts' activities programs, hike their trails, and eat at some or all of their restaurants. See "The Whitsunday Island Resorts," below, for details on where to stay. Club Crocodile Long Island is a rather noisy, unpretentious resort that nonetheless has plentiful watersports, picturesque hiking trails, wild wallabies, and a large beach-cum–tidal flat where you can laze on sun lounges. You can get to the islands on your own by ferry (see "Getting Around," earlier in this chapter), or take an organized day trip that visits one, two, or even three islands in a day. **FantaSea Cruises (℡ 1800/650 851** in Australia, or 07/4946 5111; www.fantasea.com.au) and **Whitsunday Island Adventure Cruises (℡ 07/4946 5255** for the booking agent) offer them, as do several yachts.

SCENIC FLIGHTS   Expect to pay around A$200 (US$160) for a 1-hour flight over the outer Reef (a spectacular sight from the air), about A$295 (US$236) for a seaplane flight to a private Reef pontoon to snorkel for a couple of hours, way up to A$500 (US$400) for a helicopter to drop you on a deserted coral-edged island with a champagne picnic and snorkel gear. **Hamilton Island Aviation** (© 07/4946 8249) and **Air Whitsunday** (© 07/4946 9111) both do a range of such tours. Air Whitsunday also does day trips to posh Hayman (see "The Whitsunday Island Resorts," below), the only operator to do so.

FISHING   Reef fishing is superb throughout the islands; red emperor, coral trout, sweetlip, and snapper are common catches. One of the most popular charter vessels is the 16m (52-ft.) timber cruiser *Moruya* (© 07/4946 6665, or 0415/185 653 mobile phone; www.fishingwhitsunday.com.au). Day trips depart Shute Harbour daily at 9:30am and return at 5:30pm.They include lunch, bait, fishing rods, and pickup from your accommodations. The crew will even clean your catch for you. Adults pay A$100 (US$80), seniors A$90 (US$72), children 4 to 14 A$65 (US$52), and a family of four A$265 (US$212). If you'd rather man your own fishing boat, you can rent dinghies and half-cabin cruisers, with bait and tackle, from the operators along Abel Point Marina or Shute Harbour.

ECO TOURS   Visitors to the Whitsundays can get up-close-and-personal with crocodiles in their natural habitat with **Proserpine River Eco Tours** (book through FantaSea Cruises © 07/4946 5111), which combines an open-air wagon ride through the pristine Goorganga wetlands and a boat trip on the river to learn more about one of Queensland's major crocodile-breeding grounds. This is the only place to see crocs in safety in the wild south of the Daintree. Bus pickups operate from Airlie Beach, Cannonvale, and Proserpine for the tours, which run for about 4 hours, depending on tides, and cost A$85 (US$68) adults, A$49 (US$39) kids 4 to 14, and A$219 (US$175) family of four. Back on land, you're treated to billy tea and the best damper I've ever tasted (and they'll even give you the recipe), and a talk on native wildlife over a barbecue lunch.

GOLF   Serious golfers should not miss a round on arguably Australia's best resort course, the championship **Turtle Point golf course** ★ at Laguna Quays Resort, Kunapipi Springs Road, Midge Point (© 07/4947 7777), a 45-minute drive south of Airlie Beach. An 18-hole round dodging wallabies, goannas, and kookaburras on these difficult fairways will set you back A\$66 (US\$53) midweek, A\$77 (US\$62) weekends, plus A\$33 (US\$26) for clubs and cart.

HIKING   The Whitsundays Great Walk—the first of six **Great Walks of Queensland** being developed over the next few years—covers 36km (22 miles) in Conway State Forest and **Conway National Park,** behind Airlie Beach. The trail starts in the parking lot at the end of Brandy Creek Road, a short drive from Cannonvale, and winds in three stages from Brandy Creek to Airlie Beach, with two campsites at 12km (7.5-mile) intervals. The hills here are rich in giant strangler figs, ferns, and palms, and if you're lucky you'll spot a giant blue Ulysses butterfly. Walkers should take drinking water with them, as the water in natural systems is not good for drinking.

The Queensland Parks and Wildlife Service information center (© 07/4946 7022; www.epa.qld.gov.au) on Shute Harbour Road at Mandalay Road, 2.5km (1½ miles) northeast of Airlie Beach has more information on this and other shorter walks. It's open Monday through Friday from 8:30am to 5pm and most, but not all, Saturdays from 9am to 1pm.

4 Airlie Beach: Gateway to the Whitsundays
640km (396 miles) S of Cairns; 1,146km (711 miles) N of Brisbane

The little town of Airlie Beach is the focal point of activity on the Whitsunday mainland. The town is only a few blocks long, but you will find an adequate choice of decent accommodations, a small selection of good restaurants and bars, a nice boutique or two, and facilities such as banks and a supermarket. Cruises and yachts depart from either Shute Harbour, a 10-minute drive south on Shute Harbour Road, or Abel Point Marina, a 10-minute walk west along the foreshore or a quick drive over the hill on Shute Harbour Road.

Airlie Beach has a huge artificial lagoon, offset by sandy beaches and landscaped parkland on the waterfront, which resolves the problem of where to swim in stinger season. The lagoon is the size of about six full-size Olympic swimming pools, set in 4 hectares (10 acres) of botanic gardens, with a children's pool, plenty of shade, barbecues, picnic shelters, toilets and showers, and parking.

On the edge of the Coral Sea, with views across Pioneer Bay and the Whitsunday Passage, Airlie Beach has a village atmosphere where life revolves around the beach and the marina by day, and the bars and restaurants by night. The spit of land between Airlie Bay and Boathaven Bay is home to the Airlie Beach Sailing Club. Shute

---

> ## Tips Safety
>
> Deadly marine stingers (box jellyfish) may inhabit the shore-line from October to April. The best place to swim then is in the beachfront Airlie Beach lagoon. Never swim in, or stand on the bank of, mainland rivers and estuaries in the Whitsun-days, because they are home to crocodiles.

Harbour, 11km (6¾ miles) from Airlie Beach, is one of Queensland's busiest ports, filled with yachts, cruisers, water taxis, ferries, and fishermen. For a bird's-eye view, head to the Lions Lookout.

WHERE TO STAY

Coral Sea Resort 𝒜𝒜   Set in Airlie Beach's best location, on the edge of Paradise Point, with 280-degree views of the ocean, this 6-year-old resort is one of the best places to stay on the Whitsunday mainland. There's a wide range of accommodations styles to suit everyone from honeymooners to families, and although it's relatively sprawling, the design is such that you can easily feel you're alone. All the rooms have a nautical feel, and the Coral Sea suites are divine, complete with a Jacuzzi and double hammock on the balcony. There are four styles of suites, apartments, and family units, all serviced daily. Bayview suites have a Jacuzzi inside. It's a 3-minute walk along the waterfront to Airlie Beach village.

25 Oceanview Ave., Airlie Beach, QLD 4802. 📞 **1800/075 061** in Australia, or 07/4946 6458. Fax 07/4946 6516. www.coralsearesort.com. 78 units. A$195–A$255 (US$156–US$204) double; A$275–A$335 (US$220–US$268) double suite; A$285 (US$228) double 1-bedroom apt; A$295–A$330 (US$236–US$264) double 2-bed-room apt; A$295 (US$236) family unit (sleeps 5); A$330 (US$264) 1-bedroom pent-house; A$430 (US$344) double 2-bedroom penthouse; A$595 (US$476) double 3-bedroom penthouse. Extra person A$30 (US$24). Cribs A$12 (US$9.60). Minimum 3-night stay at Easter and Dec 26–Jan 5. Ask about packages. AE, DC, MC, V. Free parking. **Amenities:** 2 restaurants; bar; 25m (82-ft.) outdoor pool; exercise room; games room; tour desk; car-rental desk; 24-hr. room service; massage; babysitting; coin-op laundry; dry cleaning. *In room:* A/C and ceiling fans, TV w/satellite and free movies, kitchenette, minibar, coffeemaker, hair dryer, iron.

Martinique Whitsunday Resort 𝒜   Your apartment in this French Caribbean–style complex high on the hill above Airlie Beach has views which make the short but very steep walk from the town well worthwhile. The one-, two-, and three-bedroom apartments are roomy and light, and each has a big balcony. The wet edge lap pool also overlooks the Coral Sea, and is surrounded by tropical gardens and waterfalls. There's a barbecue area, and you can also order kitchen supplies to be ready when you arrive. Apartments are serviced weekly, and each has a washing machine and dryer.

18 Golden Orchid Dr. (off Shute Harbour Rd.), Airlie Beach, QLD 4802. ℂ **07/4948 0401.** Fax 07/4948 0402. www.martiniquewhitsunday.com.au. A$180 (US$144) double 1-bedroom apt; A$210 (US$168) double 2-bedroom apt; A$330 (US$264) 3-bedroom apt (sleeps 6). Extra person A$25 (US$20). AE, DC, MC, V. Covered parking. **Amenities:** Outdoor lap pool; 2 Jacuzzis; exercise room; tour desk. *In room:* A/C and ceiling fans, TV, full kitchen, minibar, hair dryer, iron.

WHERE TO DINE

Clipper Bar & Restaurant MODERN AUSTRALIAN ☆☆ This is one of those places where everything on the menu looks so tempting it's almost impossible to make a decision. And thankfully, when you make it, you're in no danger of being disappointed. Stretched out beside the pool at the Coral Sea Resort (see "Where to Stay," above), this long, open restaurant is one of the best places to eat in the Whitsundays. Award-winning chef Damien Orth creates world-class fare in an open kitchen, whipping up such delights as my mouth-watering Tasmanian salmon on basil and macadamia mash with sugar cane skewers, or caramelized duck breast glazed with mandarin and star anise, with vegetable spring rolls and a Szechuan sauce. And for A$75 (US$60) per person you can indulge in a fabulous seafood platter.

In the Coral Sea Resort, 25 Oceanview Ave., Airlie Beach. ℂ **07/4946 6458.** Reservations recommended. Main courses at lunch A$11–A$25 (US$8.80–US$20), at dinner A$29–A$35 (US$23–US$28). AE, DC, MC, V. Daily 7am–9:30pm or until the last guests leave.

Mangrove Jack's Café Bar PIZZA/CAFÉ FARE Bareboat sailors, local sugar farmers, Sydney yuppies, and European backpackers all flock to this big open-fronted sports bar/restaurant. The mood is upbeat but pleasantly casual, the surrounds are spic-and-span, and the food passes muster. Wood-fired pizza with trendy toppings is the specialty. There is no table service; just place your order at the bar and collect your food when your number is called. The more than 50 wines come by the glass.

In the Airlie Beach Hotel, 16 The Esplanade (enter via Shute Harbour Rd.). ℂ **07/ 4946 6233.** Reservations recommended. Main courses A$7.90–A$20 (US$6.30–US$16). AE, DC, MC, V. Daily 10am–midnight.

5 The Whitsunday Island Resorts
VERY EXPENSIVE

Hayman ☆☆☆ This is the most luxurious, glitzy, and glamorous resort in Australia. And a A$50 million (US$40 million) redevelopment in 2003 has ensured that it is even more so. Check-in is done over a glass of bubbly aboard the resort's sleek launch that meets you at Hamilton Island airport. On arrival, you won't take long to find your way through the open-air sandstone lanais, cascading ponds, and tropical foliage to the fabulous hexagonal complex of swimming pools by the sea. Despite the luxury, Hayman is relaxed. Dress is beachwear by day, smart casual at night (but pack something elegant for dinner, if you wish). An impressive lineup of activities is available, and it's probably fair to say the staff at Hayman can organize almost anything you desire.

The Marine Centre runs dive and snorkel trips to reefs around the island shoreline (wonderful Blue Pearl Bay is just offshore), and to Bait Reef and Whitehaven Beach. It conducts introductory dives, scuba refresher courses, learn-to-dive and referral courses. Certified divers can undertake night dives.

While Hayman is renowned for the antiques, artworks, and fine objets d'art gracing its public areas, the accommodations are welcoming. Every room, suite, villa, and penthouse has a balcony or terrace, bathrobes, and valet service (and butler service in the penthouses). Pool Wing rooms with marble floors and bathrooms and tropically elegant furnishings have views over the pool, and also to the sea from the third and fourth floors. Lagoon Wing rooms overlook a lagoon and have sea views from the third floor. There are new Lagoon rooms, suites and penthouses, and 16 Retreat rooms (each with private veranda, open patios, and outdoor rinse showers), a Jacuzzi, and a contemporary beachfront restaurant. For even greater privacy, the Beach Villa, opened in late 2002, has a private Balinese style courtyard, walled gardens, its own private infinity plunge pool, and personalized concierge service.

Hayman, Great Barrier Reef, QLD 4801. © **1800/075 175** in Australia, or call The Leading Hotels of the World at © **800/745 8883** in the U.S. and Canada, 0800/181 123 in the U.K., 1800/409 063 in Ireland, 0800/44 1016 in New Zealand, or 02/9268 1888 (Sydney sales office), or 07/4940 1234 (the island). Fax 02/9268 1899 (Sydney sales office), or 07/4940 1567 (the island). www.hayman.com.au. 244 units. A$620–A$1,100 (US$496–US$880) double; A$2,000(US$1,600) suite; A$2,700–A$4,400 (US$2,160–US$3,520) penthouse; A$3,200 (US$2,560) Beach Villa. A surcharge of 10% and 4-night minimum stay Dec 24–Jan 5. Children under 13 stay free in parent's room; A$140 (US$112) children 13 and over sharing parent's room; 50% of room rate for children 12 and under in adjoining room. Children 5–12 charged 50% for all dining costs. Ask about packages. AE, DC, MC, V. Resort launch meets all flights at Hamilton Island Airport for the 55-min. transfer. Helicopter and seaplane transfers available. Hayman Island is 33km (20 miles) from Shute Harbour. **Amenities:** 4 restaurants (Asian, Italian, Australian); 2 bars; 3 swimming pools (1 saltwater and 2 heated freshwater); beachside 9-hole golf putting green; 5 day/night tennis courts (with ball machine and coaching); extensive health club with massage and sauna;

outdoor Jacuzzi; watersports (including parasailing, water-skiing, windsurfing, and catamarans; marine center offering snorkel and dive day trips, courses, and gear rental); daily kids' club for children ages 5–14, and day care for younger kids; game room; concierge; tour desk; business center and secretarial services; shopping arcade; salon; 24-hr. room service; babysitting; dry cleaning; laundry service. *In room:* A/C, TV w/free and pay-per-view movies, fax, minibar, fridge, coffeemaker, hair dryer, iron, safe.

Whitsunday Wilderness Lodge 🐘🐘

This resort was designed to show off the Whitsundays' natural beauty. Tucked in a cove under towering hoop pines and palms, it is an environmentally sensitive lodge on a national-park island for people who want to explore the wilderness in basic comfort, but without the crowds, noisy water-sports, or artificial atmosphere of a resort. It's also a great place to meet other travelers. A maximum 16 guests stay in simple but smart cabins facing the sea, each with a double and single bed, modern bathrooms, and a private deck facing the sea. Solar power rules, so there is no air-conditioning, TV, hair dryer, iron, or other appliances. There is one public phone. Social life centers on an open-sided gazebo by the beach, equipped with a natural-history library and CDs, where everyone dines together at slab tables under the Milky Way on fabulous buffet-style campfire meals. Access is only by a short but stunning helicopter flight from Hamilton Island.

Daily excursions include sailing away on the lodge's gleaming 10.2m (33-ft.) catamaran, a seaplane flight to the Outer Reef and Whitehaven Beach, sea kayaking the mangroves to spot giant green sea turtles (which are common around the lodge), snorkeling the fringing reef on uninhabited islands, or bushwalking to a magical milkwood grove no one else knows about. Or you may prefer to just laze in the hammocks, or head off with a free sea kayak and snorkel gear. The beach is more tidal flat than sand, but clean and firm enough to sunbathe on. Wildlife abounds, including Myrtle, the lodge's pet kangaroo. Those who stay on this 1,215-hectare (3,001-acre) island consider it a plus that no ferries or cruise boats call and that the lodge is inaccessible to day-trippers.

Paradise Bay, Long Island (16km/10 miles SE of Shute Harbour), Whitsunday Islands (P.O. Box 842, Airlie Beach, QLD 4802) ✆ **07/4946 9777.** Fax 07/4946 9777. www.southlongisland.com. 10 units (all with shower only). A$4,500 (US$3,600) double 3-night stay; A$5,200 (US$4,160) double 4 nights; A$5,980 (US$4,784) double for 5 nights. A$800 (US$640) double extra nights. Rates include all meals, helicopter transfers from Hamilton Island Airport, daily excursions, and equipment. Rates decrease with longer stays. On "Beachcomber Weeks," held several times a year, there's a 40% discount on 5, 6 and 7-night rates—in exchange for helping clean up the island's shores for an hour a day. MC, V. No children under 14. *In room:* Fridge, coffeemaker, no phone.

EXPENSIVE

Daydream Island Resort *Kids*   After a A$40 million (US$32 million) refurbishment, one of the Whitsunday's oldest resorts is now one of Australia's most extensive and modern spa resorts. The 16 therapy rooms have some of the most sophisticated equipment in the country and since reopening in 2001 the resort has found a new clientele while retaining many of the features—such as the outdoor cinema and kids' club—which have always made it popular with families. The state-of-the-art **Daydream Rejuvenation Spa** has an in-house naturopath and a range of computerized health analyses using equipment and tests, such as iridology and measurement of vitamin and mineral imbalances and antioxidant levels. The "village" at the southern end of the island, a short stroll along the boardwalk from the resort, has shops, cafes, a pool and bar, water activities center, and a tavern serving bistro-style meals. A rainforest walk stretches almost the entire length of the kilometer-long island, and other activities include snorkeling, sailboarding, jet-skiing, parasailing, coral viewing, reef fishing, diving and dive school, tennis, volleyball, badminton and croquet, and mini golf. Accommodation is in large, smart, comfortable rooms, with uninterrupted ocean views.

Daydream Island (40km/25 miles NE of Shute Harbour), Whitsunday Islands. (Postal address: P.M.B. 22, Mackay, QLD 4741.) ℂ 07/4948 8488. Fax 07/4948 8499. www.daydream.net.au. 296 units. A$330–A$450 (US$264–US$360) double; A$495–A$701 (US$396–US$561) suites; A$592–A$675 (US$474–US$540) family suites. Children 14 and under stay free with existing bedding. Ask about packages. AE, MC, V. FantaSea Cruises (ℂ 1800/650 851 in Australia, or 07/4946 5111) provides 15-min. launch transfers from Shute Harbour as well as from Long Island, South Molle, and Hamilton Island. **Amenities:** 3 restaurants (seafood, Australian); 3 bars; 3 freshwater outdoor pools (1 heated); 3 Jacuzzis; 2 day/night tennis courts; watersports equipment; tour desk; coin-op laundry. *In room:* A/C, TV w/pay movies and PlayStation, dataport, minibar, coffeemaker, hair dryer, iron.

Hamilton Island *Kids*   More a vacation village than a single resort, Hamilton has the widest range of activities, accommodations

---

⌠Tips⌡ Whale-Watching in the Whitsundays

Humpback whales migrate to the Whitsundays every July through September to give birth to their calves. **FantaSea Cruises** (ℂ 07/4946 5111) runs whale-watching cruises in season; it's not uncommon for whales to come right up to the boat. The cost is around A$100 (US$80) per adult and if you don't see any whales you can go again another day.

styles, and restaurants of any Great Barrier Reef island resort. Thanks to a A$56 million (US$44.8 million) refurbishment over the past 5 years, the place is looking fresh. Accommodations choices are extra-large rooms and suites in the high-rise hotel, high-rise one bedroom apartments, Polynesian-style bungalows in tropical gardens (ask for one away from the road for real privacy), and glamorous rooms in the two-story, adults-only Beach Club, which sports minimalist decor and a personal "host" to cater to every whim, as well as a choice of two-, three-, and four-bedroom self-contained apartments and villas. The best sea views come from the second-floor Beach Club rooms, from floor nos. 5 to 18 of the Reef View Hotel, and from most apartments. In-room amenities vary depending on your accommodations choice, so check when booking.

On one side of the island is a marina village with cafes, restaurants, shops, and a yacht club. The restaurants range from high-end seafood and New Australian cuisine, to more casual eateries and takeaways. On the other side are the accommodations, a large and inviting free-form pool and swim-up bar, and the wide curve of Cat's Eye Beach. Hamilton offers a huge range of watersports, fishing trips, and cruises, speedboat rides, Go-Karts, a "wire flyer" flying-fox hang glider, a pistol/clay target/rifle range, minigolf, an aquatic driving range, beach barbecue safaris in an army truck, hiking trails, an Aussie wildlife sanctuary where you can cuddle a koala or hold a baby crocodile, and an extensive daily activities program. Because the resort is split by a steep hill, you need to get around by the free shuttle (which runs half-hourly during the day, and every 15 min. 5–10pm), by golf buggy (A$35/US$28 per hr. or A$75/US$60 for 24 hr.), or on foot. Despite the price, everyone seems to go for the buggies, so the place can feel like rush hour. To get away, hit the beach or the hiking trails, because most of the 750-hectare (1,853-acre) island is virgin bushland. The biggest drawback is that just about every activity costs extra (and it's usually not cheap) so you are constantly adding to your holiday bill.

The island's dive company, **H2O Sportz** (© **07/4946 9888;** www.h2osportz.com.au), offers dive day trips to Bait Reef, 4-day diving courses up to the Advanced level, and introductory dives and snorkel safaris. Guests can also join FantaSea Cruises' day trips to the outer Reef.

Hamilton Island (16km/10 miles SE of Shute Harbour), Whitsunday Islands, QLD 4803. © **1800/075 110** in Australia, or 02/8353 8444 (reservations office in Sydney), or 07/4946 9999 (the island). Fax 02/8353 8498 (reservations office in Sydney), or 07/ 4946 8888 (the island). www.hamiltonisland.com.au. 737 units (some with shower only). A$249–A$306 (US$199–US$245) bungalow or Palm Terrace; Hotel A$340–A$410 (US$272–US$328) double; A$589 (US$471) suite. Standard villas (3-night minimum stay): A$470 (US$376) one bedroom; A$546 (US$437) 2-bedroom; A$616 (US$493) 3-bedroom. Deluxe villas (3-night minimum stay): A$687 (US$550) 2-bedroom; A$765 (US$612) 3-bedroom; A$881 (US$705) 4-bedroom. Beach Club A$547 (US$438) double. Children under 12 stay free in parents' room with existing bedding and eat free from kids' menu at 5 restaurants. No children in Beach Club rooms. Ask about packages. AE, DC, MC, V. Airlines fly into Hamilton Island Airport. Free airport-resort transfers for all guests. FantaSea Cruises (✆ **1800/650 851** in Australia, or 07/4946 5111) provides launch transfers from Shute Harbour and most other islands. **Amenities:** 10 restaurants; 7 bars; 6 outdoor pools; minigolf and driving range; day/night tennis courts; health club and spa; extensive range of watersports and activities; bike rental; child-care center for kids from 6 weeks–14 years (in 3 groups); concierge (hotel and Beach Club only); tour desk; business center and secretarial services; shopping arcade; salon; limited room service (18 hr. for Beach Club guests; 16 hr. for hotel guests); massage; babysitting; coin-op laundry; laundry service (hotel only). *In room:* A/C, TV (some rooms have VCR, some have pay movies), fax, kitchen (apts only), minibar, coffeemaker, hair dryer, iron, safe.

Peppers Palm Bay ✿   A A$7 million (US$5.6 million) upgrade in 2001 transformed this Long Island hideaway. The Balinese-style beach-front *Bures* (a kind of hut common in Polynesia) have a new glamour to them, with new decks and furnishings, and there are plans for a spa in the next few years. The resort's small swimming pool has been extended and surrounded by timber decking, and a small massage studio has opened in the former gym. This is a private and romantic spot, with no phone, radio, television, or air-conditioning in the rooms, but there's a hammock on your veranda. The large Club Crocodile Long Island resort is a 20-minute walk across the hill to the other side of the island and is completely hidden from Palm Bay, but guests at Palm Bay Hideaway can use Club Crocodile's watersports facilities. Nonmotorized watersports such as kayaks are available at Palm Bay.

Palm Bay, Long Island (16km/10 miles SE of Shute Harbour), Whitsunday Islands. (Postal address: P.M.B. 28, Mackay, QLD 4741). ✆ **1800/095 025** in Australia, or 07/4946 9233. Fax 07/4946 9309. www.peppers.com.au. 21 units. A$380 (US$304) double cabins; A$580 (US$464) double Bure; A$684 (US$547) 2-bedroom bungalows. Children charged at full adult rate. Rates include breakfast. Ask about packages. AE, DC, MC, V. FantaSea Cruises (✆ **1800/650 851** in Australia, or 07/4946 5111) provide launch transfers from Hamilton Island airport, and water taxi transfers are available from Shute Harbour. **Amenities:** Restaurant (modern Australian); bar; outdoor pool; Jacuzzi; watersports; tour desk; massage; coin-op laundry; dry cleaning/laundry service. *In room:* Ceiling fan, minibar, coffeemaker, iron, hair dryer, no phone.

INEXPENSIVE

Hook Island Wilderness Resort   This humble collection of rooms and campsites on a white sandy beach is one of the few really affordable island resorts on the Great Barrier Reef. That makes it

Island Camping

If a deserted island is your idea of paradise, you've come to the right place. You can camp in National Parks on some Whitsunday islands, with a permit. **Island Camping Connections** (✆ 07/ **4946 5255;** mobile phone 0418 786 536) will take you to one of a range of camping spots on South Molle, North Molle, Denman, Planton, Henning, Whitsunday, or Hook islands, as well as Whitehaven Beach on Whitsunday Island. Transfers leave from Shute Harbour and cost between A$45 (US$36) and A$150 (US$120) per person, depending on which island you choose. They can organize everything for you, including camping kits (A$40/US$32 for one night, A$20/US$16 for each subsequent night). They also rent inflatable kayaks and snorkeling gear, and offer a full provisioning service.

popular with backpackers and anybody who just wants to dive, rent canoes, play beach volleyball, visit the underwater observatory (free for guests), hike, fish in the four-person flat-bottom boat, laze in the pool and chill out. Good snorkeling is footsteps from shore, and the resort's dive center conducts first-time and regular dives off the beach. Hook is a national park and the second-largest Whitsunday island. The rooms are very basic, with beds or bunks sleeping six or eight. All come with fresh bed linen, but bring your own towels or rent them for A$3 (US$2.40). A store sells essentials, but try to bring everything you need.

Hook Island (40km/25 miles NE of Shute Harbour), Whitsunday Islands. (Postal address: P.M.B. 23, Mackay, QLD 4741.) ✆ 07/4946 9380. Fax 07/4946 9470. 20 tent sites; 2 8-bed dormitories; 10 rooms, 4 with bathroom (shower only). A$89 (US$71) cabin without bathroom double; extra adult A$35 (US$28), extra child 4–12 A$22 (US$18). A$130 (US$104) cabin with bathroom double; extra adult A$40 (US$32), extra child A$30 (US$24). Dorm bed A$35 (US$28) adult, A$20 (US$16) child 4–12. Tent site A$25 (US$20) adult, A$15 (US$12) child 4–12. Ask about packages. MC, V. Transfers from the mainland cost A$40 (US$29) per person, round-trip. Boat leaves Shute Harbour at 9am and leaves Hook Island for the return trip at 4.30pm (trip time: 1 hr). Book through the resort. **Amenities:** Cafe and bar; outdoor pool; watersports equipment (snorkel gear, canoes, and sea kayaks); tour desk. *In room:* A/C, minifridge.

7

The Central Queensland Coast & the Southern Reef Islands

South of the Whitsundays, the Bruce Highway travels through rural country until it hits the beaches of the Sunshine Coast just north of Brisbane. It may not be the tourism heartland of the state, but there's still plenty to discover. The most spectacular of the Great Barrier Reef islands, Heron Island, is off the coast from Gladstone. Heron's reefs are a source of enchantment for divers and snorkelers, its waters boasting 21 fabulous dive sites. In summer giant turtles nest on its beaches, and in winter humpback whales cruise by. Its close rival is nearby Wilson Island, equally beautiful and more pristine.

North of Gladstone are Rockhampton and the Capricorn Coast, named after the Tropic of Capricorn that runs through it. Rockhampton is also a stepping-stone to the resort island, Great Keppel. The island has some diving and snorkeling offshore, which you can access on a day trip from the mainland or the island. The reefs and islands off Rockhampton are not a commonly visited part of the Great Barrier Reef, yet they offer some good dive sites, most of them not far out to sea.

To the south, off the small town of Bundaberg, lies another tiny coral cay, Lady Elliot Island, which is a nesting site for tens of thousands of sea birds, and has a first-rate fringing reef. It is possible to see giant **manta rays** around the island most of the year. Bundaberg is also the departure point for another coral cay, **Lady Musgrave Island,** which snorkelers and divers can access on a day trip. It is also the only town south of the Whitsundays to offer extended live-aboard diving trips to the unspoiled and little-explored **Bunker Reef** complex.

Two little-known attractions in Bundaberg are its good shore scuba diving and a loggerhead turtle rookery that operates in summer on the beach.

For a **map** of this region, see the map on p. 159.

1 Rockhampton: Gateway to Great Keppel Island

1,055km (654 miles) S of Cairns; 638km (396 miles) N of Brisbane

You may hear Queenslanders talk dryly about "Rockvegas." Don't be fooled. "Rocky" is the unofficial capital of the sprawling beef-cattle country inland and the gateway to Great Keppel Island, but bears no resemblance to Las Vegas. Heritage buildings line the Fitzroy River, where barramundi await keen fishermen. Every Friday night at the Great Western Hotel, bull-riding cowboys take to the rodeo ring to test their skills against local Brahman bulls.

Great Keppel Island boasts a large sporty resort dedicated to the 18-to-35 market, and a couple of budget-style market resorts which are popular with families, one of which has a dive shop. Day trips to the island, or to a nearby reef with a small underwater observatory, operate from the coast, approximately 55km (34 miles) east of town.

Rockhampton has plenty of motels that provide a decent bed for the night. The **Club Crocodile Motor Inn,** Alma Street at Albert Street, Rockhampton, QLD 4700 (© **1800/816 441** in Australia, or 07/4927 7433; www.clubcroc.com.au) has doubles for A$81 to $102 (US$65–$82).

GETTING THERE   Rockhampton is on the Bruce Highway, a 3½-hour drive south of Mackay, and almost 2 hours north of Gladstone.

QantasLink (© **13 13 13** in Australia) has flights from Brisbane, Mackay, Gladstone and Sydney. **Virgin Blue** (© **13 67 89** in Australia) flies direct from Brisbane. **Jetstar** (© **13 15 38** in Australia) flies from Brisbane and Sydney.

Queensland Rail (© **13 22 32** in Queensland, or 07/3235 1122) trains call into Rockhampton daily. The trip from Brisbane takes just 7 hours on the high-speed Tilt Train; the fare is A$94 (US$75) economy class and $141 (US$113) business class.

McCafferty's (© **13 14 99** in Australia) and **Greyhound Pioneer** (© **13 20 30** in Australia) call at Rockhampton on their many daily coach services between Brisbane and Cairns. The fare is A$82 (US$66) from Brisbane (trip time: 11½ hr.) and A$127 (US$102) from Cairns (trip time: 17½ hr.).

VISITOR INFORMATION   Drop by the **Capricorn Tourism** information center at the city's southern entrance on Gladstone Road (at the Capricorn Spire; © **07/4927 2055**). It's open daily from 9am to 5pm.

The Central Queensland Coast

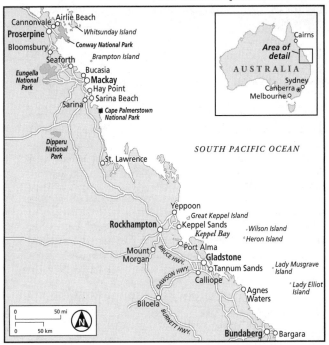

GETTING AROUND   **Avis** (© 07/4927 3344), **Budget** (© 07/4926 4888), **Hertz** (© 07/4922 2721 airport, or 07/4927 8700 city), and **Thrifty** (© 07/4927 8755) have offices in Rockhampton. The local bus is **Sunbus** (© 07/4936 2133).

2 Great Keppel Island

15km (9 miles) E of Rockhampton

This 1,454-hectare (3,591-acre) island is home to one major resort for the 18-to-35s, and a couple of smaller, family-oriented ones. You can stay at one of the resorts, or take a day trip from the mainland and pay to use many of the facilities including watersports equipment, pools, and food outlets. More grass and bushland than palmy paradise, the island's 1,454 hectares (3,591 acres) are crisscrossed with walking trails and rimmed with 17 sandy beaches, most of them appealingly deserted. It has only modest fringing coral, and the best snorkeling is around the nearby Middle Island Underwater

Observatory, a short boat trip away from the island. The observatory is also accessible by a day trip from the mainland. Certified divers won't find many deep diving opportunities around Great Keppel Island, although they can hand-feed big grouper near the observatory. The shallow waters of the island's fringing reefs are perfect for newly certified divers, however, and for anyone keen to try a first-time dive.

Day-trippers can pay to do many of the resort's watersports, eat at the cafe or restaurant, and drink at the bar. Stop by the information center to book activities and pick up a walking-trail map. Day-trippers will also find a cafe and bar operated by the island's small budget-market Keppel Haven resort. The island has a small souvenir/sundries store, a pizzeria, and an ice-creamery.

ESSENTIALS
GETTING THERE   Launches operated by **Keppel Tourist Services** (© **07/4933 6744**) and **Freedom Fast Cats** (© **07/4933 6244**) each make the 30-minute crossing from Rosslyn Bay Harbour, about 55km (34 miles) east of Rockhampton, 3 or 4 times daily. The return trip costs about A$31 (US$25) adults, A$16 (US$13) children 5 to 15, and A$78 (US$62) families of four.

From Rockhampton, take the Capricorn Coast scenic drive Route 10 to Emu Park and follow the signs to Rosslyn Bay Harbour. If you're coming to Rockhampton from the north, the scenic drive turnoff is just north of the city, and from there it's 46km (29 miles) to the harbor. You can leave your car in undercover storage at **Great Keppel Island Security Car Park** (© **07/4933 6670**) at 422 Scenic Hwy., near the harbor, for A$6.50 to A$8 (US$5.20–US$6.40) per day.

Rothery's Coaches (© **07/4922 4320**) runs a daily service from Kern Arcade on Bolsover Street in Rockhampton to Rosslyn Bay Harbour and back, three times a day. You can request a free pickup from the airport, train station, or your hotel. Round-trip fares from town are A$17 (US$14) for adults, A$14 (US$11) for seniors, students and children, or A$42 (US$34) for a family of 4. The round-trip fare to/from the airport is A$30 (US$24) for adults, A$25 (US$20) for seniors and students, A$14 (US$11) for children, and A$75 (US$60) for families.

Guests at Contiki Resort Great Keppel Island can fly from Rockhampton on a light plane, which takes about 15 minutes and costs A$138 (US$110) round-trip. Book through the resort (see below).

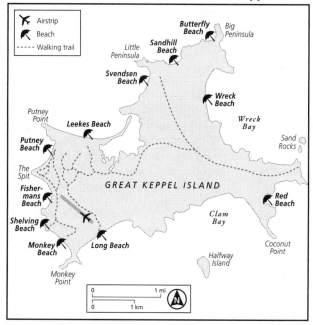

DIVING & SNORKELING GREAT KEPPEL ISLAND

Hard and soft corals, mantas, loads of reef fish, sea snakes, turtles, and other sea life can be found in the islands and reefs off Rockhampton. Rockhampton-based **Capricorn Reef Diving** (𝄞 **07/4922 7720;** www.capricornreefdiving.com) runs day trips to a choice of 40-plus dive sites around Great Keppel Island and other nearby islands in the Keppel group like Outer Rock, Man & Wife, Barren & Child Islands and the famous Egg Rock. The trips operate in a 7.5m (25-ft.) dive boat, and while they are designed for divers, 90% of the sites are suitable for snorkelers too. The company describes **Egg Rock** as a dive photographer's dream: "Some fish up to 60–70kg (130–155 lb.) in weight . . . clownfish the size of your hand in patches up to 10m (33 ft.) in diameter . . . sea snakes as thick as your arm."

The boat departs Rosslyn Bay Harbour at 9am daily, picking up passengers at Great Keppel Island en route, and returning to the mainland at 4:30pm. The day costs A$90 (US$72) with two dives, A$60 (US$48) for snorkelers, or A$145 (US$116) for two introductory dives, plus about A$40 (US$32) for gear hire. BYO lunch.

Occasionally the company runs trips beyond the Keppels to the **Swain Reef** complex on the outer Great Barrier Reef, the Capricorn Group of which Heron Island is part, or the **Bunker Group** (see "Bundaberg: Gateway to Lady Elliot Island," later in this chapter). The company also conducts PADI dive courses from open-water certification to Instructor level, and a wide range of specialty courses. Its store at 189 Musgrave St., North Rockhampton, sells, rents, and services gear.

Keppel Reef Scuba Adventures, which runs the **Keppel Island Dive Centre** (© 07/4939 5022; www.keppeldive.com), is located on Putney Beach on the island, to your left as you step off the boat. It runs a daily 10am dive trip, returning at noon, with a second trip at 12:30pm if there are bookings, getting back at 2pm. It costs A$75 (US$60) for one dive, A$55 (US$44) for two, all gear included. Anyone who has not dived in the past 12 months must do a free refresher course; if the company is unsure of your skills, you may have to pay A$99 (US$79) extra to have an instructor accompany you underwater. The shallow water around the island is perfect for introductory dives. The company offers full courses on demand only. It sells and rents snorkel gear and a few dive accessories.

Keppel Tourist Services (see "Getting There," above) does coral-viewing morning, afternoon, and full-day trips. The 9:15am morning trip departs Rosslyn Bay and picks up passengers at Great Keppel Island at 10am before heading to **Middle Island Underwater Observatory,** just offshore from Great Keppel Island. The observatory is one of those small-scale attractions common in regional areas, not a flashy modern aquarium, but it has 14 big windows through which you will see big grouper, an assortment of reef fish, and sometimes sea snakes and turtles. It features both natural reefs and an artificial reef created by scuttling an old fishing boat. You can also do coral viewing from a glass-bottom boat. At the end of the two-hour cruise, you'll be dropped off at Great Keppel to catch either the 2pm or 4:30pm launch back to the mainland.

You can take the boat to Great Keppel at 7:30am, 9:15am, or 11:30am and spend the morning on the island before joining the 2:15pm afternoon trip. This cruise takes you to snorkel nearby reefs and go **boom-netting,** the fun practice of sitting in a rope net within a sturdy frame, and getting dragged along in the water beside the boat. Half day trips cost A$48 (US$38) for adults, half price for children 5 to 14, or you can incorporate both half-day trips into a full-day that costs A$75 (US$60) adults, A$43 (US$34) kids. Ferry transfers, morning and afternoon tea, and a simple lunch at Keppel

Haven resort are all included, and you get an hour or so to explore the island after lunch. These trips are not your top Great Barrier Reef experience, but you may find them a pleasant interlude if you're driving the Queensland coast.

WHERE TO STAY & DINE

Contiki Resort Great Keppel Island   I can't tell you what it is like to stay at this resort, because I'm too old. But the word is out: If you're a young adult looking for a very good time, this is the resort for you. Following the old adage "If you can't beat 'em, join 'em," the owners and managers of this popular 30-year-old resort have closed the doors to everyone outside the ages of 18 to 35. Great Keppel made its name in Australia in the '70s with an advertising campaign that it has never managed to shake. "Get wrecked!" it screamed and they came in droves for sex, sun, and good times. Firmly stuck with an image that it later didn't deserve—for my money was once one of the best places to take a family—this resort is reverting to what made its name and was relaunched in 2002 as Australia's first Contiki Resort. About 70 water- and land-based sports are offered, and many, including catamarans, paddle-skis, and Windsurfers, are free. Activities that cost extra include scuba diving, tandem sky diving, parasailing, guided snorkeling safaris, jet-skiing, sunset champagne sails, and reef-fishing trips, to name only a few. There are three types of accommodations: Hillside Villas with sea or bush views, garden rooms, or beachfront units—my pick because of their location. If you're traveling alone, they'll even fix you up with a same-sex roommate. The whole resort was given a A$3 million (US$2.4 million) face-lift in 2001.

Great Keppel Island, QLD 4700. ✆ **1800/245 658** in Australia, or 07/4939 5044. Fax 07/4939 1775. www.contikiresorts.com. 181 units. A$504–A$784 (US$403–US$627) twin, for 2-night minimum stay; extra nights A$252–A$392 (US$202–US$314) twin. Rates include brunch and dinner. Ask about packages. AE, DC, MC, V. **Amenities:** 3 restaurants; 4 bars; 4 outdoor freshwater pools; 9-hole golf course; 2 day/night tennis courts; 2 Jacuzzis; gymnasium (7am–10pm); extensive water-sports equipment and rental; concierge; tour desk; salon; massage; coin-op laundry; laundry service; dry cleaning; nonsmoking rooms. *In room:* A/C, TV, fridge, coffeemaker, hair dryer, iron.

Keppel Haven   Not far from the ferry drop-off point at the beach is this campground-style enclave of humble but pretty cabins and tents, which is a good choice for families. Renovated in 1998, the cabins have terra cotta–look floors, bright new kitchenettes, a small double bedroom, four bunks in the living/dining area for the kids, fans, and a little porch. The permanent tents come with twin or double beds, four bunks separated by a canvas partition, and electricity. There are also two houses, each sleeping 6, with full facilities. Catamarans, windsurfers, fishing tackle, snorkel gear, and dinghies are available for hire on a pay-as-you-go basis. There's a general store selling basic groceries, and three communal kitchens and barbecues. BYO towels or rent them (towels in cabins).

Great Keppel Island via Rockhampton, QLD 4700. ✆ **1800/35 6744** in Australia, or 07/4933 6744. Fax 07/4933 6429. ktsgki@networx.com.au. 40 permanent tents, none with bathroom; 12 cabins (each sleeps 6), all with bathroom (shower only). 12 bunkhouses (with 1 bathroom per 2 rooms). Tent A$18 (US$14) per person triple or quad share, A$20 (US$16) per person twin/double, A$28 (US$22) single. Cabins A$120 (US$96) twin or double; additional person A$20 (US$16) extra. Bunkhouses A$80 (US$64) double/twin; A$220 (US$176) houses (sleep 6). A$5 (US$4) per person linen for duration of stay for tents. Cabins and bunkhouses have linen supplied. Ask about 3-day, 2-night packages with Keppel Tourist Services that include ferry transfers and a ½-day snorkeling or boom-netting cruise. MC, V. **Amenities:** Restaurant; watersports rentals; hair dryers at front desk. *In room:* Kitchenettes in cabins.

3 Gladstone: Gateway to Heron Island

550km (341 miles) N of Brisbane; 1,162 (720 miles) S of Cairns

The industrial port town of Gladstone is the departure point for beautiful Heron Island.

ESSENTIALS

GETTING THERE & GETTING AROUND   Gladstone is on the coast 21km (13 miles) off the Bruce Highway. **QantasLink** (book through Qantas) has many daily flights from Brisbane (trip time: 75 min.) and two direct flights a day from Rockhampton and Bundaberg.

Queensland Rail (✆ **13 22 32** in Queensland, or 07/3235 1122) operates trains most days to Gladstone from Brisbane and Cairns. The fare from Brisbane (trip time: 6 hr. on the high-speed Tilt Train) is A$84 (US$67); fares from Cairns (trip time: 20 hr.) range from A$151 (US$121) for a seat to A$298 (US$238) for a first-class sleeper on *The Sunlander.*

McCafferty's (✆ **13 14 99** in Australia) and **Greyhound Pioneer** (✆ **13 20 30** in Australia) operate many daily coaches to Gladstone on their Brisbane-Cairns runs. The fare is A$70 (US$56) from Brisbane (trip time: 10 hr.) and A$148 (US$118) from Cairns (trip time: 19½ hr.).

Avis (✆ 07/4978 2633), **Budget** (✆ 07/4972 8488), **Hertz** (✆ 07/4978 6899), and **Thrifty** (✆ 07/4972 5999) all have offices in Gladstone.

VISITOR INFORMATION   The **Gladstone Information Centre** is located in the ferry terminal at Gladstone Marina, Bryan Jordan Drive, Gladstone, QLD 4680 (© **07/4972 9000;** www.gladstone region.org.au). It's open from 8:30am to 5pm Monday through Friday, and from 9am to 5pm Saturday and Sunday.

WHERE TO STAY & DINE

Country Plaza International   This four-level hotel in the center of town runs a free shuttle to the wharf for guests bound for Heron Island. Gladstone's largest and best hotel, it caters primarily to business travelers, so it has ample facilities—spacious rooms with balconies, modern bathrooms, an upscale seafood restaurant, and a pool and sun deck. Most rooms have views over the port or the city. There are six three-bedroom apartments and one two-bedroom apartment.

100 Goondoon St., Gladstone, QLD 4680. © **07/4972 4499.** Fax 07/4972 4921. www.plazahotels.com.au/gladstone.htm. 80 units. A$130 (US$104) double; A$140–A$150 (US$112–US$120) apts. AE, DC, MC, V. Free covered parking. **Amenities:** Restaurant (seafood); bar; outdoor pool; business center; free transfers from airport, coach terminal, marina, and train station; 24-hr. room service; laundry service; dry cleaning. *In room:* A/C, TV w/free movies, fax, dataport, minibar, coffeemaker, hair dryer, iron.

4 Heron Island: Coral, More Coral, Turtles & Whales ✮✮✮

72km (45 miles) NE of Gladstone

This is, quite simply, one of the most magical places in the world, I think. The difference between Heron Island and others is that once there, you have no need to travel further to the reef. Step off the beach, and you enter magnificent fields of coral that seem to stretch for miles. And the myriad life-forms which abound are accessible to everyone through diving, snorkeling, reef walks at low tide, or aboard a semisubmersible vessel which allows you to view the ocean floor without getting wet. When geologist Joseph Bette Jukes named this piece of paradise in 1843, he overlooked the turtles for which it is now famous and favored the reef herons that populated the island. There has been a resort on Heron Island since 1932, and in 1943 the island was made a National Park. It is a haven for wildlife and people alike, and an experience of a lifetime is almost guaranteed at any time of year. Heron Island is a rookery for giant green and loggerhead turtles. Resort guests gather on the beach from late November to February to watch the female turtles lay eggs, and from February to mid-April to see the hatched babies scuttle down the sand to the water. Humpback whales pass by June through September.

Three days on Heron Island gives plenty of time to see everything. The island is so small you can walk around it at a leisurely pace in about half an hour. Snorkeling and reef walking are major occupations for visitors—if they're not diving, that is, for the island is home to 21 of the world's most stunning dive sites.

Guided island walks include a visit to the research station based on the island. As for the reef walk, just borrow a pair of sandshoes, a balance pole, and a viewing bucket, and head off with a guide at low tide. The walk can take up to 90 minutes, so if it gets too hot you can head back to the resort.

A fishing trip should also be on the agenda, even for the most inexperienced. The reef fish seem to just jump onto the hook!

GETTING THERE   A courtesy coach meets flights at 10:30am to take guests to Gladstone Marina for the launch transfer to the island (trip time: 1hr., 40 min); it departs 11am daily (except Christmas). Round-trip transfers aboard the sleek new 130-seater catamaran *Heron Spirit* costs A$180 (US$144) for adults, half price for kids 3 to 14. Make sure you take seasickness medication, as this trip can be rough, especially on the outward bound journey. Helicopter transfers can be arranged for A$291 (US$233) per person one-way. A 15kg (33-lb.) luggage limit applies on the helicopter (one soft suitcase per person only). Excess bags are stored free at Gladstone Airport.

WHERE TO STAY & DINE

Heron Island Resort ★★★ *Kids*   This lovely, low-key resort has been transformed over the past few years, and changes to the accommodations mix continue alongside cosmetic changes. The latest are the chic new Wistari Suites, each with a private garden and veranda. But new accommodations, a revamped central complex, and a stylish, contemporary new look have not changed the focus on the outdoors. The brilliant colors of the island's surrounding water and Reef are reflected in the interiors, and everything is light-filled and breezy. Heron's central complex is equal parts grand Queenslander home and sophisticated beach house, with smart bar and lounge areas open to ocean views and sunsets. Duplex-style Turtle Rooms are designed for couples or families, both with en-suite bathrooms, casual living area, and a shady veranda, or you can go for greater luxury in the suites or the private beach house. The **Aqua Soul Spa** opened in late 2003, offering double treatment rooms, therapies designed for two and usual spa treatments and pampering

The Spa complex is in a secluded spot on the edge of the Island's pisonia forests, removed from the main resort.

Mantas, plentiful turtles, gorgonian fans, moray eels, shark, huge coral "bommies" (outcrops), millions of colorful reef fish, gutters, and swim-throughs—Heron Island's dive sites have loads to offer. Divers can make only three dives per day, two in the morning and one in the afternoon, which you may find frustrating if you're keen to hit the water as many times as possible and don't want to gear up twice a day. All dives are from a guided boat. Dive packages are available for A$50 (US$40) per dive for one to four dives, A$35 (US$28) for each after that. You can also do night dives for A$75 (US$60), or join a A$1,500 (US$1,200) day trip to dive rarely explored reefs farther afield from Heron. First-timers can make an introductory dive for A$150 (US$120). Three-day referral courses start every Monday (for which you have to arrive Sunday) and cost A$400 (US$320). The dive shop sells and rents gear.

Heron Island, via Gladstone, QLD 4680 (P&O Resorts, G.P.O. Box 5287, Sydney, NSW 2001). ℂ **1800/737 678** in Australia, 800/225-9849 in the U.S. and Canada, 020 7805 3875 in the U.K., 02/9257 5050 or fax 02/9299 2477 (Sydney reservations office). www.poresorts.com. 109 units (some with shower only). Turtle Rooms A$480 (US$384) double; Reef Suite A$560 (US$448) double; Heron Beachside Suite A$700 (US$560) double; Point Suite, Wistari Suite, or private Beach House A$940 (US$752) double. Extra adult A$150 (US$120), extra children 3–14 A$90 (US$72). Free crib. Rates include all meals and many activities. Ask about special packages. AE, DC, MC, V. No children allowed in Point suites or Beach House. **Amenities:** Restaurant (Australian); bar; outdoor pool; 2 day/night tennis courts; Jacuzzi; Spa; limited watersports equipment rental; Heron Kids Junior Rangers program (7–12 only) in Australian school vacations; game room; activities desk; babysitting; coin-op laundry; lounge with TV; public phones; Internet access. *In room:* Ceiling fan, fridge, coffeemaker, hair dryer, iron, no phone (except in 4 Point Suites and Beach House).

5 Bundaberg: Gateway to Lady Elliot Island

384km (238 miles) N of Brisbane; 1,439km (892 miles) S of Cairns

The sugar town of Bundaberg is the last point south (or the first point north) from which you can explore the Great Barrier Reef. It is the gateway to the wonderful diving and snorkeling on **Lady Elliot Island,** a Great Barrier Reef resort where you can stay overnight or visit on an aerial day trip. Snorkeling and diving day cruises run to **Lady Musgrave Island,** an uninhabited Great Barrier Reef coral cay. Divers can also visit a few wrecks and other sites in the area, and experience some of Australia's best **shore diving** off Bundaberg's beaches. If you visit the area between November and March, plan an evening at the **Mon Repos Turtle Rookery.**

Moments   **Up Close & Personal with a Turtle**

The egg in my hand is warm, soft, and about the size of a Ping-Pong ball. At our feet, a giant green turtle sighs deeply as she lays a clutch of about 120 eggs in a pear-shaped chamber dug from the sand. A large tear rolls from her eye. In the distance the wedge-tailed shearwaters call eerily to each other, backed by the sound of the ocean.

The egg-laying ritual of the turtles is central to a trip to Heron Island in the summer months. At night and in the early morning, small groups of people gather on the beaches to witness the turtles lumber up the beach, dig a hole in the sand, and lay their eggs. (The turtles are not easily disturbed, and you can get very close.) Every night during the season, volunteer guides from the University of Queensland research station based on the island are on hand; you can watch and ask questions as the researchers tag and measure the turtles before they return to the water. The laying season runs December through February, and only 1 in 5,000 hatchlings will live to return in about 50 years to lay their own eggs.

Another good place to watch the turtles nesting is at Mon Repos Beach, outside Bundaberg. Mon Repos Conservation Park is one of the two largest loggerhead-turtle rookeries in

ESSENTIALS

GETTING THERE & GETTING AROUND   Bundaberg is on the Isis Highway, 50km (31 miles) off the Bruce Highway from Gin Gin in the north and 53km (33 miles) off the Bruce Highway from just north of Childers in the south.

QantasLink (𝄐 **13 13 13** in Australia) flies from Brisbane daily and from Gladstone three times a week.

Queensland Rail (𝄐 **13 22 32** in Queensland, or 07/3235 1122) trains stop in Bundaberg every day en route between Brisbane and Cairns. The fare is A$59 (US$47) from Brisbane economy class on the Tilt Train; fares range from A$163 (US$130) for a seat to A$316 (US$253) for a first-class berth on *The Sunlander* from Cairns.

McCafferty's (𝄐 **13 14 99** in Australia) and **Greyhound Pioneer** (𝄐 **13 20 30** in Australia) call here many times a day on their the South Pacific. The visitor center by the beach has a great display on the turtle life cycle and shows films at approximately 7:30pm each night in summer. Visitors can turn up anytime after 7pm; the action goes on all night, sometimes until as late as 6am. Nesting happens around high tide; hatching usually occurs between 8pm and midnight. Try to get there early to join the first group of 70 people, the maximum allowed at one laying or hatching. This is important if you have children; on one visit, we gave up at midnight with two small children and went to bed without making it to the beach. Take a flashlight if you can.

The **Mon Repos Turtle Rookery** ⚘ (© 07/4159 1652 for the visitor center) is 14km (8½ miles) east of Bundaberg's town center. Follow Bourbong Street out of town toward Burnett Heads as it becomes Bundaberg–Bargara Road. Take the Port Road to the left and look for the Mon Repos signs to the right. Admission to the visitor center is free April through November (9am–4pm), but when the turtles start nesting, you pay A$5 (US$4) for adults, A$2.50 (US$2) for children. November through March, the center is open from 7pm until midnight.

coach runs between Brisbane and Cairns. The 6½ hour trip from Brisbane costs A$46 (US$37). From Cairns it is a 21½ hour trip, for which the fare is A$154 (US$123).

Avis (© 07/4152 1877), **Budget** (© 07/4153 1600), **Hertz** (© 07/4155 2403), and **Thrifty** (© 07/4151 6222) all have offices in Bundaberg.

VISITOR INFORMATION The **Bundaberg Region Visitor Centre** is at 271 Bourbong St. at Mulgrave Street, Bundaberg, QLD 4670 (© **1800/308 888** in Australia, or 07/4153 8888; www.bundabergregion.info). It's open daily from 9am to 5pm.

DIVING & SNORKELING THE REEF
MAJOR REEF SITES
The southern reefs of the Great Barrier Reef are just as prolific, varied, and colorful as the reefs farther north off Cairns. However,

because this part of the coast is less settled, fewer snorkel and dive boats exist to visit them. Many are the virgin reefs in these parts that have never seen a diver.

The only reef visited by snorkelers and divers on a daily basis from Bundaberg is pretty **Lady Musgrave Island,** a vegetated 14-hectare (35-acre) national-park coral cay, 52 nautical miles off the coast. It is surrounded by a lagoon 8km (5 miles) in circumference, filled with hundreds of corals and some 1,200 of the 1,500 species of fish and other marine creatures found on the Great Barrier Reef.

Lady Musgrave Island is one of the **Bunker Group** of islands and reefs, which lie approximately 80km (50 miles) due north of Bundaberg. Actually, they are due east of Gladstone and closer to that town, but no boats visit them from there. Little explored by divers, these vividly colored reefs are some of the most pristine on the Great Barrier Reef. Farther south of Bunker Group is **Lady Elliot Island.** Although it lies outside the borders of the Great Barrier Reef Marine Park, Bundaberg's **Woongarra Marine Park** offers the best shore diving in Queensland; it's common for divers visiting the Reef to drop in on it. This small park hugs the town's coastline in an area known as Bargara, and has loads of soft and hard corals, nudibranchs, wobbegongs, epaulette sharks, sea snakes, some 60 fish species, and frequent sightings of green and loggerhead turtles. Most of this is in water less than 9m (30 ft.) deep, and you can walk right into it off the beach.

Beyond Woongarra, 2.5 nautical miles offshore, is **Cochrane artificial reef,** where a few Mohawk and Beechcraft aircraft have been dumped to make a home for fish. Other sites off Bundaberg in about 23m (75 ft.) of water include the **manta "cleaning station"** at Evan's Patch, a **World War II Beaufort bomber** with lots of marine life, and others.

Remember to add the A$4.50 (US$3.60) Environmental Management Charge (EMC), or "reef tax," to the fare of every passenger over 4 years old.

DAY-TRIP DIVE & SNORKEL BOATS & SHORE DIVING

Lady Musgrave Barrier Reef Cruises (*℗* **1800/072 110** in Australia, or 07/4159 4519; www.lmcruises.com.au) operates day trips to **Lady Musgrave Island** using one of two 24m (78-ft.) air-conditioned boats, either the 140-passenger *Lady Musgrave* catamaran or the 70-passenger *Spirit of Musgrave* trimaran. During the 2½-hour journey—which can be rough so take seasick medication if you think you need to—the crew play a video briefing on the Reef's ecosystem, and give a snorkel briefing to first-timers. Flotation vests are available for snorkelers who want them. The pontoon has change rooms and seating. At the lagoon, you can swim, snorkel, or take semisubmersible and glass-bottom boat rides over coral. After lunch, tender boats run you to and from the island if you want to walk the beach (it's coral rubble underfoot, so wear old shoes) or take a guided walk around the island to learn more about its seabird colonies. Keep an eye out for sea turtles laying eggs or hatching on the beach between November and March, though this mostly happens at night.

In total, you get around 4 hours on the coral. First-time divers can try an introductory dive inside the lagoon, which, unlike many coral cay lagoons, is quite deep (an average 6m/20 ft.), which raises your chances of seeing bigger fish. Certified divers dive 2 of about 20 sites located around the outside edge of the lagoon's continuous reef wall. You may see turtles, mantas, eagle rays, and moray eels, and you will see plenty of reef fish and corals. Visibility is excellent. An underwater dive camera is available for rent. Book dives ahead.

The day costs A$140 (US$112) adults, A$72 (US$58) for children 4 to 14. Introductory dives cost A$70 (US$56) extra for one dive, or A$105 (US$84) for two; certified dives cost A$58 (US$46) for one dive, or A$80 (US$64) for two. Prices include snorkel and dive gear, and lunch. Wet suits, which you will want between June and August this far south, are also available for rent. The boat departs Monday, Thursday, Saturday and Sunday, from Port Bundaberg, a 20-minute drive from the city. The vessel leaves the jetty at 8am and returns to shore at about 5:45pm. Transfers to the jetty from town are available for an extra A$10 (US$8) per person, round-trip.

One of the cheapest and best ways to dive in Bundaberg is to walk in to **Woongarra Marine Park** right off the shore. **Hoffman's Rocks** and **Barolin Rocks** are two of the best sites, both about a 20-minute drive due east of town, south of Mon Repos beach. **Salty's Dive Centre** (see below) will rent you dive gear for A$45 (US$36) per day, and will even give you a lift down to the beach. The company also runs **day trips** to Cochrane artificial reef for A$100 (US$80) including all gear.

LIVE-ABOARD EXCURSIONS

Salty's Dive Centre (✆ **1800/625 476** in Australia, or 07/4151 6422; www.saltys.net) runs a 3-day, 3-night excursion to the **Bunker** group. The boat spends the first day diving Lady Musgrave Island, then heads north over the following 2 days to dive rarely visited reefs and islands such as **Fairfax and Hoskyn. Manta Ray Bommie, Coral Canyon** and **The Entrance Bommie** are among the sites you'll dive at. The trips depart every Tuesday and Friday at 9pm. The cost is A$495 (US$396), including up to 10 dives and all meals, plus A$65 (US$52) for gear rental. A double cabin is available for A$595 (US$476). Night dives are included in the price. You travel in the 22m (72-ft.) *Venus II,* which has been refitted and has 4 air-conditioned quad-, triple-, or twin-share cabins, all with en suite bathrooms. There's room for sunbathing on the little upstairs deck, and the crew are friendly and well-organized.

LEARNING TO DIVE

Salty's Dive Centre is one of the longest-established dive centers in Bundaberg. It does 5-day open-water certification courses, which incorporate the 3-day trip to the Bunker group (see "Live-Aboard Excursions," above) into the final 3 days. These cost A$580 (US$464). Already certified divers can obtain Advanced certification during the trip for an extra A$85 (US$68). A 4-day shore-based course featuring 2 days of shore diving is just A$169 (US$135), though, of course, you'll have to budget for accommodations. The learn-to-dive courses start every Monday and Thursday. Salty's also does dive master and instructor courses, and specialty diver courses.

USEFUL DIVE-RELATED BUSINESSES

Salty's store at 208 Bourbong St. (see above) is the biggest dive outfit in town. It rents, sells, and services dive gear.

WHERE TO STAY

Acacia Motor Inn This tidy motel is a short stroll from the town center. It has undergone a complete refit inside and out two years ago, with new furniture, carpets and TVs, as well as a repaint and the addition of shade sails around the pool area. The rooms are clean and well-kept, extra-large family rooms at a decent price. Local restaurants provide room service, and many are within walking distance. The five family units have kitchenettes.

248 Bourbong St., Bundaberg, QLD 4670. ℂ **1800/351 735** in Australia, or 07/4152 3411. Fax 07/4152 2387. acabund@fc-hotels.com.au. 26 units (all with shower only). A$72 (US$58) double. Additional person A$11 (US$8.80) adults, A$6 (US$4.80) children under 12. A$5 (US$4) crib. AE, DC, MC, V. Covered parking. **Amenities:** Outdoor saltwater pool; nearby golf course; access to nearby health club; bike rental; tour desk; limited room service; in-room massage; coin-op laundry; same-day dry cleaning; nonsmoking rooms. *In room:* A/C, TV/VCR w/pay movies, dataport, minibar, coffeemaker, hair dryer, iron.

6 Lady Elliot Island

80km (50 miles) NE of Bundaberg

The southernmost Great Barrier Reef island, Lady Elliot is a 42-hectare (104-acre) coral cay ringed by a wide shallow lagoon filled with dazzling coral life.

Reef walking, snorkeling, and diving are the main reasons people come to this coral cay that's so small you can walk across it in 15 minutes. You may snorkel and reef-walk only during the 2 to 3 hours before and after high tide, so plan your schedule accordingly. You will see dazzling corals and brilliantly colored fish, clams, sponges, urchins, and anemones. Divers will see a good range of marine life, including green and loggerhead turtles (which nest on the beach Nov–Mar). The island is renowned for its giant **manta rays** up to 4m (13 ft.) across—they sometimes pop up right next to divers unexpectedly. Whales pass by June through September.

Lady Elliot Island is a sparse, grassy island rookery, not a lush tropical paradise, so don't expect white sand and palm trees. Some people will find it too spartan; others will relish chilling out in a beautiful, peaceful location with reef all around. Just be prepared for the smell and constant noise of those birds.

GETTING THERE   You reach the island by a 30-minute flight from Bundaberg or Hervey Bay. Book your air travel along with your accommodations. Round-trip fares are A$175 (US$140) for adults and A$88 (US$70) for children 3 to 12. There is a 10-kilogram (22-lb.) luggage limit. **Seair Pacific** (✆ **07/5599 4509;** www.seairpacific.com.au) operates day tours from Brisbane and the Gold Coast for A$599 (US$479) or from the Sunshine Coast for A$449 (US$359), which include flights, snorkel gear, glass-bottom-boat ride, lunch, and guided activities. Day trips from Hervey Bay and Bundaberg cost A$219 (US$175) adults and A$110 (US$88) kids aged 3 to 12.

Tips Heads Up!

When you land on the grass airstrip at Lady Elliot Island during nesting season, you'll think you're on the set of Hitchcock's *The Birds*. The air is thick with thousands of swirling noddy terns and bridal terns that nest in every available branch and leave their mark on every available surface, including you (so bring a big cheap straw hat for protection).

WHERE TO STAY

Lady Elliot Island Resort ℛ   Accommodations here are fairly basic, but visitors come for the reef, not the room. Top of the range are the Island Suites, which have one or two separate bedrooms, and great sea views from the deck. Most Reef rooms have a double bed and two bunks, and a deck with views through the trees to the sea. Shearwater bunk rooms sleep up to six, and all room types have modern private bathrooms. The cool, spacious tent cabins have four bunks, electric lighting, and timber floors, but share the public toilets and showers used by day guests. All accommodations have fans. The limited facilities include a boutique, a dive shop, and an education center. There is no air-conditioning, no keys (secure storage is at front desk), no TVs, no radio, and one public telephone. The food is basic. A low-key program of mostly free activities is run, including glass-bottom boat rides, badminton, guided walks, and beach volleyball, and because of the relatively low number of guests, you pretty much get the reef to yourself.

Divers have six major sites to choose from. Visibility is often beyond 20m (65 ft.). Guided shore and boat dives are available (A$51/US$41 and A$62/US$50 respectively), as well as night dives (A$82/US$66) for certified divers. Introductory dives cost A$121 (US$97). The dive shop also runs open-water certification, Advanced, and Rescue courses.

Great Barrier Reef via Bundaberg. (P.O. Box 206, Torquay, QLD 4655). ℭ **1800/072 200** in Australia, or 07/5536 3644. Fax 07/5536 7285. www.ladyelliot.com.au. 40 units, 20 with bathroom (shower only). A$290 (US$232) double for tent cabins; A$330 (US$264) double for Shearwater bunk rooms; A$390 (US$312) double for Reef units; A$450 (US$360) double for 1 bedroom or A$480 (US$384) double for 2-bedroom Island Suites. A$75 (US$60) extra child 3–12. Minimum 3-night stay Dec 24–Jan 5. Ask about 2-, 4-, 5-, and 7-night packages, and dive packages. Rates include breakfast and dinner. AE, DC, MC, V. **Amenities:** Cafe/bistro and dining room; saltwater pool; children's program for children 3–12 (on Queensland school holidays only). *In room:* Ceiling or wall fans, no phone.

8

Fraser Island & The Sunshine Coast

North of Brisbane lies the aptly named **Sunshine Coast**—more white sandy beaches, crystal-clear waters, and rolling mountains dotted with villages. It lies outside the Great Barrier Reef Marine Park, but offers similar opportunities for outdoor adventures and chances to see native wildlife.

Don't miss the wild beauty of the largest sand island in the world, World Heritage–listed **Fraser Island.** Each year from August to October, humpback whales frolic in the sheltered waters between Fraser Island and Hervey Bay—if you're in the area you won't want to miss out on the opportunity of experiencing the whales firsthand.

1 Fraser Island: Eco-Adventures & Four-Wheel-Drive Fun

1,547km (959 miles) S of Cairns; 260km (161 miles) N of Brisbane; 15km (9¼ miles) E of Hervey Bay

The biggest sand island in the world, this 162,000-hectare (400,140-acre) World Heritage–listed island off the central Queensland coast attracts a mix of ecotourists and Aussie fishermen. Fraser is a pristine vista of eucalyptus woodlands, dunes, clear creeks, ancient rainforest, blue lakes, ochre-colored sand cliffs, and a stunning 121km (75-mile) long beach. For four-wheel-drive fans though, Fraser's true beauty lies in its complete absence of paved roads. On weekends when the fish are running, it's nothing to see 100 four-wheel-drives lining 75-Mile Beach, which is an authorized road. Pedestrians should beware!

You'll need more than a day here to see everything and to truly appreciate how stunning this place is. Allow at least 3 days to soak it all up, and to allow for the slow pace dictated by the sandy trails that call themselves roads.

ESSENTIALS

GETTING THERE Hervey (pronounced "Harvey") Bay is the main gateway to the island. Take the Bruce Highway to Maryborough, then the 34km (21-mile) road to Hervey Bay. If approaching from the north, turn off the highway at Torbanlea, north of Maryborough, and cut across to Hervey Bay. Allow 3 hours from the Sunshine Coast, a good 5 hours from Brisbane.

Guests at Kingfisher Bay Resort (p. 180) can get to the resort aboard the Kingfisher Bay Fastcat, which departs Urangan Boat Harbour at Hervey Bay at 8:30am, noon, 4pm, 6:30pm (7pm Fri–Sat) and 10pm. Round-trip fare for the 40-minute crossing is A$44 (US$35) adults and A$22 (US$18) kids 4 to 14. The resort runs a courtesy shuttle from Hervey Bay's airport and coach terminal to the harbor. You can park free in the open at the Fastcat terminal. Drive to the terminal first to unload your luggage at the Kingfisher Bay reception desk, then return to the parking lot and walk back (only 100m/328 ft.). **Fraser Coast Secure Vehicle Storage,** at 629 The Esplanade (© **07/4125 2783**), a 5-minute walk from the terminal, has covered parking for less than A$10 (US$8) per 24 hours.

Both **McCafferty's** (© **13 14 99** in Australia) and **Greyhound Pioneer** (© **13 20 30** in Australia) coaches stop several times a day in Hervey Bay on their Brisbane-Cairns-Brisbane routes. The 5-hour trip from Brisbane costs A$34 (US$27). From Cairns, the fare is A$180 (US$144) for an almost 24-hour trip.

The nearest train station is in **Maryborough West,** 34km (20 miles) from Hervey Bay. Passengers on the high-speed **Tilt Train** (Sun–Fri) can book a connecting bus service to Pialba via **Queensland Rail** (© **13 22 32** in Queensland, or 07/3235 1122). The fare from Brisbane for the 3½-hour Tilt Train trip is A$52 (US$42) economy class and A$78 (US$62) business class, plus nominal bus connection fare. Fares are A$175 (US$140) in a seat and A$334 (US$267) in a first-class sleeper from Cairns (trip time: about 27 hr.). Train passengers from the north take a courtesy shuttle to Maryborough Central, then the next available local bus to Pialba.

GETTING THERE & AROUND BY FOUR-WHEEL-DRIVE 🐾
Four-wheel-drives are the only permissible mode of vehicle transportation on the island. Many four-wheel-drive-rental outfits are based in Hervey Bay. You must be 21 or over to rent a 4WD. You'll pay about A$110 and A$195 (US$88–US$156) a day, plus around A$20 to A$35 (US$16–US$28) per day to reduce the deductible, which is usually A$4,000 (US$3,200), plus a bond (typically A$500/

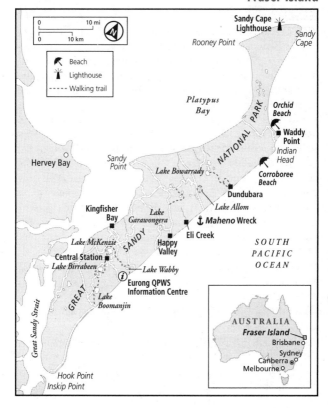

US\$400). You must also buy a government Vehicle Access Permit, which costs A\$30 (US\$24) from your rental-car company, Urangan Boat Harbour, or the River Heads boat ramp; or A\$40 (US\$32) from a Queensland Parks and Wildlife Service office on the island. Both **Bay 4WD Centre** (✆ 07/4128 2981; www.bay4wd.com.au) and **Ausbay 4WD Rentals** (✆ 1800/679 479 in Australia or 07/4124 6177) rent four-wheel-drives; offer camping and accommodated four-wheel-drive packages; rent camping gear; organize Vehicle Access Permits, barge bookings, camping permits, and secure storage for your car; and pick you up free from the airport, coach terminal, or your hotel. **Kingfisher Bay 4WD Hire** (✆ 07/4120 3366; www.kingfisher-bay-4wdhire.com.au) within Kingfisher Bay Resort (see below) rents four-wheel-drives for A\$195 (US\$156) a day, plus a A\$30 (US\$24) Fraser Island driving permit and a A\$2,000

(US$1,600) security deposit (by credit card) held until return of the vehicle in the same condition as hired. They allow 1-day rentals. Book well in advance.

Four-wheel-drives transfer by **Fraser Venture** barge (✆ **07/4125 4444**), which runs three times a day (four times on Saturdays) from River Heads, 17km (11 miles) south of Urangan Boat Harbour. The round-trip fare for vehicle and up to 4 occupants is A$115 (US$92), plus A$6 (US$4.80) per extra passenger. Kingfisher Bay Resort (see below) also runs a barge from River Heads, costing A$110 (US$88) round-trip for the vehicle and four passengers, A$6 (US$4.80) per extra passenger. It is a good idea to book a place for the 45-minute crossing.

Fraser Island Taxi Service (✆ **07/4127 9188**) is another option for getting around, and they use 4WDs, of course. It's based at Eurong on the island's eastern side. A typical fare, from Kingfisher Bay Resort across the island to go fishing on 75-Mile Beach, for example, is A$65 (US$52). The taxi seats five.

VISITOR INFORMATION   Contact the **Hervey Bay Tourism Bureau,** Urraween Road at Maryborough-Hervey Bay road, Pialba (P.O. Box 8, Hervey Bay, QLD 4655; ✆ **1800/811 728** in Australia, or 07/4124 2912; www.herveybaytourism.com.au). A better source for Web-connected travelers is www.hervey.com.au. The **Marina Kiosk** (✆ **07/4128 9800**) at Urangan Boat Harbour is a one-stop booking and information agency for all Fraser-related travel. Several Queensland Parks and Wildlife Service information offices are on the island.

There are no towns and very few facilities, food stores, or services on the island, so if you're camping, take all supplies with you.

ECO-EXPLORING THE ISLAND

Fraser's turquoise lakes and tea-colored "perched" lakes in the dunes are among the island's biggest attractions. The brilliant blue **Lake McKenzie** is beautiful; a swim here may be the highlight of your visit. Lake Birrabeen is another popular swimming spot. Don't miss a refreshing swim in the fast-flowing clear shallows of **Eli Creek.** Wade up the creek for a mile or two and let the current carry you back down. You should also take the boardwalk through a verdant forest of palms and ferns along the banks of Wanggoolba Creek.

The **Fraser Island Great Walk** (✆ **07/5459 6114;** www.epa. qld.gov.au) follows a continuous winding track from Dilli Village to Lake Garawongera. The main trail is 85km (53-mile) long and takes 6 to 8 days to complete, but there are offshoots that provide short, full day, overnight, and 2- to 3-day walks. The walk takes you to many of the island's landmarks such as Lake McKenzie, Central Station, Wanggoolba Creek, Valley of the Giants, and Lake Wabby.

Don't swim at **75-Mile Beach,** which hugs the eastern edge of the island—there are dangerously strong currents and a healthy shark population. Instead, swim in the **Champagne Pools** (also called the Aquarium)—pockets of soft sand protected from the worst of the waves by rocks. The bubbling seawater turns the pools into miniature spas. The pools are just north of **Indian Head,** a 60m (197-ft.) rocky outcrop at the northern end of the beach.

View the island's colored sand in its natural setting—the 70m (230-ft.) cliffs called **the Cathedrals,** which stretch for miles north of the settlement of Happy Valley on the eastern side of the Island.

Some of Queensland's best fishing is on Fraser Island. Anglers can throw a line in the surf gutters off the beach. (Freshwater fishing is not allowed.) Bream, whiting, flathead, and swallowtail are the beach catches. Indian Head is good for rock species and tailor; and the waters east off **Waddy Point** yield northern and southern reef fish. **Kingfisher Bay Resort** (see below) offers free fish clinics, rents tackle, and organizes half-day fishing jaunts.

August through October, tour boats crowd the straits to see humpback whales returning to Antarctica with calves in tow. Kingfisher Bay Resort runs a whale-watching cruise from Urangan Harbour.

WHERE TO STAY

Fraser Island Retreat ⟨ (Finds) This is the wild side of Fraser Island, just minutes from 75-Mile Beach. Don't come expecting a luxury resort, but one that has comfortable timber cottages and all the amenities you need. There's a small swimming pool, surrounded by a deck and deck chairs, and each cottage has a small veranda. The rooms all have fans, limited cooking facilities, and a VCR. (You can rent videos.) The bar/bistro is open for all meals, but be warned that day-tour buses stop here for lunch so it can be crowded at that time. If you want to cook for yourself, there's a general store selling food and liquor. The store also has fuel, ice, and gas for campers. You can also hire a four-wheel-drive from the resort. There's a public phone to use. The only access is by plane (**Air Fraser Island,** ℂ **07/4125 3600**) or bus. **Fraser Island Tours** (ℂ **07/4125 3933**) will transfer guests to the resort from Hervey Bay and also runs day tours of the island for A$99 (US$79) adults and A$55 (US$44) children 4 to 14.

Happy Valley, Fraser Island, QLD 4650. (C) 07/4127 9144. Fax 07/4127 9131. www. fraserislandco.com.au. 9 units (all with shower only). A$125–A$160 (US$100– US$128) 1-bedroom lodge (sleeps 3); A$160–A$200 (US$128–US$160) family lodge (sleeps 5). Ask about package deals. AE, MC, V. **Amenities:** Restaurant (Bistro); bar; outdoor pool; tour desk; car-rental desk; babysitting; coin-op laundry. *In room:* TV/VCR, kitchenette, small fridge, no phone.

Kingfisher Bay Resort 🐾🐾 *Kids*   This sleek, environment-friendly eco-resort lies low along Fraser's west coast. Hotel guest rooms are smart and contemporary, with a Japanese-style screen opening onto a balcony looking into the bush, but my pick is the two- and three-bedroom villas just a short walk from the main resort area and pools. The hillside villas, which have Jacuzzis on their balconies, are fairly luxurious, but there's that long haul up the hill to contend with. An impressive lineup of eco-educational activities includes daily four-wheel-drive tours with a ranger to points of interest around the island, free guided walks daily, and an excellent free Junior Eco-Ranger program on weekends and school vacations. You can also join bird-watching tours, guided canoe trips, sunset champagne sails, and dolphin and dugong (manatee) spotting cruises. Wildlife videos play continuously in the lobby, and the on-site ranger office lists the animals and plants you are most likely to spot.

Fraser Island (PMB 1, Urangan, QLD 4655). (C) **1800/072 555** in Australia, or 07/ 4120 3333. Fax 07/4120 3326. www.kingfisherbay.com. 262 units. A$270 (US$216) double for hotel rooms; A$816–A$1,080 (US$653–US$864) 3 nights in 2-bedroom villa (sleeps 5); A$969–A$1,260 (US$775–US$1,008) 3 nights in 3-bedroom villa (sleeps 6); minimum 3-night stay in villas. Additional person A$22 (US$18). Free crib. Ask about package deals. AE, DC, MC, V. **Amenities:** 3 restaurants (bush tucker, modern Australian, buffet); 4 bars; 4 outdoor saltwater pools (heated main pool has water slide for the kids); day/night tennis courts; Jacuzzi; watersports equipment and fishing tackle for hire; kids' club; game room; tour desk, babysitting. *In room:* A/C (hotel rooms only), TV, kitchen (villas only), fridge, coffeemaker, hair dryer, iron, washing machine and dryer (villas only).

2 The Sunshine Coast

Warm weather, miles of pleasant beaches, trendy restaurants; and a relaxed lifestyle attract Aussies to the Sunshine Coast in droves. Despite some rather unsightly commercial development in recent years, the Sunshine Coast is still a great spot if you like lazing on sandy beaches and enjoying a good meal.

The Sunshine Coast starts at **Caloundra,** 83km (51 miles) north of Brisbane and runs all the way to **Rainbow Beach,** 40km (25 miles) north of **Noosa Heads** 🐾, where the fashionable crowd goes.

The Sunshine Coast

Australia Zoo **3**
Big Pineapple **1**
Underwater World **2**

Information (i)
Lighthouse 🗼

Inskip Point

Tin Can Bay

Rainbow Beach

Tin Can Bay

AUSTRALIA
Area of Detail
Sydney
Canberra

Great Sandy National Park

Teewah Coloured Sands

Forty Mile Beach

Wolvi

Bruce Highway

Mary River

4WD

Kinaba Information Centre (i)
Lake Cootharaba

Noosa River

Laguna Bay

Noosa Heads
Noosa National Park

Tewantin
Noosaville
Sunshine Beach

Cooroy

Eumundi

Mary River

Coolum

Yandina

Sunshine Coast Motorway

Mapleton Falls National Park
Nambour (i)

Sunshine Coast Airport
Mudjimba

Obi Obi Creek
BLACKALL RANGE

Mapleton
Flaxton
Blackall Ranges Tourist Drive 23
1 Woombye
Maroochydore (i)
Mooloolaba **2**

Conondale National Park

Kondalilla Falls National Park

Montville

Buderim

JIMNA RANGE

CONONDALE RANGE

Blackall Ranges Tourist Drive 23

Maleny

Landsborough

(i) Caloundra

0   10 mi
0   10 km

Glass House Mountains

Beerwah **3**

Bruce Highway

Bribie Island

There's a wide range of accommodations, from inexpensive motels and holiday apartments to five-star hotels and resorts.

SUNSHINE COAST ESSENTIALS

GETTING THERE   If you're driving from Brisbane, take the Bruce Highway north to Aussie World theme park at Palmview, then exit onto the Sunshine Motorway to Mooloolaba, Maroochydore, or Noosa Heads. The trip takes about 2 hours.

QantasLink (© **13 13 13** in Australia) has two or three flights daily (trip time: 30 min.) from Sydney and Melbourne to the Sunshine Coast Airport in Maroochydore, 42km (26 miles) south of Noosa Heads. **Virgin Blue** (© **13 67 89** in Australia) and **Jetstar** (© **13 15 38** in Australia) both also fly from Melbourne and Sydney. **Henry's Airport Bus Service** (© **07/5474 0199**) meets all flights; door-to-door transfers to Noosa Heads are A$18 (US$14) for adults and A$10 (US$8) for kids 4 to 14, one-way. Bookings are not necessary for arrival pickups but should be made for transfers back to the airport about 24 hours ahead.

The nearest train station to Noosa Heads is in **Cooroy,** 25km (16 miles) away, to which **Queensland Rail** (© **13 22 32** in Queensland, or 07/3235 1122) operates two daily services from Brisbane on its **CityTrain** (© **07/3235 5555**) network. The trip takes about 2½ hours and the fare is A$18 (US$14) including bus connection to Noosa Heads. Queensland Rail's long-distance trains departing Brisbane pick up but do not drop off passengers in Cooroy, with the exception of the high-speed **Tilt Train** (which runs Sun–Fri). The fare is A$28 (US$22). *The Sunlander* makes several trips from Cairns each week; the fare is A$183 (US$146) for a seat, A$345 (US$276) for a first-class sleeper. Local bus company **Sunbus** (© **13 12 30** or 07/5450 7888) meets most trains at Cooroy station and travels to Noosa Heads; take bus no. 12.

Several coach companies have service to Noosa Heads from Brisbane, including **Sun-air** (© **1800/804 340** in Australia, or 07/5478 2811) and **Suncoast Pacific** (© **07/5443 1011** on the Sunshine Coast, or 07/3236 1901 in Brisbane). **McCafferty's** (© **13 14 99** in Australia) and **Greyhound Pioneer** (© **13 20 30** in Australia) have many daily services from all major towns along the Bruce Highway between Brisbane and Cairns. Trip time to Noosa Heads is 2 hours and 35 minutes from Brisbane, and just over 27 hours from Cairns. The single fare is A$19 (US$15) from Brisbane and A$187 (US$150) from Cairns.

VISITOR INFORMATION   Write to **Tourism Sunshine Coast Ltd,** P.O. Box 264, Mooloolaba, QLD 4557 (℗ **07/5477 7311;** fax 07/5477 7322; www.sunshinecoast.org) for information. In Noosa, drop into the **Noosa Tourist Information Centre** (℗ **07/5447 4988;** fax 07/5474 9494) at the eastern roundabout on Hastings Street where it intersects Noosa Drive. It's open daily from 9am to 5pm. Other tourist information centers are: **Maroochy Tourism** at Sunshine Coast Airport (℗ **07/5448 9288**) or at Sixth Avenue and Aerodrome Rd., Maroochydore, (℗ **07/5479 1566**); and **Caloundra Visitor Information Centre,** 7 Caloundra Rd., Caloundra (℗ **07/5491 9233**).

GETTING AROUND   Major car-rental companies on the Sunshine Coast are **Avis** (℗ **07/5443 5055** Sunshine Coast Airport, or 07/5447 4933 Noosa Heads), **Budget** (℗ **07/5448 7455** airport, or 07/5474 2820 Noosa Heads), **Hertz** (℗ **07/5448 9731** airport or 07/5447 2253 Noosa Heads), and **Thrifty** (℗ **07/5451 8426** airport, or 07/5447 2299 Noosa Heads). Many local companies rent cars and four-wheel-drives, including **Trusty** (℗ **07/ 5491 2444**).

The local bus company is **Sunbus** (℗ **07/5450 7888,** or 13 12 30 in Australia).

EXPLORING THE AREA

HITTING THE BEACH & OTHER OUTDOOR FUN   Main Beach, Noosa Heads, is the place to swim, surf, and sunbathe. If the bikini-clad super-model look-alikes are too much for you, head to Sunshine Beach, just behind Noosa Junction off the David Low Way, about 2km (1¼ miles) from Noosa Heads. It's just as beautiful. Both beaches are patrolled 365 days a year.

Learn to surf with two-time Australian and World Pro-Am champion **Merrick Davis** (℗ **0418/787 577** mobile phone; www.learn tosurf.com.au), who's lived in Noosa for about 10 years. Merrick and his team run 2-hour lessons on Main Beach daily for A$40 (US$32), 3-day certificate courses for A$110 (US$88), and 5-day courses for A$150 (US$120). They will pick you up and drop you off at your accommodations, and also rent surfboards, body boards, and sea kayaks.

If you want to rent a Windsurfer, canoe, kayak, surf ski, catamaran, jet ski, or fishing boat that you can play with on the Noosa River, or take upriver into Great Sandy National Park (see below), check out the dozens of outfits along Gympie Terrace between James Street and Robert Street in Noosaville.

The **Aussie Sea Kayak Company** (© 07/5477 5335; www.aussea kayak.com.au), at The Wharf, Mooloolaba, runs a 2-hour sunset paddle on the Maroochy River every day for A$45 (US$36)—including a glass of champagne on your return as reward for all the hard work! Half-day tours run every day for 3 to 4 hours at Mooloolaba (A$65/ US$52), day tours for 6 hours, Tuesday, Friday, and Saturday at Noosa (A$110/US$88). The company also runs overnight adventures to Moreton and North Stradbroke Islands, and to Fraser Island and the Whitsundays for up to 6 days.

EXPLORING NOOSA NATIONAL PARK   A 10-minute stroll northeast from Hastings Street brings you to the 432-hectare (1,067-acre) **Noosa National Park.** Anywhere you see a crowd looking upwards, you're sure to spot a koala. They're often seen in the unlikely setting of the car park at the entrance to the park. A network of well-signposted walking trails leads through the bush. The most scenic is the 2.7km (1½-mile) coastal trail. The shortest trail is the 1km (just over ½-mile) Palm Grove circuit; the longest is the 4.8km (3-mile) Tanglewood trail inland to Hell's Gates—definitely worth the effort.

GREAT SANDY NATIONAL PARK   Stretching north of Noosa along the coast is the 56,000-hectare (138,320-acre) Great Sandy National Park (often called Cooloola National Park), home to forests, beach, and freshwater lakes, including the state's largest, Lake Cootharaba. A popular thing to do is cruise the Everglades formed by the Noosa River and tributary creeks. The park's information office, the **Sir Thomas Hiley Information Centre** (© 07/5449 7364; daily 9am–3pm), is on the western shore of Lake Cootharaba, about 30km (19 miles) from Noosaville. It has a display on the area's geography and a mangrove boardwalk to explore; it's accessible only by boat, which you can rent from the numerous boat-rental outfits in Noosaville. There are several half-day cruises into the Everglades, and guided kayak tours explore the park's lower reaches.

The other option is to take a four-wheel-drive along 40-Mile Beach, a designated highway with traffic laws, for a close-up view of the Teewah colored sand cliffs. This is a great place to get away from the crowds and enjoy nature's wonders. Lifeguards do not patrol the beach, so do not swim alone, and take care. Tours are available, or you can rent a four-wheel-drive and explore on your own. To reach the beach, cross Noosa River on the ferry at Tewantin, then take Maximilian Drive for 4km (2½ miles) to the beach. Stock up on water, food, and gas in Tewantin. The ferry (© 07/5447 1321) costs A$10 (US$8) per vehicle round-trip; it operates from 5:30am to 10:15pm Sunday through Thursday, and 5:30am to midnight Friday and Saturday.

WILDLIFE PARKS & THEME PARKS Small theme parks seem to thrive on the Sunshine Coast. Don't expect thrill rides, but you might find some of them a pleasant way to spend a few hours.

A transparent tunnel with an 80m (262-ft.) moving walkway that takes you through a tank filled with sharks, stingrays, groupers, eels, and coral is the highlight at **Underwater World** (℗ 07/5444 8488; www.underwaterworld.com.au), at The Wharf, Mooloolaba. Kids can pick up starfish and sea cucumbers in the touch pool, and there are displays on whales and sharks, shark breeding, freshwater crocodile talks, an otter enclosure, and a 30-minute seal show. You can also swim with the seals (A$75/US$60), or dive with the sharks (A$125/US$100 for certified divers, including gear, or A$145/US$116 for non-divers). It's open daily from 9am to 6pm (last entry at 5pm). Closed Christmas. Admission is A$23 (US$18) for adults, A$15 (US$12) for seniors, A$16 (US$13) for students, A$13 (US$10) for children 3 to 15, and A$59 (US$47) for a family of five. Allow 2 hours to see everything, more if you attend all the talks.

At the **Big Pineapple** (℗ 07/5442 1333; www.bigpineapple.com. au), 6km (3¾ miles) south of Nambour on the Nambour Connection Road in Woombye—don't worry, you can't miss the 16m (52-ft.) tall monument—you can take a train ride through a working pineapple plantation, ride through a rainforest and a macadamia farm in a macadamia-shaped carriage, and take a boat ride through a hydroponics greenhouse. The park also has a baby animal farm, kangaroos, koalas, a rainforest walk, a small but excellent nocturnal house called "Creatures of the Night," and a gift shop. It's open 365 days a year from 9am to 5pm (opens later on Christmas and Anzac Day; call for exact time). Entry is free; each tour is priced separately so you can do all or just one, but the best option is to buy a family pass to all tours, which costs A$75 (US$60) for two adults and up to four children aged 4 to 14. Allow half a day if you do everything.

Farther south on Glass House Mountains Tourist Drive 24 at Beerwah, off the Bruce Highway, is crocodile hunter Steve Irwin's **Australia Zoo** (℗ 07/5436 2000; www.crocodilehunter.com). Steve and his wife, Terri, stars of the *Crocodile Hunter* television shows, are renowned for handling dangerous saltwater crocs and are often around to say hello. The zoo is in the process of a A$40 million (US$32 million) upgrade, which will expand it from 20 hectares

(50 acres) to 100 hectares (251 acres) in the next 5 years. Look for new themed sections displaying animals from around the world including Madagascar, South East Asia, Africa, the Americas, and Asia. Demonstrations and feedings are held regularly throughout the day, but the highlight is the saltwater croc show at 1:30pm. You can also hand-feed 'roos, pat a koala, check out foxes and camels, and watch (even hold!) venomous snakes and pythons. Admission is A$23 (US$18) for adults, A$19 (US$15) for seniors and students, A$14 (US$11) for kids 3 to 14, and A$65 (US$52) for a family of five. The park is open daily from 8:30am to 4pm. Closed Christmas. Courtesy buses pick you up and return you to Beerwah and Landsborough railway stations or from Noosa, Maroochydore, Alexandra Headlands, Mooloolaba, and Caloundra.

WHERE TO STAY
EXPENSIVE

Hyatt Regency Coolum 🐨🐨 A couple of hours under the expert care of the therapists at the **Sun Spa** and you'll feel years younger! This is one of the reasons the well-heeled flock to this sprawling bushland resort. The other is its 18-hole Robert Trent Jones, Jr.–designed golf course. The Sun Spa (there are entrance fees of around A$13/US$10 a day as well as the cost of treatments) does everything from aromatherapy baths to triglyceride checks (130 treatments in all) and has massage rooms, aqua-aerobics, yoga, a 25 meter (82 ft.) lap pool, and much more. An almost-6-hour body detox costs A$400 (US$320), but you can get a mini-facial or a half-hour massage for A$60 (US$48). Australian Golf Digest rated the golf course as one of Australia's top five resort courses in 2000. Golf widows and widowers can play tennis; take the twice-daily free shuttle into Noosa to shop; and surf at the resort's private beach. A nightly shuttle runs to Noosa Heads restaurants for A$15 (US$12) per person, round-trip.

So spread out are the low-rise accommodations that guests rent a bike to get around, wait 15 minutes for the two free resort shuttles (frustrating when you're in a hurry!), or get into the healthy swing of things and walk. Accommodations all sport contemporary decor and come as "suites" (a single room divided into living and sleeping quarters); two-bedroom President's Villas with a kitchenette; villas within the Ambassador Club, which has its own concierge, pool, tennis court, and lounge; and two-story, three-bedroom Ambassador Club residences boasting rooftop terraces with a Jacuzzi.

The **Village Square** is just that: a cluster of shops, restaurants, bars, and takeout joints that provides the heart of the resort.

Warran Rd., off David Low Way (approx. 2km/1¼ miles south of town), Coolum Beach, QLD 4573. ℭ **1800 266 586** in Australia, 800/633-7313 in the U.S. and Canada, 0845/758 1666 in the U.K. or 020/8335 1220 in London, 0800/44 1234 in New Zealand, or 07/5446 1234. Fax 07/5446 2957. www.coolum.regency.hyatt.com. 323 units (some with Jacuzzis). A$220–$395 (US$176–$316) double; A$320–$1,400 (US$256–$1,120) villa; A$1,030–$2,200 (US$824–$1,760) Ambassadors residence. Rates include continental breakfast. Extra person A$45 (US$36). Children under 13 stay free in parents' room using existing bedding. Ask about golf, spa, and other packages. AE, MC, V. Valet parking A$18 (US$14) or self-parking. Resort shuttle meets all flights at Sunshine Coast Airport for A$18 (US$14) per person, one-way. Town car transfers from Brisbane Airport A$79 (US$63) per person, one-way (shared service with other guests); limousine transfers available. **Amenities:** 4 restaurants; 3 bars; 9 outdoor pools (main pool and lap pool are heated); golf course; 9 night/day tennis courts; health club and spa; watersports equipment rental; bike rental; children's programs daily for kids 6 weeks to 12 yr. old (for a fee); concierge; tour desk; car-rental desk; business center; shopping arcade; limited room service; massage; babysitting; same-day dry cleaning; nonsmoking rooms; executive rooms. *In room:* A/C, TV w/pay movies, fax, dataport, kitchenette, stocked minibar, coffeemaker, hair dryer, iron, safe.

Sheraton Noosa Resort & Spa 𝕬𝕬𝕬 Another great place to enjoy a day spa by the sea is at Noosa's first AAA-rated five-star resort. Right in the heart of Hastings Street, the Sheraton has a prime spot among the chic boutiques and restaurants. There are several different styles of rooms, but the best in my book are those with views away from the beach but looking right down the Noosa River to the mountains. Sit on the balcony at sunset and drink it in. All the rooms are extra-large, and all have Jacuzzis. You'll pay more for the two-level poolside villas, which have private access to the pool area, but there's no view. Some rooms have ocean (but not beach) views. The **Aqua Day Spa** has a Roman-bathhouse feel to it and offers a wide range of treatments in its seven treatment rooms. The hotel restaurant, **Cato's**—named for Australian novelist Nancy Cato, who lived in Noosa until her death a few years ago—fronts onto Hastings Street and is a great place to watch the world go by.

Hastings St., Noosa Heads, QLD 4567. ℭ **1800/073 535** in Australia, 888/625-5144 in the U.S., or 07/5449 4888. Fax 07/5449 2230. www.sheraton.com. 169 units. A$280–A$530 (US$224–US$424) double low season; A$535–A$650 (US$424–US$520) double high season (Dec 25–Jan 4). Secure covered parking and valet parking. **Amenities:** Restaurant (brasserie); 2 bars; outdoor heated pool; health club and sauna; spa; Jacuzzi; game room; concierge; tour desk; limited room service; massage (poolside and in-room); babysitting; laundry/dry cleaning service or use of free guest laundry. *In room:* A/C, TV w/free and pay-per-view movies, kitchenette with microwave, minibar, fridge, coffeemaker, hair dryer, iron, safe.

MODERATE

Noosa Village Motel *(Value)* All the letters from satisfied guests pinned up on the wall here are a testament to owners John and Mary Skelton's hard work in continually sprucing up this clean, bright little motel in the heart of Hastings Street. The pleasant rooms are spacious and freshly painted, with a cheerful atmosphere. There's no air-conditioning, but the rooms all have ceiling fans. And at these rates, it's one of Hastings Street's best values.

10 Hastings St., Noosa Heads, QLD 4567. ℂ **07/5447 5800.** Fax 07/5474 9282. http://www.austourism.com.au/nvc/resort/noosavillagemotel.html. 11 units (9 with shower only). High season (Dec 24–Jan 14) A$195 (US$156) double, A$260 (US$208) family suite; low season A$110–A$120 (US$88–US$96) double, A$165 (US$132) family suite. Additional person A$10–A$15 (US$8–US$12). Ask about May/June specials. MC, V. Free parking. **Amenities:** Bike rental; tour desk; car-rental desk; room-service breakfast; babysitting; coin-op laundry; nonsmoking rooms. *In room:* TV, kitchenette, fridge, hair dryer.

WHERE TO DINE

Noosa's Hastings Street comes alive at night with vacationers wining and dining at restaurants as sophisticated as those in Sydney and Melbourne. Just stroll along and see what appeals to you—but you will need reservations during high seasons. For a great breakfast try **Café Le Monde** at the southern end of Hastings Street (opposite the back of the Surf Club), or **Bistro C,** one of the few restaurants that still has beachfront dining. Noosa Junction is a less attractive place to eat, but the prices are cheaper. There are about 90 restaurants at Mooloolaba to choose from.

Ricky Ricardo's *(R)* MODERN AUSTRALIAN Owners Leonie Palmer and Steven "Stef" Fisher, stalwarts of the Noosa restaurant scene, named their latest not for a Latin TV idol, but for Stef's great-uncle Ricky, a "gentleman scallywag" whose zest for life is reflected here. I'd choose it for lunch over dinner simply because of the fantastic setting; the food is sensational at any time. You can sit over a long lunch drinking in the view across the Noosa River while nibbling from an innovative tapas menu or something more sub-stantial. The menu is Mediterranean style, with fresh seafood and regional produce used throughout, and changes seasonally.

2/2 Quamby Place (inside the shopping center), Noosa Sound, QLD 4567. ℂ **07/ 5447 2455.** Reservations recommended. Main courses A$17–A$33 (US$14–US$26). AE, DC, MC, V. Daily noon–midnight.

Season *(R)* MODERN AUSTRALIAN With one of the few beachfront restaurant locations, this is one of Noosa's most popular restaurants. Former Sydney chef Gary Skelton has maintained his following, with vacationers from southern states rediscovering Season, and even if the locals balk at the A$10 (US$8) corkage for BYO wine there's no question the food remains superb. Breakfast dishes start from A$4 (US$3.20) for muffins or you can indulge yourself with buttermilk and banana pancakes (with palm sugar butter and maple syrup) for A$12 (US$9.60). For dinner? How about the pan-fried reef fish filet with crushed pinkeye potatoes, leek, and tomato, or even simpler, the barbecued seafood antipasto. Smoking is not permitted.

25 Hastings St., Noosa Heads, QLD 4567. ℂ **07/5447 3747.** Reservations accepted on the day you dine only. Main courses A$21–A$26 (US$17–US$21). AE, DC, MC, V. Daily 8am–10pm.

Index

See also Accommodations and Restaurants indexes below.

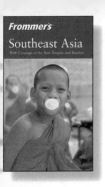

Frommer's

Southeast Asia

With Coverage of the Best Temples and Beaches

The only guide independent travelers need to make smart choices, avoid rip-offs, get the most for their money, and travel like a pro.

Frommer's Alaska
Frommer's Alaska Cruises & Ports of Call
Frommer's Amsterdam
Frommer's Argentina & Chile
Frommer's Arizona
Frommer's Atlanta
Frommer's Australia
Frommer's Austria
Frommer's Bahamas
Frommer's Barcelona, Madrid & Seville
Frommer's Beijing
Frommer's Belgium, Holland & Luxembourg
Frommer's Bermuda
Frommer's Boston
Frommer's Brazil
Frommer's British Columbia & the Canadian Rockies
Frommer's Brussels & Bruges with Ghent & Antwerp
Frommer's Budapest & the Best of Hungary
Frommer's California
Frommer's Canada
Frommer's Cancun, Cozumel & the Yucatan
Frommer's Cape Cod, Nantucket & Martha's Vineyard
Frommer's Caribbean
Frommer's Caribbean Cruises & Ports of Call
Frommer's Caribbean Ports of Call
Frommer's Carolinas & Georgia
Frommer's Chicago
Frommer's China
Frommer's Colorado
Frommer's Costa Rica
Frommer's Cuba

Frommer's Denmark
Frommer's Denver, Boulder & Colorado Springs
Frommer's England
Frommer's Europe
Frommer's European Cruises & Ports of Call
Frommer's Florence, Tuscany & Umbria
Frommer's Florida
Frommer's France
Frommer's Germany
Frommer's Great Britain
Frommer's Greece
Frommer's Greek Islands
Frommer's Hawaii
Frommer's Hong Kong
Frommer's Honolulu, Waikiki & Oahu
Frommer's Ireland
Frommer's Israel
Frommer's Italy
Frommer's Jamaica
Frommer's Japan
Frommer's Las Vegas
Frommer's London
Frommer's Los Angeles with Disneyland® & Palm Springs
Frommer's Maryland & Delaware
Frommer's Maui
Frommer's Mexico
Frommer's Montana & Wyoming
Frommer's Montreal & Quebec City
Frommer's Munich & the Bavarian Alps
Frommer's Nashville & Memphis
Frommer's Nepal
Frommer's New England
Frommer's Newfoundland & Labrador
Frommer's New Mexico
Frommer's New Orleans
Frommer's New York City
Frommer's New Zealand
Frommer's Northern Italy
Frommer's Norway
Frommer's Nova Scotia, New Brunswick & Prince Edward Island
Frommer's Oregon

Frommer's Ottawa
Frommer's Paris
Frommer's Peru
Frommer's Philadelphia & the Amish Country
Frommer's Portugal
Frommer's Prague & the Best of the Czech Republic
Frommer's Provence & the Riviera
Frommer's Puerto Rico
Frommer's Rome
Frommer's San Antonio & Austin
Frommer's San Diego
Frommer's San Francisco
Frommer's Santa Fe, Taos & Albuquerque
Frommer's Scandinavia
Frommer's Scotland
Frommer's Seattle
Frommer's Shanghai
Frommer's Sicily
Frommer's Singapore & Malaysia
Frommer's South Africa
Frommer's South America
Frommer's Southeast Asia
Frommer's South Florida
Frommer's South Pacific
Frommer's Spain
Frommer's Sweden
Frommer's Switzerland
Frommer's Texas
Frommer's Thailand
Frommer's Tokyo
Frommer's Toronto
Frommer's Turkey
Frommer's USA
Frommer's Utah
Frommer's Vancouver & Victoria
Frommer's Vermont, New Hampshire & Maine
Frommer's Vienna & the Danube Valley
Frommer's Virginia
Frommer's Virgin Islands
Frommer's Walt Disney World® & Orlando
Frommer's Washington, D.C.
Frommer's Washington State

Frommer's

WILEY

Available at bo   everywhere.

Frommer's Portable Guides

Destinations in a Nutshell

- Frommer's Portable Acapulco, Ixtapa & Zihuatanejo
- Frommer's Portable Amsterdam
- Frommer's Portable Aruba
- Frommer's Portable Australia's Great Barrier Reef
- Frommer's Portable Bahamas
- Frommer's Portable Berlin
- Frommer's Portable Big Island of Hawaii
- Frommer's Portable Boston
- Frommer's Portable California Wine Country
- Frommer's Portable Cancun
- Frommer's Portable Cayman Islands
- Frommer's Portable Charleston
- Frommer's Portable Chicago
- Frommer's Portable Disneyland®
- Frommer's Portable Dominican Republic
- Frommer's Portable Dublin
- Frommer's Portable Florence
- Frommer's Portable Frankfurt
- Frommer's Portable Hong Kong
- Frommer's Portable Houston
- Frommer's Portable Las Vegas
- Frommer's Portable Las Vegas for Non-Gamblers
- Frommer's Portable London
- Frommer's Portable London from $90 a Day
- Frommer's Portable Los Angeles

- Frommer's Portable Los Cabos & Baja
- Frommer's Portable Maine Coast
- Frommer's Portable Maui
- Frommer's Portable Miami
- Frommer's Portable Nantucket & Martha's Vineyard
- Frommer's Portable New Orleans
- Frommer's Portable New York City
- Frommer's Portable New York City from $90 a Day
- Frommer's Portable Paris
- Frommer's Portable Paris from $90 a Day
- Frommer's Portable Phoenix & Scottsdale
- Frommer's Portable Portland
- Frommer's Portable Puerto Rico
- Frommer's Portable Puerto Vallarta, Manzanillo & Guadalajara
- Frommer's Portable Rio de Janeiro
- Frommer's Portable San Diego
- Frommer's Portable San Francisco
- Frommer's Portable Savannah
- Frommer's Portable Seattle
- Frommer's Portable Sydney
- Frommer's Portable Tampa & St. Petersburg
- Frommer's Portable Vancouver
- Frommer's Portable Vancouver Island
- Frommer's Portable Venice
- Frommer's Portable Virgin Islands
- Frommer's Portable Washington, D.C.

Frommer's

 WILEY

 Available at

DARE TO BE...

IRREVERENT guide to **Walt Disney World & Orlando**
fourth edition
"Like being taken around by a savvy local."
—*The New York Times*

IRREVERENT guide to **Manhattan**
fifth edition
"Like being taken around by a savvy local."
—*The New York Times*

IRREVERENT guide to **New Orleans**
fourth edition
"Like being taken around by a savvy local."
—*The New York Times*

IRREVERENT guide to **Amsterdam**
fifth edition
"Like being taken around by a savvy local."
—*The New York Times*

IRREVERENT guide to **San Francisco**
fifth edition
"Like being taken around by a savvy local."
—*The New York Times*

...Different

Irreverent Guide to Las Vegas
Irreverent Guide to London
Irreverent Guide to Paris
Irreverent Guide to Boston
Irreverent Guide to Los Angeles

Irreverent Guide to Rome
Irreverent Guide to Seattle & Portland
Irreverent Guide to Vancouver
Irreverent Guide to Washington, D.C.
Irreverent Guide to Chicago

Frommer's
A Branded Imprint of WILEY
Now you know.

Available at bookstores everywhere.

Frommer's Budget Guides

Frommer's
ENGLAND
FROM $75 A DAY

Free
Foldout
Map!

Plan Your Trip Online at Frommers.com

Live Large
and
Spend Little

*The guide that shows you
how to have lots of
fun without spending too
much cash.*

- Australia from $50 a Day

- California from $70 a Day

- England from $75 a Day

- Europe from $85 a Day

- Florida from $70 a Day

- Hawaii from $80 a Day

- Ireland from $80 a Day

- Italy from $70 a Day

- London from $90 a Day

- New York City from $90
  a Day

- Paris from $90 a Day

- San Francisco from $70
  a Day

- Washington, D.C. from $80
  a Day

Frommer's

⊛ **WILEY**

Available at bookstores everywhere.

Frommer's® National Park Guides

Algonquin Provincial Park
Banff & Jasper
Family Vacations in the National
  Parks

Grand Canyon
National Parks of the American
  West
Rocky Mountain

Yellowstone & Grand Teton
Yosemite & Sequoia/Kings
  Canyon
Zion & Bryce Canyon

Frommer's® Memorable Walks

Chicago
London

New York
Paris

San Francisco

Frommer's® With Kids Guides

Chicago
Las Vegas
New York City

Ottawa
San Francisco
Toronto

Vancouver
Walt Disney World® & Orlando
Washington, D.C.

Suzy Gershman's Born to Shop Guides

Born to Shop: France
Born to Shop: Hong Kong,
  Shanghai & Beijing

Born to Shop: Italy
Born to Shop: London

Born to Shop: New York
Born to Shop: Paris

Frommer's® Irreverent Guides

Amsterdam
Boston
Chicago
Las Vegas
London

Los Angeles
Manhattan
New Orleans
Paris
Rome

San Francisco
Seattle & Portland
Vancouver
Walt Disney World®
Washington, D.C.

Frommer's® Best-Loved Driving Tours

Austria
Britain
California
France

Germany
Ireland
Italy
New England

Northern Italy
Scotland
Spain
Tuscany & Umbria

The Unofficial Guides®

Beyond Disney
California with Kids
Central Italy
Chicago
Cruises
Disneyland®
England
Florida
Florida with Kids
Inside Disney

Hawaii
Las Vegas
London
Maui
Mexico's Best Beach Resorts
Mini Las Vegas
Mini Mickey
New Orleans
New York City
Paris

San Francisco
Skiing & Snowboarding in the
  West
South Florida including Miami &
  the Keys
Walt Disney World®
Walt Disney World® for
  Grown-ups
Walt Disney World® with Kids
Washington, D.C.

Special-Interest Titles

Athens Past & Present
Cities Ranked & Rated
Frommer's Best Day Trips from London
Frommer's Best RV & Tent Campgrounds
  in the U.S.A.
Frommer's Caribbean Hideaways
Frommer's China: The 50 Most Memorable Trips
Frommer's Exploring America by RV
Frommer's Gay & Lesbian Europe
Frommer's NYC Free & Dirt Cheap

Frommer's Road Atlas Europe
Frommer's Road Atlas France
Frommer's Road Atlas Ireland
Frommer's Wonderful Weekends from
  New York City
The New York Times' Guide to Unforgettable
  Weekends
Retirement Places Rated
Rome Past & Present

Travel Tip: He who finds the best hotel deal has more to spend on facials involving knobbly vegetables.

Hello, the Roaming Gnome here. I've been nabbed from the garden and taken round the world. The people who took me are so terribly clever. They find the best offerings on Travelocity. For very little cha-ching. And that means I get to be pampered and exfoliated till I'm pink as a bunny's doodah.

travelocity®

1-888-TRAVELOCITY / travelocity.com / America Online Keyword: Travel

004 Travelocity.com LP. All rights reserved. TRAVELOCITY, the Stars Design and The Roaming Gnome are trademarks of Travelocity.com LP. CST# 2056372-50.

Travel Tip: Make sure there's customer service for any change of plans — involving friendly natives, for example.

One can plan and plan, but if you don't book with the right people you can't seize le moment and canoodle with the poodle named Pansy. I, for one, am all for fraternizing with the locals. Better yet, if I need to extend my stay and my gnome nappers are willing, it can all be arranged through the 800 number at, oh look, how convenient, the lovely company coat of arms.

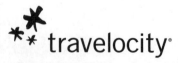

travelocity®

1-888-TRAVELOCITY / travelocity.com / America Online Keyword: Travel